*History and the Social Web*
A COLLECTION OF ESSAYS

# HISTORY

## *and the* SOCIAL WEB

*A Collection of Essays by*

AUGUST C. KREY

THE UNIVERSITY OF MINNESOTA PRESS

Minneapolis

PUBLISHED IN GREAT BRITAIN, INDIA, AND PAKISTAN BY
GEOFFREY CUMBERLEGE: OXFORD UNIVERSITY PRESS, LONDON, BOMBAY, AND KARACHI

TO

*George Clarke Sellery*

SCHOLAR, TEACHER, AND FRIEND

# Preface

$S$OME five years ago the authorities of the University of Minnesota Press proposed the publication of a collection of my essays for which there was a continuing demand. Their suggestion came in part from the fact that the one which they had published, "A City That Art Built," had been out of print for some time and they were repeatedly being urged to make it available again. They expressed the hope that I would prepare such a collection before I retired from active teaching. This book is the result.

Except for two papers prepared for professional historians, all these essays were addressed to a general audience, and these two professional papers are included here because of their wider interest. All but two have been published in one or another form, mostly in periodicals, at irregular intervals over a span of more than thirty-five years. All of them as they appear here have undergone more or less extensive revision for the purpose of integrating them into a book that would have a reasonable measure of unity and continuity. The separate essays have, I hope, been transformed into successive chapters of continued thought, so that the book presents my interpretation of the period of European history from 300 to 1600 A.D. and the importance of its study in modern times.

It would be quite impossible to make adequate acknowledgment of all the assistance received in the preparation of these essays. The books read, the discussions with colleagues, the contributions of teachers over all these years, are too numerous even to be catalogued. Let me single out those to whom I feel most deeply indebted. First in this list I would place my instructors at the University of Wisconsin, who started my interest in history as a profession and apparently determined the direction of that interest: Dana Carleton Munro, who introduced me to medieval history; George Clarke Sellery, who interested me in the Renaissance; and Frederick Jackson Turner, whose comprehensive view of society and brilliant interpretation of its operation have been a continuing inspiration to me. To them, too, I owe my abiding interest in the pedagogy of the profession, which several of these essays reflect, for my first course on the teaching of history was conducted by D. C. Munro, with some collaboration from the other two as well.

More than half of these essays were first read before the Gown-in-Town Dining Club, whose membership reflects the varied academic interests of the University of Minnesota. The club members' custom of friendly criticism and suggestion usually rendered such exposure very profitable. Nearly all the essays were submitted to the critical scrutiny of my wife, Laura Krey, whose unusual feeling for word and sentence was of inestimable benefit. And the staff of the University of Minnesota Press, including its director, Helen Clapesattle, gave me much skillful aid in arranging the individual papers in logical sequence for book publication.

Specific acknowledgment is made with each essay to the publisher or periodical that first issued it, but I should like to express my thanks here to all the publishers and editors who so graciously granted me permission to draw upon their publications.

AUGUST C. KREY

# Table of Contents

# PART ONE

*The Long Road Back*

# 1

# A Society without Education

$T$HIS is an experimental age. The wonders wrought through technology have been so marvelous as to incline all classes of society to scientific experimentation. Inspired by this support, scholars in fields of learning other than the sciences have been led to undertake varied programs of controlled research. This is notably true in education in this country and in our own time. Any idea, new or old, if dressed up as an experiment, is sure of a welcome somewhere in our educational world.

No one, however, has suggested that we try the experiment of omitting education altogether. Yet, it would be interesting to observe a whole society like our own operating without any of what might be called formal training. Our society, which has advanced so much farther than any other in the direction of universal education, would seem to offer an unrivaled opportunity for comparison. And the experimentalists might be tempted to endorse the scheme for its very magnitude. Certainly it would rank as the world's greatest experiment in education.

Not many persons are aware that such an experiment *has* been tried, or so nearly tried that most of the consequences can be anticipated with a high degree of certainty. Few realize that a society quite as large as our own, with as many or more people

NOTE: This essay appeared in somewhat different form, under the title "The World's Greatest Educational Experiment," in *Social Education*, October 1938.

and with a culture or civilization in some respects as high or higher, once gave up schools and educational work.

True, the circumstances surrounding the occurrence did not perfectly meet all the demands of the suggested experiment. The venture was not undertaken deliberately as a social and educational experiment; education was not given up all at once; and there were a few isolated spots in which formal schooling was not quite entirely abandoned. Yet these spots were so few, the amount of education they preserved so meager, and the absence of education over the rest of the area so complete that perhaps the most exacting experimentalist would admit that the results tend to indicate the probable consequences of a more perfect experiment.

I am referring, of course, to the Roman Empire, or rather to that portion of it lying west of the Greek peninsula, though that peninsula itself might very well be included.

That Rome did once have widespread education every schoolboy who ever divided Gaul into three parts or castigated Catiline with the blistering rhetoric of Cicero has good reason to suspect. That it was good as well as widespread is attested by the fact that before the first century *anno Domini* was ended, the conquered provinces, Spain and Gaul, were already contributing leaders to Roman literature. Northern Africa and Britain, too, reflected the efforts of Roman educators. Theirs was not a system of compulsory education in our sense, or even one of public education. Most of the training was offered by private teachers, though with some municipal and imperial support. Education was being carried on in the army and in rural districts, but its chief center was in the towns. During the century or more which spans the golden and silver ages of Latin literature, interest in education ran deep and wide through the population of Rome.

I must leave to students of ancient history the task of explaining just how the Romans, who occupied the Italian peninsula south of the Apennines, succeeded in spreading education throughout conquered territory with a population and an extent many times greater than those of the conquering state. The undertaking was so thoroughly successful, however, that its effects are still noticeable in the language of the people living in most of this region today.

Yet those same Romans, after accomplishing this miracle of education, after assimilating this vast barbarous population to their own culture, gave up their educational efforts. The steps in this process of abandonment are numerous, many of them probably scarcely perceptible. Those too fall largely in the field of the ancient historian, and I shall therefore not attempt to indicate them in detail here. It is possible, however, to follow the decline of education step by step from the second century to the sixth, when the process was complete.

We can see the progress of decay most clearly revealed in the career and writings of Apollinaris Sidonius, who lived in Gaul from about 430 to 490 A.D.—that is, through most of the fateful fifth century.

For the Western world that century meant the end of "the grandeur that was Rome." To St. Jerome, then living on the edge of the desert at Bethlehem, the news of the sack of Rome by Alaric and the Visigoths in 410 marked also the end of the world, and he therefore urged all his friends to espouse the ascetic life and prepare their souls for eternity. At Hippo St. Augustine labored for the next twenty years on his *City of God* as a refutation of the lament which many refugees to Africa were making that the invasion of Rome had been due to the wrath of the pagan gods at being forgotten or neglected.

But the tragedy of 410 was mild compared to those that were to follow. Britain was abandoned, soon to be taken over by the Anglo-Saxons; southern Gaul was recognized by 415 as the home of the Visigoths, northern Africa by 430 as the possession of the Vandals. Each then spreading their control, the Visigoths advanced into Spain and the Vandals to Carthage, the islands of the western Mediterranean, and finally in 455 to a more thorough sack of Rome than Alaric's. By 462 the Burgundians had moved into eastern Gaul and held Lyons as their capital. In their wake the Allemani soon occupied both banks of the Upper Rhine, while

5

the Franks began edging their way southward to the Loire; and the year 476, when Romulus Augustulus was deposed without a successor, has often been seized upon as the symbol of the end of the Roman Empire in the West.

The life of Sidonius spanned most of these critical events. His family belonged to the great landed nobility of Gaul. His father, his grandfather, and ancestors even more remote had climbed the ladder of Roman imperial administration to the prefecture of Gaul, and that was the career to which he too aspired and for which he was educated. He did enter the administrative service and his political activity took him to the very center of imperial affairs. He became prefect of Gaul, was at Rome during the brief period when his father-in-law, Avitus, was emperor, and later was prefect of Rome under the emperor, Anthemius.

Sidonius ended his days in the ecclesiastical office of bishop of Clermont, and it is probable that to this later dignity, together with the reputation of sainthood which local legend soon ascribed to him, we owe the preservation of his writings. But it is also true that he fancied himself as a writer, and was supported in this opinion by the fulsome flattery of his friends, who no doubt persuaded him to collect and publish his various works. This he did in the leisure of his declining years, after he had become bishop; and to what extent his later status may have conditioned the selection and revision of these earlier writings can probably never be determined. Their matter, however, and even their literary embellishment indicate that they have come down to us largely as they were originally written, and as such they constitute our chief guide to the progress of events during this ominous and momentous century.

Literary critics agree in condemning Sidonius' labored rhetoric and his overgenerous use of synonyms, metaphors, and literary allusions, which he probably employed in more or less conscious accord with the conventional standards of the period. Certainly his style will not bear comparison with that of Ambrose, Ausonius, Symmachus, Jerome, or Augustine of Hippo, all of whom had received their education before 400 A.D. and completed their writing careers by 430. Yet to Sidonius' fifth-century contemporaries he seemed to possess the most gifted pen of his time. Nor have the students of Latin literature been able to find any better writer of the late fifth century; and this fact in itself must be interpreted as reflecting a sharp decline in the cultural level of the age in which he lived.

The relatively high standard of culture reflected in the writings of Ausonius, Symmachus, and the three great Latin Church fathers may be explained by the widespread interest in education which prevailed in the later fourth century. Seldom had education been more highly esteemed. Famous teachers were honored with high public office, Ausonius being elevated to the consular dignity while many others were given positions as vicars, prefects, and court officials. Emperor Gratian further showed his appreciation of education by issuing an edict to improve the salaries of teachers of grammar and rhetoric. All municipalities were expected to maintain schools, and the imperial treasury supplemented the resources of the cities. Such cities as Treves, Lyons, Bordeaux, Arles, Milan, Rome, and Carthage were flourishing centers of learning, and numbered among their citizens thousands of students.

It was not so in Sidonius' time. Writing in the year 478 to his friend Johannes, a grammarian who had just opened a school at Bordeaux, he congratulated him "for deferring the *decease* of literature" and told him, "in this tempest of war which has wrecked the Roman power, you are the *sole* master in Gaul who has brought the Latin tongue safely into port." Perhaps hopefully he adds: "Since old grades of rank are now abolished which once distinguished the high from the low, in the future culture must afford the sole criterion of nobility" and "I shall owe to your school and your teaching the certainty of an understanding audience."

If taken literally, all these statements would seem to imply that education, which was flourishing in Gaul at the end of the fourth century, had dwindled in that area by the last quarter of the fifth century to only one school and one teacher. Even allowing for

7

rhetorical exaggeration, all that Sidonius has to say on the subject indicates at best a catastrophic decline of education in general.

But there is little evidence in Sidonius' writings that he thought anything was wrong with the schools of the day. In the letter in which he invited his old schoolteacher to spend a summer at his country estate he seems to take the educational system for granted. Among his own political activities there were several strenuous and, on the whole, successful efforts to prevent the levying of taxes upon the people of his class, but there was evidently no connection in his mind between this reluctance to be taxed and education. He does deplore the fact that not all members of his class show a proper interest in either politics or learning and that there is little learning among those who surround the Visigothic chieftain.

The most striking sign of the times, however, is afforded by Sidonius' interest in his son's education, to which he alludes in his letters. We find him apparently trying to teach his boy himself. Whether he did this because he liked to do so, or because the teachers were no longer good, or because he could find no satisfactory teachers is not clear. Perhaps all three of these factors played a part. At any rate the boy was not well educated.

Throughout western Europe, the abandonment of education was virtually complete by 600 A.D., and our evidence can be drawn from the greatest scholars of the day. Italy had no greater mind nor one more cultivated than that of Pope Gregory I. He was still aware that there were rules of grammar, but he was no longer able to follow them too closely. The greatest scholar in Gaul, so far as we know, was Gregory, bishop of Tours, who apologizes for the poor writing of his ecclesiastical history because "culture was on the wane or rather perishing" and no accomplished writer could any longer be found in all Gaul.

The most pathetic evidence of the decline, however, appears in the career of Isidore of Seville, the most learned man of that time in Spain. Braulio, a bishop of Spain, wrote to Isidore asking him to provide men like himself with a work which would furnish knowledge on all subjects. If the request seems astonishing,

8

how much more so is Isidore's unhesitating compliance with it!
Isidore found time, in the spare moments that his duties as bishop
of Seville permitted, to complete the work within a few years.
When Braulio had received it, he wrote that a frequent reading
of this book would leave the reader "ignorant of neither Divine
nor human learning." It was an encyclopedia, and the whole in
about the space of an ordinary textbook.

If these three men represented the most highly educated group
of the time, what must have been the condition of the rest?
Towns were no longer offering education, the state no longer
supported it, nor were private individuals of any class maintaining teachers. Very few monasteries, still fewer bishoprics, were
even making a pretense of education except in the forms of
priestly practice, and that chiefly by imitation and by ear. Academic education had practically been abandoned. Book learning
had ceased to be.

The books were still there. There were many collections of
books at the time, enough to provide Italy, Gaul, Spain, northern
Africa, and Britain with nearly all the valuable literature and
learning of the ancient world. They merely were not used. The
people among whom they existed did not know how to use them.
Worse still, these people were probably unaware that the books
contained anything that could possibly be of value to them. The
books, therefore, were regarded as outmoded furniture, and, like
other old furniture, they were exposed to the customary forces
of attrition, dust, vermin, and ignorance, passive or active. For
most of the collections of books in these regions this process of
neglect had started long before 600 A.D. Thereafter it merely proceeded with accelerated force.

Under such conditions what happened to the ordinary activities
of society—to the processes of government, for example?

Government was in the hands of the military, chiefly of Teu-
tonic origin. Their military training even under the Romans had
not included academic education. Now even their Roman advisers and lieutenants had none.

The kings therefore were unaware of any good reason why

they should not divide their kingdoms among their sons, of whom they usually had several. Nor did the vassals of these sons see any reason why they themselves should not rule over their own districts at will, deferring at first to occasional military demands from their superiors. Their immediate subjects, in turn, took the same attitude toward them, until the whole region tended to be governed by the physically most powerful individual in each small neighborhood. His active life was spent in maintaining his control over the locality and in resisting all efforts of similar individualists to encroach upon his sovereignty.

Thus society had reached the rock bottom of dispersion of political authority. The unit of government was almost the smallest area which could support a single person whose chief concern was to keep from supporting himself. And this state of affairs required constant fighting, whether against those whom the local lord forced to work for him or against nearby rivals. Neighborhood and private warfare became chronic.

The pages of Gregory of Tours show how far government in Gaul had already moved in this direction before 600 A.D., and there is no reason for assuming that conditions in Italy, Spain, and northern Africa were much different. This tendency increased after 600 A.D. Either superior force or organized persuasion might have prevented it from reaching its logical conclusion, but the superior force did not appear. The possibility of persuading the individual fighters that they might enjoy more and greater material blessings if they yielded some of their individual sovereignty for the sake of wider cooperation was also missing, for that kind of persuasion presupposed education. And now men no longer knew of conditions before their own parents' days and doubtless assumed that existence had always been just as they were finding it in their own lifetime.

In any consideration of human activities, it is natural to consider government and law in sequence. During the centuries under examination, justice was of a summary kind administered arbitrarily by the fighting head of the community. The sword or battle-ax took the place of the imperial code, and even where the weapon was not directly employed, the threat of its use was always present. Precedents were invoked when remembered, though not many were remembered for more than two generations, and even then they were not allowed to interfere seriously with the wishes of the local lord. Law books, like other books, still existed, but nearly all were allowed to gather dust. The legal profession disappeared from western Europe. Those who would experience vicariously a society without lawyers can do so by gazing upon the history of western Europe during the five centuries following 600 A.D. Administration was conducted without record. Usually the local lord was able to forget all dues which he owed and to remember all those due him. In case of disputed recollection, his memory was usually decisive.

Economic and social life as well as law were at the mercy of the strong arm, thick neck, and low brow. Since each locality lived in a state of constant suspicion of its neighbors, usually in the more acute forms of fear or anger, there could be little effective intercourse between even immediate neighborhoods. Each community had therefore to provide for all its own needs and learn to live on what the neighborhood produced.

City life was impossible on any large scale. Perhaps it is more correct to say that it ceased. In some places, as in Rome, large areas of the city were leveled and converted into arable land. Probably most of the larger towns with walls and monumental buildings were thus transformed into small self-sufficient communities like those in the more rural areas. Smaller towns, especially those that had grown up to supply the luxuries of life around natural baths or in the hills, were completely abandoned. Even before the close of the sixth century forests had invaded such places, as St. Columban found when he established his monasteries at Anagray and Luxeuil in eastern Gaul. Commerce dwindled to such commodities as could be carried in a pack, or ceased altogether.

Those who today cherish the ideal of economic self-sufficiency or the totalitarian state would have found their ideal almost as fully in operation as it has ever been in a society that once was civilized. Each neighborhood virtually had to provide for all its needs entirely within its own confines.

Food, of course, received first attention. The soil was either turned to satisfy the full range of required crops, or the people were forced to modify their needs to accord with the natural production. Agriculture confined to local neighborhoods for centuries may afford the modern geneticist more food for thought than it gave the medieval peasant for sustenance. The harvest was pitifully small in relation to the seed. Centuries later, when life had become somewhat more settled and the interchange of ideas less confined, it was still deemed proper to reckon five families of peasants or serfs necessary to supply the family of one knight or fighting man.

Animals, like grain and other agricultural crops, were dependent upon local strains for their perpetuation. Only a successful foray upon the stock of the nearest neighbors afforded any opportunity for crossbreeding. And since most of the cattle had to be slaughtered each fall because there was not fodder enough to tide them over the winter, it must have been a strain, often too great a strain, on the spirit of self-denial to preserve the best for breeding. Four centuries of more or less haphazard inbreeding must have resulted in kinds of livestock, grains, fruits, and other foodstuffs quite unlike those to which we are accustomed today. The miniatures of the early Middle Ages that depict cattle much smaller than human beings may in many instances have been much more literally accurate than most of us have supposed.

Whether human stature also was affected by the character of the food produced under these conditions is a question which the absence of any large suits of armor in European museums would seem to answer in the affirmative. The small yields of various kinds of foodstuffs, together with the uncertain and inadequate means of preserving any except the hardiest for even a few months, gave the average community a very slender margin of safety in unfavorable seasons. It is probably for this reason that famines are among the most common calamities recorded in the meager chronicles of the time—death-dealing famine in one neighborhood, when others not more than a hundred miles away might be enjoying relative plenty.

Social life became restricted, not merely because intercourse was confined to small neighborhoods, but even more because most available energy was absorbed in providing the elemental necessities.

At least 80 per cent of the population was engaged in agriculture, most of it on a semiservile basis. The serfs had to till the fields, contribute labor, and in their spare moments repair houses, tools, and furniture as well as share in the task of making various articles of apparel. The lot of the women was, of course, more arduous than that of the men. They were all expected to marry. When married, they regularly bore as many children as was biologically possible. They prepared the food for their families, and made most of the clothing. They often helped with the work in the fields, and contributed labor to the local lord. They did not know what it was to suffer from unemployment. There was work enough for them to fill every hour of the waking day. Probably the only relief from unremitting toil was afforded by religious celebrations, and it required a long hard struggle by the clergy to ensure even this.

The remaining 20 per cent or less of the population included the fighters and the clergy. To gain a bare living, the average priest probably had to supplement the thin offerings of his flock with his own labor. Meanwhile professional duties were probably in great demand, for, in addition to the formal church services, he had also to minister to the sick and the needy and the dying. Baptism, marriage, and burial, certainly the first and last, made more frequent demands upon his time than in more modern periods. And the priesthood was much less numerous than it later became.

Life was not much more leisurely for the fighters. Fighting itself occupied a portion of every year, and the preparations for fighting most of the rest of the time. Hunting, which tended to be a monopoly of this group, was less a social diversion than an essential occupation to supply the family table. The care of horses and weapons, the construction and repair of fortifications

13

involved an amount and variety of work which could not all be delegated. Nor can it be forgotten that the main business of this class was hand-to-hand warfare requiring large as well as skillful muscle. Most of their days were probably spent in what today even the most romantically inclined would be forced to describe as manual labor.

The wives of these fighters were probably no less occupied than were their husbands, and with cares and duties not much more elegant than those of the peasant women. For the four centuries after 600 A.D. there was no leisure class in this portion of Europe.

Children were numerous. After they were weaned there was probably little interference with their activities by their parents, and there were no teachers. So far as the child was concerned, he could live a perfectly child-centered, uninhibited existence. He was free to follow his own interests until he bumped into someone else, ate poisonous substances, or fell down a well. Many other hazards that beset childhood in those days are indicated by the folklore of this period which has come down to us. Comparatively few children survived the period of infancy and fewer still reached adult age to beget children of their own. Those who did had run the gantlet of all the ills and accidents to which an unguided life could subject them.

Let the eugenists find what comfort they can in the thought that for several centuries only the physically fit survived and begot children. If such is their dream of an ideal society, they will find it to have been nearly realized in western Europe in the four or five centuries after 600 A.D.

There were no sweeping epidemics of disease. Medical history, which recounts the sweep of the plague over the Mediterranean world in the sixth century, must wait until the fourteenth before it finds an epidemic of equal scope. This does not, however, betoken the absence of disease of epidemic potentialities. It merely reflects the lack of extensive intercourse among the peoples of Europe. The epidemics that did occur soon spent themselves within restricted areas.

# A Society without Education

Doubtless most of the diseases known in that region today occurred then. The method of warfare in an age in which antisepsis was unknown permitted the prevalence of all the ills invited by open wounds. In addition, there were a host of diseases now almost unknown, like St. Anthony's Fire, which resulted from the consumption of tainted food. Other afflictions that thrive on insanitary conditions of living, chiefly of skin and scalp, were much more common then than now. On the whole, the incidence of disease was probably greater than it had been before or was to be later, and there were probably few persons who passed middle age without exhibiting some of the deformities of tooth or limb that untreated illness so often leaves.

Medicine was practiced, but not studied. The rough surgery of the battlefield was usually performed by amateurs, and fevers and pains were usually treated with such herbs and medicaments as feminine folklore reputed to be beneficial. Superstitious beliefs and practices were, however, the common resort of most people for most ailments. Our best glimpse into the medical practice of these centuries is afforded by that curious volume in the *Rolls Series* entitled "Leechdoms, Wortcunning, and Starcraft of Early England." As the title indicates, astronomical phenomena were thought to be as efficacious in their influence on health and disease as on the processes of agriculture.

Theology was but little known. The offices of the Church were conducted in many instances on the basis of imitation alone and the verbal formulas were repeated with awed reverence, if not with accuracy. Bishops were often no more enlightened than priests. In Gaul, where before the end of the sixth century it had become customary to choose bishops without regard to their knowledge of theology, the priests under such supervision found little incentive or opportunity to increase their own knowledge. Direct inspiration was doubtless relied upon by many in emergencies, and the priests were thus ill-fitted to oppose those individuals who professed to have been divinely called to practice religion in various capacities. Such individuals continued to appear here and there, more or less sincere in their belief in their mission and more or less successful in gaining adherents.

Other aspects of culture underwent changes equally important, though there is less direct testimony about them. Doubtless some literature was produced, although the lack of leisure allowed little time either for its production or its consumption. What there was must have been preserved, as well as communicated, orally. This may be inferred from the popular literature like *Beowulf*, the *Nibelungenlied*, and the *Chanson de Roland* which a later, more literate age put into writing.

The circulation of this material, however, must have been seriously impeded by diversities in language. Whatever progress had been made under Roman rule toward the development of a common language had been entirely checked, or rather reversed. Language continued to change, but its change was determined by the populace, not by a learned group. Each community developed its own idioms, its own variations of vocabulary and pronunciation to suit its own needs and circumstances. After four centuries of such development persons living only a few miles apart in some cases found it almost impossible to understand one another. These local dialects—themselves the product of the isolation which political organization brought about—were in turn to serve as the greatest obstacle to wider unification when that again became possible.

This general account of conditions which followed the sixth century, when formal education had been virtually abandoned, may seem somewhat extreme, but it would not be difficult to substantiate it by instances of actual occurrence in some portion or other of western Europe throughout these centuries. Those times and places when conditions were better, as in Gaul under Charlemagne, in Germany and Italy under Otto the Great, and in Britain under Alfred, may almost be dismissed as exceptions. Historians have been so intent upon tracing the beginnings of modern culture and institutions that these exceptional instances have loomed disproportionately large and have distorted our views of the more prevalent state of affairs. Institutionally and culturally the exceptions are the more important of course, but how quickly did Gaul revert to its former ways after Charlemagne, and Germany after Otto the Great! If we view this development without the bias of interest in modern civilization, we cannot doubt the essential correctness of the description here given.

But at this point it is well to remember that conditions were not perfect for the experiment of a society without education. There were from the outset a few isolated spots in which education had not been completely abandoned.

We need not concern ourselves with the persistence of education in the eastern Mediterranean or even with its revival among the Moslems who swept around the southern Mediterranean and well up into Spain. Neither of the states involved was in a position to extend its educational work west or north, and the religious differences only served to accentuate the barrier between them and western Europe. Both Constantinople and Baghdad, Byzantium and the Caliphate, may therefore safely be ignored as active factors in our problem during the four centuries just described.

We cannot, however, ignore two other spots, southern Italy and Ireland. The work of old Cassiodorus in the sixth century illustrates how formal education barely escaped extinction in Italy and adjacent regions. After a full life as a sort of prime minister for several Gothic kings, he sought to end his years on his estate in southern Italy. Piously he built on his estate two monasteries, one for old men like himself, the other for younger men. Doubtless he expected to spend his last years in reading and in edifying conversation with his old cronies, but when he gathered his young men together in the other monastery, he found many of them practically illiterate. Instead of enjoying a life of leisure, he was faced with the task of becoming a schoolmaster. Undaunted, he set to work to prepare primary textbooks for these men, even writing a little manual of orthography.

It is a common notion, for which there is little support, that the rising Christian Church stood eagerly by to grasp the torch of learning from the faltering hand of the dying Empire and thus saved it for future centuries. We forget that until after 300 A.D. Christianity was a forbidden religion and that the chief work of conversion of the Romans in the West was done after that time. People came into the Church already educated. The experience of Ambrose, Jerome, and Augustine, who were fully educated before they took up the religious life, is typical. The priests of the time confined their educational efforts to instruction in religion, spiritual and moral. That they must someday also undertake instruction in letters probably did not occur to them. Even as late as the sixth century education in letters was still assumed to be a secular function, of the State rather than of the Church.

This had been the view even of Cassiodorus when as prime minister he addressed edicts to town authorities requesting them to pay the salaries of grammarians and rhetoricians. That the Church finally assumed an interest in common education was in no small measure due to examples such as he himself afforded in his later days. His almost accidental discovery of the illiteracy of the young men in his monastery and the providential extension of his life were factors largely responsible for bringing the problem to the attention of at least some of the churchmen.

What Cassiodorus did, the kind of textbooks and educational treatises he wrote, do not impress us today. But his efforts represented the best that an old man who had never been a schoolteacher could do. Perhaps his work was not much more than the feeble recollection of the educational process through which he had passed as a youth. Even so, it was dynamic in its effect and was to point the way for centuries. A generation after the death of Cassiodorus, Gregory the Great sent the monks of Monte Cassino to carry on his work among the heathen Anglo-Saxons.

Not less important was the work of the Irish. This non-Roman people had become converted to Latin Christianity at least a century and a half before the death of Cassiodorus. The introduction of this religion carried with it the obligation to teach Latin and Greek letters as well as theology. As a result, while the Roman world was abandoning education the Irish were taking it up, so that by the time of Cassiodorus the Irish had already acquired as much learning as Cassiodorus still remembered, or more. Had the Irish kept these blessings to themselves, we might disregard their work outside the Roman world. As is well known, however, the zeal of the Irish was too great, their altruism too expansive for them to confine their efforts to Ireland alone. They carried both their religion and their education first to Great Britain and then to the continent of Europe, even to northern Italy.

The heathen Anglo-Saxons who felt the impact of both forces, from Italy and from Ireland, were fired to similar endeavor, as Bede and Boniface and Alcuin so brilliantly testify. But it is unnecessary to trace that development in detail. It is a familiar story which every textbook in medieval history repeats, for it throws light on modern institutions of learning and intellectual activity.

By the end of the eleventh century, contact with the Byzantine and even the Moslem East was again established and the churchmen, who thus far had carried the burden of education alone, now received substantial help in their task from merchants. The advance made by the thirteenth century has justly commanded the enthusiastic admiration of all later ages. More was to follow in the next two centuries, at the end of which exploration had extended men's knowledge to the ends of the earth. Viewed solely in terms of its own development, this educational effort is marvelously impressive. Apparently its influence is to be seen and felt in ever widening and deepening circles.

From that point of view, the two centers in which education had not been completely abandoned had been influential indeed—had in fact damaged the perfection of our experiment considerably.

Admitting this impairment, however, we can learn a great deal from an inventory of the extent to which, as a result of all this effort, learning and civilization had been recovered by the end of the thirteenth century.

Theology was the chief interest of the scholars who followed the work of Cassiodorus and the Irish. It was the subject to which they devoted their most strenuous labors. Yet it was not until the time of Anselm of Canterbury, at the very end of the eleventh century, that leading theologians clearly perceived that the *Magna moralia* of Gregory the Great did not meet all the demands of theology. A century and a half later it was commonly recognized that the great Church fathers of the fourth and early fifth centuries had not completed their task, that they had been intent primarily upon the establishment of the separate items of doctrine. The work of fitting these separate items into a consistent statement of theology still remained to be done. This was the contribution of the great theologians of the thirteenth century and was most nearly achieved in the *Summa theologica* of Thomas Aquinas, who died in 1274. By the end of the thirteenth century, churchmen had caught up fully with the great fathers of the fourth century and in their knowledge of supporting philosophy had reached back to the days of Aristotle and Plato. Thus the systematic organization of theology which, if education had not been abandoned, might normally have been accomplished within a single generation, or two at the most, after Augustine had to wait nearly eight hundred years.

Teaching was naturally a close second to theology in the concern of the scholars of these centuries. Yet it was not until the time of John of Garland in the thirteenth century that teachers composed textbooks better than those Cassiodorus wrote or recommended. And it was not until the time of Vittorino da Feltre and Guarino of Verona, two centuries later, that they devised a system of instruction as good as, or better than, that of Quintilian, the best of the Roman educators. That represents an interval of more than thirteen hundred years.

The book of ready reference, the encyclopedia, for which Bishop Braulio asked in the time of Isidore of Seville, continued to be needed through all this period. No one was able to provide a better reference manual until the Dominican, Vincent of Beauvais, royal librarian and tutor for the children of Louis IX of France, compiled his *Speculum mundi* about the middle of the thirteenth century. It should be said that in this achievement he had the help of many bright young Dominicans who were studying in Paris, perhaps St. Thomas among others. Even so, we must wait three hundred years more before we find an encyclopedist whose knowledge of nature would have commanded the respect of Pliny, from whom Isidore derived much of his lore. That is an interval of more than fourteen hundred years.

Law is another obvious field of scholarly interest. Church law, which was naturally growing during this period, was given its first systematic treatment by Gratian in the twelfth century, the more authoritative codification of canon law coming in the thirteenth century with the work of Gregory IX and Boniface VIII. Additions made in the fields of customary and maritime law were being written down in the fourteenth century. In civil law Justinian's code was not used in full in western Europe until the time of Irnerius in the twelfth century, and it is difficult to say just when Europe had a group of lawyers comparable to those who drew up the Justinian code. Perhaps not until the seventeenth century.

Medicine had again become a subject of study, appearing in Salerno and Montpellier during the twelfth century, possibly somewhat earlier at Salerno. Yet Galen, in his epitomes, remained the great authority until the sixteenth century, when Vesalius, Fracastoro, and Paracelsus advanced beyond him. Their work marks an interval of more than thirteen hundred years before the best of the Romans was equaled and exceeded.

We might similarly examine what happened to the development of other branches of learning, theoretical and applied, including the practical arts of architecture and agriculture. While these matters were not directly of concern to theology and the schools, they were a part of civilization and the monastic scholars by no means overlooked them. Such a study would demonstrate that in each field there was retardation to equal that which we have observed in theology, teaching, law, and medicine.

In other words, with all the help that the work of the monasteries, the renewal of contact with Constantinople and the East, and the extension of trade around the world could give, it required more than a thousand years for people to regain the degree of civilization which had been theirs before they gave up education. And what a millennium that had been! During the first five hundred years there was warfare everywhere and nearly all the time; famine, disease, and chronic afflictions flourished; superstition and blind fears were ready to break out in orgies at any time. When we contemplate these obstacles, the work of the monks, for so many centuries the only agency of enlightenment, assumes its truly heroic proportions. It is little wonder that against such a background the advance that they had achieved by the thirteenth century should have won the extravagant acclaim of nearly every historian who has studied this period.

It might be more generous on our part to blame the sufferings our ancestors had to endure during all those centuries upon some outside force rather than upon their voluntary abandonment of education. We might, for example, ascribe all that happened to the overwhelming incursion of barbarous invaders. But we are denied this comfort; for, in less than two centuries while education was still being supported, Rome had transformed the semi-barbarous inhabitants of all Gaul and Spain and adjacent lands into Latin-speaking loyal subjects, leaders of Roman culture in fact. The so-called barbarians with whom Rome dealt in the fifth and sixth centuries were not nearly so numerous as the Gauls and Celt-Iberians had been. Most of them had been in close contact with the Roman Empire since the early fourth century and had lived within the Empire from the early fifth century. During most of this time they were actually in the employ of the Empire and, on the whole, eager and willing to learn its ways.

They respected Roman law and Roman institutions, and this attitude is most fully revealed in the acceptance of the Roman religion by the entering tribes, who had nearly all been previously converted to the Arian doctrine when that was still in free debate. But by the opening of the fifth century Arianism had been outlawed and the Athanasian Creed had become the official and sole religion of the Roman Empire. If the attitude of the "barbarians" toward the Empire and its institutions had been less respectful, this difference in religion might well have aroused genuine hostility against the orthodox Romans. Instead, we find a policy of toleration consistently maintained by the kings even when the imperial policy was one of persecution of Arians. So little, indeed, were these kings inclined to fanatical opposition that they even permitted the orthodox to convert members of their court and royal families, so that by 500 A.D. the orthodox Roman religion enrolled all the Franks and many Burgundians, Visigoths, Vandals, and Ostrogoths also. In view of this favorable attitude of the "barbarian" kings toward Roman law and religion, we might expect a similar attitude toward Roman education. And as a matter of fact there is no evidence of any hostility to education on the part of the "barbarian" kings, who fell more and more, as they lived among the Romans, into the custom of using the Latin tongue and of issuing their royal edicts in that language. Certainly the opportunities for educating these barbarians were vastly superior to those which had existed for the Romans in their dealings with the earlier Gauls, Celt-Iberians, and Britons. That the later groups were not educated must therefore be regarded as due to lack of wish and purpose. In spite of the respectful attitude of the kings in Gaul toward the Roman Empire, its laws, language, religion, and culture, none of these kings was induced to maintain the Roman educational system. And considering the fact that somewhat later, in Italy, Roman nobles at the court of Theodoric the Ostrogoth did awaken to the danger of neglecting the schools and did persuade that king to lend his support to education, the Gallic nobility, Sidonius among them, must be charged with some degree of blame, either for shortsightedness or indifference.

The explanation lies not in any overthrow of the Roman Empire, but in the unconscious abandonment of education.

The situation is almost exactly symbolized by the picture of Sidonius, ex-prefect of Gaul and late in life bishop of Clermont, hearing his son recite his lessons. Sidonius and the others of his class were not opposed to education. They were only opposed to taxation. Though Sidonius firmly believed in academic education and fervently desired its continuance, there is no record of his having taken any practical step either as a courtier with the "barbarians" or as bishop of the Church to ensure this. And if he who so sincerely believed in it did nothing to maintain the educational system, there is little reason to expect his fellows to have done any more. Indeed, there is in all his writings no record that any of his colleagues, either in the civil service or in the episcopal office, ever took any practical step toward this end. They could, or thought they could, provide the necessary education for their own children. Sidonius was the first of his line to have to educate his son himself, however, and when he assumed the task, the end was in sight.

The leaders of the senatorial nobility had taken education for granted. It had not occurred to them that people cannot provide for their own education, cannot in fact even provide for the education of their children except to pay the teachers for the work. The persons who teach children must be of the same generation as the parents and provision for their training must be the task of the grandparents of the pupils. The parents of Sidonius and of the senatorial nobility of his time had failed to make that provision. They had done nothing to train teachers, and as a result, when the son of Sidonius was growing up there were no competent teachers.

I sometimes wonder whether this essential fact of education has been pondered as much as it should be today. How many of our curriculum-makers realize, in their anxiety to acquaint pupils with immediate, current problems, that they are preparing the next generation to deal with their own problems, for which some solution will have been found, but neglecting to prepare it to deal with those of its forebears, which may recur.

It would be strange to think that demands for money to pay teachers and for other needed improvements inclined the nobility of Rome to intrigue for the overthrow of the Ostrogothic administration. If they had hoped thus to avoid taxation, they were soon bitterly disillusioned, for the Greeks to whom Justinian entrusted the administration of Italy proved to be extremely skillful and quite insatiable in their levying of taxes. The Roman nobility turned again to the Ostrogoths, but too late. The devastating wars of the next twenty years made education of any formal kind impossible for most of Italy. It is all the more remarkable that

# A Society without Education

Cassiodorus persisted in his concern about education despite discouragement from members of his own class and despite the ravages of war. That he lived to accomplish what he did was, in the light of later events, hardly less than providential.

Such is the story of the world's greatest educational experiment. As an experiment it was not perfect because, owing to the efforts of Cassiodorus and the Irish missionaries, it was not quite complete. But had the experimental conditions been more nearly perfect, perhaps neither you nor I would know about what happened —or care.

# 2

## The Return to Law: The International State of the Middle Ages

So MUCH has been said during the last few years about an international organization which shall bring peace and order to the people of the world and so little about previous efforts of society to achieve the same result that it seems not inappropriate to sketch again the outlines of one of the most successful of those attempts.

It might appear rather rash, certainly visionary, to propose that the United Nations be empowered not only to administer territories gained by joint conquest, but also to recruit armies and levy taxes directly from the people, without the intermediation of national governments; to act as a supreme court, with original jurisdiction in cases arising between nations or against rulers of nations and with appellate jurisdiction in all cases whether of nations or individuals; and to execute its judgments whether against individuals or against states, even to the extent of making war upon an obstinate state. That would seem a very dangerous array of powers indeed, and yet this is but a sober summary of

NOTE: This essay is an amalgamation of materials from two separate papers: "The International State of the Middle Ages and Some Reasons for Its Downfall," first published in *The American Historical Review*, October 1922; and "Can Law Supplant Force in International Affairs?" which was first published in *The Pacific Spectator*, Winter 1947.

the powers actually exercised by such an international authority through nearly two centuries of medieval history.

The road to this achievement began at the opening of the tenth century in southern and southeastern France, in a joint effort of churchmen and laymen, society in short, to re-establish peace and decency out of the chaos into which Europe had been thrown by a series of devastating wars.

The empire of Charlemagne had included most of western Europe, but the quarrels among his grandsons and great-grandsons had broken that empire to pieces. The turmoil of their rivalry had been made more chaotic still by the raids of the Vikings on the west, the Moslems from the south, and the Hungarians from the east. And under the cover of local defense, which these calamities had necessitated, had arisen a menace of indiscriminate and almost universal private warfare which continued after the external danger had subsided.

Almost all the restraints of orderly society were destroyed. Rule was wholly by force; there was no longer any appeal to law. Some 80 per cent of the people got such living as they could from agriculture and the rest of the population were either warriors (about 19 per cent) or clergymen (1 per cent or less). Only the clergy made any pretense to literacy; the 99 per cent could neither read nor write. Each little landlocked community looked after itself, never knowing when some band of raiders would come over the hill or water from north or south or east or west to steal their crops and herds, violate their women, and kill their men.

There was no recognized ruler. Each generation had to determine its leaders from among its warriors, and this was done as much by fighting each other as by resisting raiders from the neighboring locality. Warfare was hand to hand with sword and battle-ax, spear and lance. Those who could get them had helmets and armor for protection as well as shields, and in larger neighborhoods they built heaps of heavy masonry within which to hold out against superior numbers of raiders. Those stone piles are not the romantic castles of the thirteenth century that we read about in our childhood. These fortresses of the earlier, iron age of feudalism were gloomy piles without windows, only narrow slits through which arrows might be shot, and with parapets at the top from which heavy stones and other missiles could be hurled at the attackers below. Fighting was continuous, and every warrior was expected to engage in at least one campaign against neighboring fighters every year, and usually got some practice in battling with his fellows also. There was no respect for private property. The warriors took what they needed or wanted. The diet of most persons was little above the starvation level most of the time, and since each neighborhood was chronically at war with every other neighborhood that touched it there was no commerce. The sword and battle-ax were the chief, almost the only, medium of exchange in all transactions whether of land, possessions, family relations, or personal grievances. No records were kept. Any help that experience might give was confined to the oral transmission between three generations, grandparents to grandchildren at the most. The task of mere survival under such conditions took up all the time and energy anyone could muster.

Luchaire, who probably knew the history of France during these centuries more thoroughly than any other scholar, summed up the condition of the times thus: "The living reality as it stands forth from the chronicles and documents of the time shows that brute force dominated everything. The feudal obligations were performed, the feudal contracts were respected, the feudal customs were observed, only when the suzerain was powerful enough to compel obedience. The bond of vassalage became weaker as the noble rose in the hierarchy. But at the bottom as at the top, it was ceaselessly broken, and good faith was constantly violated by vassal and lord alike. The ineradicable habits of a military people, the instinctive hatred of the neighbor, the conflict of rights which were ill-defined and of interests which were poorly adjusted, caused perpetual struggles. There was no feudatory who was not at loggerheads with his different suzerains, with the bishop and abbots of the country around, with his peers, and with his vassals. War raged not only between the possessors of the fiefs but in the bosom of the family. Quarrels between relatives over inheritance heaped up the measure of strife." [1]

There is no reason to suppose that such conditions were not as deeply resented by our ancestors as they would be by ourselves. The sense of outraged humanity must have been just as prevalent then as now, but the great majority of people doubtless felt utterly helpless to correct it. There were others, however, less numerous but more fervent and less docile, who were determined to correct the situation. These, we may be certain, appeared among both the nobility and the peasantry. But what could they do?

They could expect no help from the papacy, for the papacy was submerged in the mire of Roman party strife, nor from other secular clergy, most of whom were similarly mired in the welter of feudal competition. Nor could they look for any help from kings whose power did not extend beyond their petty feudal domains. Their chief hope must rest in themselves, in their local cooperation, their own activity as a self-determining society.

Fortunately nearly all of western Europe by this time had been converted to Christianity, a religion which had come to them from ancient Rome and in the Latin language. The belief in the immortality of the soul and the idea that life on earth was a preparation for eternity were generally accepted. In moments when there was no fighting this belief was widely remembered, and in times of illness even the most truculent warrior thought of it. Hence unarmed clergy, especially if they had no property, enjoyed a certain measure of immunity from the armed violence and could move about unmolested. It was, therefore, by joining this profession that the determined humanitarian could best hope to improve the lot of his fellow man.

Records show that both nobles and peasants entered upon the monastic career. The immunity from the operation of brute force which their unselfish and propertyless state accorded them gave them the opportunity to study and to learn that there had been a time when disputes were settled by law instead of force and bloodshed. It also enabled them to wander beyond the confines of the locality and to communicate with other members of the clergy, both monastic and secular, who shared their feelings and their knowledge.

Relatively few persons in Europe knew in 980 A.D. that a gathering of churchmen at Charroux in southeastern France had passed a resolution condemning to eternal damnation those who "broke into churches, did violence to churchmen or stole the possessions of the poor." This was known as the "Peace of God." Under the conditions of the time this enactment represented real courage on the part of the participating clergy. More startling is the fact that another Church council less than thirty years later enacted a resolution proclaiming the period from Saturday noon until Monday morning as sacred from the profanation of private warfare. This was known as the "Truce of God." Both enactments were extremely modest and were obviously intended to permit people to engage in the practice of their religion. Yet both represented a real encroachment upon the unrestrained profession of arms. Thus were born these two institutions, the Peace of God and the Truce of God, which were to be promulgated in ever widening circles and with expanded force for the next three centuries.

The complete story of the regeneration of orderly society out of this chaos of brute force would be too long to tell here, but its main outlines can be quite fully illustrated in the story of one institution, the monastery of Cluny in eastern France. This monastery was founded in the year 910 by the joint efforts of William, duke of Aquitaine, and a Benedictine monk very much concerned about the disordered state of society. William, who had won and held his position through his fighting ability, may have become acquainted with this high-minded monk during a period of illness and been so impressed with his sincerity and integrity that he decided to grant him an outlying piece of land on which the monk and other like-minded men might carry on their work for the benefit of society.

The deed to this land itself is interesting for it shows that William well understood the conditions of the time. He threatened

not only with eternal damnation but with his own physical pun-
ishment anyone "whether noble, bishop, king or pope" who might
dare to violate the peaceful life of these monks. The community
was to be exempt from the jurisdiction of the local bishop and
count, be subject only to the head of the Church, and be free of
all secular interference. William himself lived eight years longer,
and during that time saw the monastery well founded. It lived
up to the rule of St. Benedict on the highest plane of its founders'
intentions and the younger men who joined the community were
so well trained that they were able, as called upon, to teach its
ideals to others.

As nearby regions became aware of the high order of life and
service practiced by these monks, they sought to have similar
communities in their own neighborhoods and therefore petitioned
to have either the abbot or one of his monks establish or reform
an existing monastery on the same basis. This quickly became a
fashion, and the monastery at Cluny soon found itself the head
of a series of monasteries which became known as the Congregation of Cluny. The story of each of these foundations or affilia-
tions was almost always the same. One of the greater nobles lent
his support to the movement, invited the monks to his territory,
and supported them in their good work against any encroach-
ments. The mother monastery of Cluny maintained a supervisory
control over these subsidiary houses either through annual visits
of the abbot or by the appointment of priors trained in the mother
house; usually both.

The rapid growth and spread of the Congregation of Cluny is
well illustrated by the fact that when William the Conqueror
asked for monks of Cluny to establish branch houses in England
the abbot was forced to reply that he could not immediately com-
ply with the request because all his trained monks were already
out on similar missions elsewhere. By the year 1000 A.D. the Congregation of Cluny had spread to northern France and southern
Germany, throughout southern France, and into Spain and northern Italy. The travel necessary to keep these communities in touch

with each other also kept the officials of Cluny in touch with more secular society, especially with bishop, nobles, and townspeople.

Perhaps the most striking feature of the monastery of Cluny was its ability to maintain its original ideals consistently for more than two centuries and to impart them to its subsidiary houses. History records few instances in which institutions, religious or secular, have been able to maintain their initial ideals so long beyond the lifetime of their founders.

Part of Cluny's success was undoubtedly due to a policy adopted shortly after the death of the first abbot. It became the regular practice of the monks to choose one of the younger monks as successor to the deceased abbot. As a young man he would naturally rely upon the advice of the elder brethren in his management of affairs and would thus continue to learn wisdom in administration so that when the last of the elder brethren had died he would be able to continue with all that acquired wisdom. Thus from 927, when the first abbot died, until 1109, when Abbot Hugh died, there had been really just four abbots. It was this practice that permitted Cluny to maintain a consistent policy throughout the two centuries and to act as the sustaining nucleus of persistent humanitarianism in European society.

Naturally, the monastery and Congregation of Cluny attracted to its membership an unusually large proportion of persons anxious to improve the disturbed conditions of society. Its members were called upon not only to establish new monasteries and reform old ones but also to serve as bishops, archbishops, and finally as popes. There were men of Cluny present at Charroux where the Peace of God was first proclaimed and also at the council which proclaimed the Truce of God. And we can be quite certain that they were instrumental in spreading these ideas to all the regions in which the Congregation of Cluny was found. Their advice was sought by both the king of France and the emperor of the Holy Roman Empire; and surely with their approval if not at their urging, the emperor, Henry II, before the middle of the eleventh century required all newly made knights not only to swear loyalty to their feudal lords but also to take an oath to support the Peace and Truce of God. This combination marks the beginning of the code of chivalry.

It has usually been assumed that the Peace and Truce of God were not enforced and that the tortures of the damned were too remote to deter the easily aroused passion for private and neighborhood warfare. That they were repeatedly violated cannot be denied, but possibly some historians like Gibbon and Bury have judged too hastily from the violations. Other historians, notably Maitland, perhaps the greatest of English legal historians, goes so far as to deem them the most important preliminary to the development of modern criminal law. Maitland's view is cordially supported by Luchaire and Haskins, the greatest medievalists of France and the United States respectively.

There was scarcely a Church council of any consequence during the eleventh century which did not re-enact the Peace and Truce of God, and these re-enactments usually involved expansion of the original provisions. Thus in 1095, at the Council of Clermont, it was proclaimed that "every man above the age of twelve, whether noble, burgess, villein, or serf, was required to take the oath of adherence to the Truce of God every three years." And the Peace of God was extended until in the thirteenth century it exempted from the ravages of private and neighborhood warfare "all church buildings and their environs, all clergy, merchants, women, and peasants as well as orchards, seeds, cattle, and agricultural implements." The Truce of God was extended sometimes to periods of several months and regularly included all days from Thursday noon until Monday morning, all festival days, and certain special occasions—which left, all told, less than a fourth of the year to the unabated practice of private warfare.

The enforcement of these two institutions was not limited to this series of spiritual injunctions alone. Their champions, even the purely ecclesiastical, like the monks of Cluny, showed an astonishing amount of practical wisdom. It was early discovered that the vast majority of violations arose from the material ambitions of petty knights and vassals. The greater lords had less to gain and more to lose by the incessant practice of violence. At least they could afford to scorn the temptation to pillage mere peasants, small merchants, and priests. Their own dangers came chiefly from their lesser vassals, who did yield only too frequently to such petty temptations. This cleavage among the promoters of private warfare was easily seized upon and the greater lords, especially the kings, were invited to lend their material support to the measure.

What a boon it was to them! To have the noncombatant productive population thus welded together in the support of the Peace and the Truce of God would furnish them an anvil upon which they could hammer the flaming ambitions of their troublesome vassals into some degree of obedience. Some of the great nobles saw the light very quickly, others were helped to it by the sage counsel of the abbot of Cluny or other churchmen. The pious monarchs Robert of France and Henry II of Germany were able to recommend the measure most heartily, and soon other nobles took up the idea and lent their endorsement to the proclamations. Then the hotheaded vassal who so far forgot himself as to risk the remote danger of eternal damnation was likely to cool off somewhat at the prospect of an immediate foretaste from his overlord.

Few persons, I presume, would seriously urge that the Crusades were instituted as a war to end war, as a means to universal peace, at least among Christian peoples. And yet that thought was certainly a factor in the First Crusade. We must remember that the Council of Clermont at which the First Crusade was preached in 1095 was called by Pope Urban II, a monk of Cluny, and Urban had an extended visit with his old mentor, the abbot of Cluny, before the meeting of the Council nearby. All the reports of Urban's speech at the Council that have come down to us emphasize his lament at the spectacle of Christians shedding Christian blood, thus endangering their own salvation. Out of it grew the slogan "If you must fight, go fight the Infidel," which proved a powerful deterrent to private warfare and was so used throughout the next two centuries. King and noble and commoner alike were compelled to stay their violence against the possessions or families of those who had marked themselves with the cross.

The tremendous response to Urban's appeal for the crusade is in itself a tribute to the success of the campaign for the Peace and the Truce of God. Those measures had been so successful in curbing private warfare that they had created a condition we would now call "technological unemployment." The warriors, trained only for warfare and finding that the clergy with the help of the greater nobility had limited their opportunity for practicing this profession, welcomed the new opportunity afforded by the crusade and for the next two hundred years crusading drained off much of the surplus fighting energy from Europe.

The progressively successful campaign for the Peace and Truce of God transformed western Europe. Farmers could once more count on harvesting their crops. Their surplus could be traded, and merchants could again travel the highways. Money supplanted the sword as the medium of exchange. Trades developed to supply the farmer with many articles that he hitherto had had to make for himself, leaving him free to plant and harvest larger and larger crops. Towns grew up or grew bigger. Schools were again established and the proportion of literate and educated people gradually increased. While education was still solely a function of the Church and all students were considered prospective churchmen, as the term *cleric* still implies, many new learned professions were created, and these afforded opportunities for men who would otherwise have been limited to the profession of arms.

It was in the solution of disputes, however, that the most remarkable advance was made. Canon law had never wholly disappeared during this period. It showed the way to a peaceable settlement of conflicts, and as neighborhood warfare was progressively curbed the saving provision in canon law that permitted recourse to the Roman civil law helped to deal with the types of disputes thus salvaged from private violence.

The study of Roman civil law, thus resumed, was enormously promoted as a result of the Crusades. As men signed themselves with the cross to go on the crusade or took up the pilgrim staves to follow in the wake of the crusaders, the Church assumed guardianship of their families and property, and disputes arising about either had to be settled by Church courts and according to Church law. Consequently, as a result of the First Crusade archbishop and bishop found themselves overwhelmed by the additional judicial business and many of them sent their archdeacons to Bologna where the "new" law (i.e., the old Roman civil law) was taught. These archdeacons, trained in law, returned to their episcopal courts and managed the new judicial business so well that many who were neither crusaders nor pilgrims came to prefer to submit their disputes to the bishop's courts rather than settle them on the battlefield.

It was not long after this that the shrewder kings like Henry II of England and Frederick Barbarossa discovered the advantages of court solutions of disputes about lands, property, and person. Both these monarchs and other kings after them took into their employ churchmen trained in the law schools of the Church, first as prime ministers and finally in many other administrative positions as well. The profession of law was thus reborn and its modern birth may be dated about the middle of the twelfth century. The ecclesiastical origin of the profession is still reflected in the robes worn by the judiciary.

For another century and a half it looked as though law might be completely substituted for force in the solution of disputes between individuals and even between nations. By the time of Innocent III the Church with the papacy at its head had become an international state. It had everything a state has—and more. It could raise funds by direct taxation and raise armies equally directly. It controlled education, controlled the agencies of publicity, and controlled the courts. It applied its laws equally to peasant and king and it executed judgments against both. The social cares of charity and public health were in its hands. And on top of all this, it wielded the awful power of eternal life or death. It now could prevent not only nobles but kings from making war upon each other and it did so.

The advance to this point had been accompanied by constant

struggles and setbacks, but in practically every conflict the papacy appeared as the champion of the common needs and desires of society against the selfish interests of individuals or groups. The popes displayed a willingness to undergo discomforts and dangers in upholding the justice of their cause, and society rewarded them by ever increased confidence and delegations of power. Never before or since in history have the moral forces of so vast a society been so thoroughly concentrated and so effective.

For a century after Innocent III his successors maintained the papacy at this height of effective international power. Then the beginnings of the decline became noticeable. The causes for the collapse have often been studied and chief among them, it is generally agreed, was the rise of the national states. That is another story, but it is pertinent here to mark the fact that these new units of power disrupted the international state of the Middle Ages, not because they functioned as political organizations—Innocent III had clearly shown that the papacy had ample resources to cope with such organizations—but because the national state built up a moral force opposed to the papacy.

Now that six centuries have convinced society that unrestrained national warfare is just as devastating and destructive and scarcely less direct than the neighborhood warfare of feudal times, we are again groping toward some form of international control. And this parallel from history suggests that we need not be too despondent about the possibility of substituting law for force in the settlement of disputes between nations. The League of Nations and the United Nations are not nearly so fantastic as the Peace and the Truce of God must have seemed when they were proclaimed. This story from the past would seem to suggest that to ensure the prospect of enduring peace the United Nations must rally as much of the moral and humanitarian force of the world as came eventually to support those two medieval institutions.

### NOTES

[1] A. Luchaire, "The Realities of Feudalism," translated in D. C. Munro and G. C. Sellery, *Medieval Civilization*, pp. 173–74 (New York: The Century Co., 1910).

# 3

# The Rebirth of the Medical Profession

I MUST at once disclaim any technical knowledge of either medicine or surgery. My interest in this subject is that of a historian whose yearly task it is, figuratively, to patrol the history of western Europe from 300 to 1600 A.D. watching all the activities of society, of which the practice of medicine is not the least important.

At the beginning of my chronological journey the medical profession is one of great dignity and honor. It is possessed of a vast literature accumulated during an unbroken continuity of more than a thousand years, perhaps even several millenniums. Hippocrates, who was born about 460 B.C., had many antecedent writings to help him, and Galen, who died in 201 A.D., more than 600 years later, left voluminous works drawn from vast reading as well as his own observation. Dioscorides, who in the first century A.D. had assembled all previous knowledge of plant, animal, and mineral medicines, had already become the standard authority in pharmacology. These works on medicine were supplemented by the scientific writings of such scholars as Aristotle, Pliny, and Ptolemy.

I have mentioned only the most distinguished authors, whose

NOTE: This essay was published, in slightly different form, in *Surgery* for February 1955 under the title, "Medicine and Surgery A.D. 600–1600: the Rebirth of the Medical Profession in Western Europe."

works though voluminous were only a part of the accumulated literature on these subjects. All this was available throughout the Roman world in 300 A.D. and there were distinguished teachers and flourishing medical schools in various parts of the Empire. By 600 A.D. however, there was no medical profession in western Europe. Why?

The Roman Empire, which had included nearly the whole of the civilized Western world for many centuries, had begun to decline in power. It had failed to solve the problem of peaceful succession in the imperial office, leaving the way open for ambitious individuals to intrigue or fight for it, and invariably it was the person who could control the military of the Empire that won out. Unfortunately the Empire had adopted a dangerous military policy of relying chiefly upon mercenaries drawn from the barbarian tribes on its borders. In the course of time even the commanders of the army were drawn from these tribes. And the Roman Empire seems to have made little effort to civilize, or rather Romanize, these barbarians even after they were enlisted in the army. Since service in the army was a lifetime profession they were trained only as soldiers, a purely physical occupation. Their incentive to service was pay, not patriotism—pay and power.

Another unfortunate development arose from the imperial adoption of Christianity as a state religion, for the emperors lent their support to uniformity of doctrine and outlawed those who were declared heterodox or heretical. In the great division of opinion over the nature of the Trinity, the Arians were declared heterodox and were persecuted. Many of these Arians sought refuge among the barbarian tribes, whom they converted to their form of Christianity. This led to the anomalous situation that the soldiers upon whom the Empire depended were legally outlaws.

In the contact between these Arian troops and the more numerous orthodox Christians of the Empire the Arians were gradually being converted and would in the course of time all have been won, as happened in Spain. But the emperor, Justinian, who fancied himself as a theologian, became impatient and thought to speed up the conversion by embarking upon a series of ruinous wars in northwest Africa, Italy, and part of Spain. These wars dragged on for over twenty years, with the result that the West was alienated from the East, and that the Roman Empire, which had been centered at Constantinople ever since the time of Constantine, was barely strong enough to hold its own in a suicidal war with Persia. This war, ending in 628, left the contestants so thoroughly weakened that they fell easy prey to the new Arab empire just started by Mohammed.

Life in western Europe, now left to itself, rapidly degenerated under a semibarbaric military caste whose every captain sought to make himself autonomous ruler of his immediate neighborhood. These rulers had no tradition of learning. They regarded hand-to-hand warfare as the only honorable occupation for a freeman and consequently physical training for that occupation was the only form of education they supported. They maintained no schools as the civil government of the Roman Empire had done. Formal education ceased.

There is no evidence of hostility to the profession of medicine on the part of these rulers, nor of any deliberate effort to destroy the vast literature in which the accumulated medical knowledge was preserved. But by 600 A.D. practically no layman could read those books. Thus without conscious intent on anyone's part, the medical profession as a learned profession was dead in western Europe.

Its demise occurred within the span of the period from 525 to 600 A.D. There were still laymen, especially in Italy, as late as 525 A.D. who were sufficiently educated to read and understand the medical literature. By 600 A.D. there were practically none.

It is from this point that I begin my story of the thousand years it took to revive medicine as a learned profession. In attempting to cover so vast a sweep of time in these few pages, I shall be forced to make rather wide-reaching generalizations, which I would qualify were there more space. The general impressions, however, I believe to be sound.

The one bright ray of hope for the ultimate revival of the medical profession came from the fact that so large a portion of the people of western Europe had been won to at least a nominal acceptance of Christianity. The language of Western Christianity was Latin, and the Bible, the service books, and the commentaries by the great Church fathers were all written in that language. The Church officials therefore had to take over the task of educating their priests sufficiently to be able to carry on the services. This involved some attention to elementary instruction in the seven liberal arts, which had formerly been provided by the State.

The secular clergy, bishop and priests, who were engaged in the practice of their profession had little time to spare for teaching, especially in such turbulent times. Fortunately, however, St. Benedict of Monte Cassino had devised a rule for the government of communities of deeply devout Christians which permitted survival even under the worst conditions, and these communities afforded sheltered spots in which education was still possible.

These two providential accidents, that the language of Christianity was Latin and that Benedictine monasticism was already founded before 600 A.D. are of vital importance to our story.

Let us now look at the status of medicine in the West at this time. There was no organized profession of medicine. There were no medical schools. The books were still there but the only persons who could read them were the clergy, and their intellectual interests were directed toward theology. But people still suffered illness and needed help.

Gregory the Great, unquestionably the most highly educated man in Italy at this time, was elected pope in the midst of an epidemic which had carried off his predecessor. Almost his first act was to order the people to repair to the churches to pray for divine intervention and the faithful to march in religious procession to the various shrines in the city. Many persons fell dead along the line of march or in the churches but the plague shortly abated and the people were convinced that their prayers had been answered. Many of the miracles recounted by Gregory in his *Dialogues on Italian Saints* were concerned with healing, and many visitors to the papal court were favored by him with presents of precious relics of Roman saints and martyrs to be carried back to their own churches, presumably there to perform miracles of healing.

Gregory, bishop of Tours, probably the most learned man in all Gaul, has left an account of a personal experience. He had suffered a severe toothache and appealed to two physicians for help without avail. Finally he went to the tomb of St. Martin, scraped some of the dust from the top of it and applied this to his tooth—and gained almost immediate relief.

Isidore of Seville, the most learned man in Spain, included a brief section on medicine in his *Etymologiae*, which served as the standard encyclopedia for western Europe for many centuries. In this section he poses the question why medicine is not included among the liberal arts and answers it by saying that "the liberal disciplines embrace separate subjects whereas medicine embraces all. He, the physician, must know grammar . . . rhetoric . . . logic . . . arithmetic . . . geometry . . . music [here he cites David's cure of Saul from an unclean spirit and "Ascalepiades'" cure of one subject to frenzy] and astronomy . . . because our bodies change, too, along with the qualities of the heavens." Hence "medicine is called a second philosophy for as the soul is cured by the first [theology] so is the body by the other, for both disciplines claim the whole man." [1]

That is certainly a high tribute to the profession, but in Isidore's day it was merely a reminiscence and many centuries were to pass before it again became a fact. But his statement helped to keep alive a pleasant memory and a hope.

For a century and a half after 600 A.D. conditions went from bad to worse. Then for a century there was an upswing, thanks to the fact that the Carolingian line produced four strong rulers in succession who not only brought peace and security to Frankland but extended their Empire north and east and south. Many monasteries sprang up and learning was again encouraged. The greatest of this line, Charlemagne, even encouraged the laity to take up learning. Physicians are again mentioned. For instance, Einhard, Charlemagne's secretary and biographer, records that in later life Charlemagne came to hate his physicians because they insisted that he eat boiled meat rather than roasted, which he much preferred. Who these physicians were and how they were trained is not explained.

But this Carolingian Empire afforded only a brief interlude. Charlemagne's descendants lacked the strength of their forebears, and his grandsons engaged in unholy civil wars, first against their father and then against each other. The military caste took advantage of this turmoil to gain local independence. The resultant political disintegration was made more chaotic by the Viking invasions, which affected all of western Europe along the seaboard. Moslem pirates from Africa raided Italy and southern France. A new Asiatic migration of Hungarians moved up the Danube valley and Slavs pressed in from the northeast. Heathens all, they found the churches and monasteries especially attractive prey, beacon lights pointing to the richest plunder, and thus destroyed much of the civilization built up by the Carolingian Empire. The British Isles were hardest hit but only a little more than western France, Italy, and eastern Germany.

Thus was inaugurated the iron age of feudalism, which lasted for nearly two centuries, from 850 to about 1050. Such medicine as was practiced was strictly of the homemade variety—obstetrics and pediatrics being the concern of the older women, the wise women of the neighborhood, and surgery done by the man in the community most skillful with a knife. We get some notion of what this medicine was like from that curious volume in the English *Rolls Series* entitled "Leechdoms, Wortcunning, and Starcraft of Early England"—"wort," of course, being the Anglo-Saxon term for roots and including herbs or "yarbs."

A few rays of light began to appear in this darkest part of the Middle Ages toward the second half of the tenth century. A strong line of rulers in German Saxony then brought peace to a considerable portion of Europe, and the Vikings, now settled down, had been converted to the Christian religion and promised soon to become zealous protectors rather than destroyers of civilization. Church councils enacted and gradually found ways to enforce the Peace and the Truce of God so as to curb the incessant private warfare that was the major curse of the age. Monasteries were reformed and sought to maintain their standards by some degree of affiliation in clusters like the Congregation of Cluny.

There was even progress in the study of medicine. The rule of St. Benedict required its followers to take care of the sick, but usually this involved only the monastic community and its immediate neighborhood because each monastery was a purely local institution. The monks supplemented their spiritual therapy with such material remedies as they could discover, and most of them cultivated medicinal plants and even acquired books on healing where possible.

One such instance is recorded by the monk, Richer of Rheims, in the year 991. Heribrand, a member of the cathedral chapter of Chartres, had acquired a copy of the *Aphorisms* of Hippocrates, which he invited Richer to come and read with him. The journey, which would require little more than two hours by auto today, took Richer three harrowing days to make, so bad were the conditions of roads at the time. Arrived at Chartres, to quote him, "I entered diligently into the study of the Aphorisms of Hippocrates with my master Heribrand, a man of much culture and learning. But in this work I learn only the ordinary symptoms of diseases and such knowledge of ailments not being sufficient for my desires, I begged him to read with me the book on the concord of Hippocrates, Galen and Suranus. He granted my request for he was a very skillful man in his art and well acquainted with pharmaceutics, botany and surgery." [2]

Think of one book—a very little one at that—combining the lore of Hippocrates, Galen, and Suranus! Even the *Aphorisms* which he had read with Heribrand was only an epitome. But the episode does indicate some progress.

These fingers of light fused together into full dawn when the reformed monks and clergy regained control of the papal office and thus ensured unified leadership over the whole of Latin Christendom, as they did about 1050. This drive for reform which had started north of the Alps had acquired terrific momentum.

# The Rebirth of the Medical Profession

The local variations in the conduct of church services and practices which had developed under feudalism were being eliminated and the idea of one unified and uniform Church under the firm headship of the pope at Rome had become the battle cry of the reform party.

In southern Italy this party encountered some communities of Greek Christians who regarded Constantinople as their center. The centuries of separation had resulted in the development of important differences between the Greek and Latin Christendom, and it was only logical that the reform party, which had ironed out so many local variations in the West, should undertake to eliminate these differences also. Negotiations were undertaken with Constantinople, looking toward the unification of all Christendom under the Roman papacy. Though the Greeks were not at all willing to accept the headship of the pope, the rising power of the Seljukian Turks led them to court the assistance of the West. This was granted in 1095 when Pope Urban II launched the First Crusade for the rescue of the Christian churches in the East from the hand of the Infidel.

Thus intimate contact between East and West, which had been broken in the sixth century, was to be effectively re-established in the twelfth century. And it would be hard to overestimate the importance of this resumption of connections with the East.

The knowledge of medicine had never sunk so low in the East during these centuries as it had in western Europe. Constantinople survived successive attacks by the Arabs and preserved its libraries, and the Greeks who peopled it had a high regard for learning, which was resumed when conditions permitted. So too did the Nestorian Christians and the Jews of Syria. Even the Arabs, though they lacked the tradition of scholarship, were an able people whose ancestors had lived on the edge of all the great civilizations of antiquity, and they respected erudition. Once firmly in control of a vast empire, the Moslems supported learning, and the great caliphs, including Haroun-al-Raschid, had camel caravans laden with Greek and Latin books brought to Baghdad, where they engaged Nestorians and Jews to translate these works into Arabic. Great schools arose at Baghdad, at Cairo, and finally at Cordova in Spain.

Next to the Koran, medicine was a favorite subject of advanced study in these schools, for the lusty, pleasure-loving Arab rulers were most anxious to prolong their enjoyment of life as much as possible and the advance of medical knowledge seemed to be the surest means to that goal. The Arabs not only helped to preserve the ancient knowledge of medicine but seem to have made important additions to it.

What resumption of contact with this East might mean for the West had already been foreshadowed by what happened in Salerno, the Italian town famous for its healing waters. The improvement in the condition of Western society, the lessening of neighborhood warfare, the increase in trade, the return to a money economy, all made possible wider and more frequent travel. The Normans, hybrid descendants of the Northmen, seemed to have inherited all the vigor of their Viking forebears. Having adopted Christianity, they added to their natural urge for travel the additional impulse of pious pilgrimage to the Holy Land. Thus they became acquainted with southern Italy, of which they soon made themselves masters.

The population over which they ruled was highly heterogeneous, including Greeks, Jews, and even Moslems as well as Latins. Being practical-minded they developed a policy of tolerance toward all these subjects, and Salerno, which lay within their territory, again became a health resort for those who could afford it. Some brought doctors with them, and these doctors, along with their apprentices, exchanged information, so that there grew up in Salerno in the eleventh century an informal school of medicine.

The Normans soon came to realize that educated physicians could be more helpful than the uneducated, and they passed this word along to their relatives in France and England, with whom they had kept in touch. Thus Robert of Normandy, eldest son of William the Conqueror, repaired to Salerno to be cured of a troublesome wound incurred on the First Crusade.

Montpellier in southern France had a similar though less spec-

## The Rebirth of the Medical Profession

tacular development. There too the rulers practiced tolerance, and learned doctors of Jewish or Arab background became the nucleus around which a medical school grew up. Both Salerno and Montpellier had become centers for the study as well as the practice of medicine by the opening of the twelfth century.

The astounding success of the First Crusade in its capture of Edessa, Antioch, and Jerusalem and the establishment of the Latin states of Syria won all Latin Christendom to acceptance of the leadership of the Church. Crusaders, pilgrims, and merchants could now travel in relative safety from the most remote parts of the West to the Holy Land and did so. With all this came a tremendous quickening of the peaceful activities of society—agriculture, commerce, industry, building—which Dean C. H. Haskins of Harvard called a renaissance. The Church, which had done so much to cut down the amount of neighborhood warfare, now did as much to substitute law for force in the settlement of disputes. More men of learning were required to man the courts, and schools became crowded with students, not all of whom intended to join the clergy. Some, after taking instruction in the liberal arts, went off to Bologna to study law, while still others went to Salerno or Montpellier to study medicine. Kings, princes, prelates, and even towns bid for the services of educated physicians, and Jewish doctors were to be found at many of the courts. Physicians became quite numerous by the middle of the century, and in some places, Florence for one, they organized themselves in guilds. And so there was again an organized medical profession in western Europe.

The quality of the medicine they practiced, however, left much to be desired even in such favored regions as the Holy Land, where there was contact with the best of Eastern medicine. We have the following description of practice there in the second half of the twelfth century from two scholars, one an Arab, the other a Latin archbishop. The Arab scholar, Usamah, whose uncle was ruler of Shaizar, tells of a Latin noble who sent a request to this uncle for a physician.

"My uncle sent him a Christian physician named Thabit. Thabit was absent but ten days. So we said to him 'How quickly hast thou healed thy patients!' He said, 'They brought before me a knight in whose leg an abscess had grown and then a woman afflicted with imbecility. To the knight I applied a small poultice until the abscess opened and became well; and the woman I put on a diet and made her humor wet. Then a Frankish physician came to them, and said "This man knows nothing about treating them." He said to the knight "Which wouldst thou prefer, living with one leg or dying with two?" The latter replied "Living with one leg." The physician said bring me a strong knight and a sharp axe. A knight came with the axe. And I was standing by. Then the physician laid the leg of the patient on a block of wood and bade the knight strike his leg with the axe and chop it off with one blow. Accordingly he struck it—while I was looking on, but the leg was not severed. He dealt another blow, upon which the marrow flowed out and the patient died on the spot. He then examined the woman and said "This is a woman in whose head there is a devil which has possessed her. Shave off her hair"—Her imbecility took a turn for the worse. The physician then said "The devil has penetrated through her head." He therefore took a sharp razor, made a deep cruciform incision in it, pulled off the skin at the middle of the incision until the bone of the skull was exposed and rubbed it with salt. The woman also expired instantly.' "

Usamah was willing to praise Western medicine when he could, as he did in the case of a man who had an infection develop in a leg wound. This infection opened in fourteen places and every time one closed another would open. "A Frankish physician . . . removed all the ointments which were on the leg and began to wash it with very strong vinegar. By this treatment all the cuts were healed and the man became well again. He was up again like a devil." [3]

The Latin scholar, William, archbishop of Tyre, makes these telling comments on the relative merits of Eastern and Latin medicine.

Writing of Baldwin III, king of Jerusalem, he says: "Desiring to take a physic before the approach of winter, as was his custom, he obtained certain pills from Barac, the physician of the count [of Tripoli], a part of which were to be taken at once and the rest after a short interval. For our Eastern princes, through the influence of their women, scorn the medicines and practices of our Latin physicians and believe only in the Jews, Samaritans, Syrians and Saracens. Most recklessly they put themselves under the care of such practitioners and trust their lives to people who are ignorant of the science of medicine. It was rumored that these pills were poisoned [they tried the rest of the medicine on a dog who died within a few days]. As soon as the king had taken the pills he was seized with a fever and dysentery which developed into consumption from which he never recovered."

King Baldwin was succeeded on the throne by his brother Amaury. "Amaury suffered a severe attack of dysentery—and a violent fever came on, although the dysentery yielded to the physician's skill. After suffering intolerably from the fever for several days he ordered physicians of Greek, Syrian and other nations noted for skill in diseases to be called and insisted that they give him some purgative remedy. As they would not consent to this he had Latin physicians called and made the same request of them adding that whatever the result might be he would take the responsibility upon himself." [4] He did. He died.

While these quotations indicate that medical knowledge was still far from what it had been in ancient Roman days, they do reveal the presence of a recognized profession, and this was a real gain.

By the end of the twelfth century and the beginning of the thirteenth, so many students had congregated at certain centers, notably Paris and Bologna, that it was necessary to organize higher education at these places apart from monasteries and bishoprics. Thus universities came into being and within them appeared four faculties, arts and theology but also law and medicine. Montpellier, which already had a medical school, added the other faculties and became a university. Padua soon became a university. Salerno never did, its medical school being absorbed by the University of Naples.

All these schools were educating physicians, but the supply was still lagging far behind the demand and this afforded extraordinary opportunities for charlatans, quacks, and impostors of all kinds. Snake oil and cure-all vendors were to be found at the fairs and market places and roundabout in the towns. Fraud appeared also in the field of supernatural healing. Possession of the Holy Land provided a rich field for the acquisition of sacred relics and these became an important and profitable article of commerce. Pilgrim travel went not only to the Holy Land but also to famous shrines such as Rome, Compostella, and the tomb of Thomas à Becket at Canterbury. These pious pilgrims in quest of health or the easing of their consciences were favorite prey for vendors of fraudulent relics. Glib impostors sold rusty nails, splinters of wood, and bones of doubtful origin to the credulous along the pilgrim highways. Church councils sought to check the fraud by requiring authentication of the relics.

The problems of the medical profession were more complex. As early as 1140 the ruler of the two Sicilies, in which Salerno was located, enacted requirements for the licensing of physicians, and by the end of the century there were enough trained doctors to justify the prohibition of the practice of surgery by the clergy. Sharper definitions of the relations of apothecaries, leeches, barber-surgeons, wise-women, and midwives to the practice of medicine were enacted. With the establishment of the universities and the guilds of physicians, the requirements for a medical degree and a license to practice were pushed higher and higher.

If medical students regard the present requirements as rather trying, they might be reminded of those laid down by Emperor Frederick II in 1240 for anyone who would practice in his kingdom of the Sicilies: "An Arts course of three years to the baccalaureate, then five years in the medical school, followed by a year of practice with a reputable physician, another year if the candidate desired to practice surgery as well as Medicine." Ten years all told. Nor was that all. The candidate must then present letters of recommendation from physicians and present himself for examination. If successful, he was authorized by the ruler to practice. Only such were legally permitted to practice medicine and surgery in that region.[5]

By the end of the thirteenth century and the beginning of the fourteenth, there were famous teachers and a growing body of writings on medicine and surgery. There were, to mention only a few: Mondino, whose book on anatomy was to become the standard text on that subject; Pietro d'Abano, who not only was recognized in his own day as the greatest Latin authority in medicine, but who also spent some years in Constantinople learning Greek and brought back with him to Padua a number of Greek classics in medicine, notably the pharmaceutical work of Dioscorides; and Guy de Chauliac, professor at the medical school of Montpellier and personal physician of the popes at nearby Avignon, whose book on surgery became a standard textbook. This accumulation of writings by Western medical scholars continued at a fairly rapid pace until the middle of the fourteenth century, when the Black Death appeared in Europe.

The Black Death—which, I am told, a student in a public health course once spelled out as the "bourbonic" plague!—caused a severe setback in all activities of society, but probably most in medicine. Too few physicians had the courage of Guy de Chauliac, who was ministering to Pope Clement VI at the time. To quote this good doctor:

"So contagious was the disease, especially that with bloodspitting, that no one could approach or even see a patient without taking the disease. The father did not visit the son, nor the son the father. Charity was dead and hope abandoned. . . . For self-preservation there was nothing better than to flee the region before becoming infected and to purge oneself with pills of aloes, to diminish the blood by phlebotomy and to purify the air by fire and to comfort the heart with senna and things of good odor and to soothe the humors with Armenian bole and resist putrefaction by means of acid things. For the cure, bleedings, evacuations and electuaries and cordials were used. The external swellings were softened with figs and cooked onions, peeled and mixed with yeast and butter, then opened and treated like ulcers. Carbuncles were cupped, scarified and cauterized. As for me, in order to avoid infamy, I did not dare absent myself, but with continuous fear preserved myself so that I was able to apply the above said remedies; nevertheless, toward the end of the epidemic I fell ill with a continuous fever and a swelling in the groin and was ill for six weeks. I was in such danger that my companions believed that I would die, but the abscess became ripe and was treated as I have said and I escaped by the grace of God." [6]

Guy brought Pope Clement safely through the epidemic, and a part of his treatment was to keep His Holiness within an area completely surrounded by charcoal burners. He did it doubtless to purify the air by fire, but it certainly helped to keep rats and their fleas away from the patient.

Few physicians, as I have said, had the courage of Guy. Most of the people were left unattended and the plague swept away a large fraction of the whole population of Europe. Many of the laity who survived blamed the doctors for this, and Petrarch, the most famous literary figure of the time, who had lost his beloved Laura and his chief benefactor, Cardinal Colonna, as well as many other friends, was especially bitter in his hatred. He wrote numerous letters denouncing the whole medical profession. "With them —not as with other trades—it is sufficient to be called a physician to be believed to the last word and yet a physician's lie harbours more danger than any other." He was willing to urge that society do away with physicians entirely and quoted Cato to the effect that Rome had got along well without them for six hundred years. [7]

The learned explanation of the Black Death at the time was that it was due to the conjunction of Jupiter, Saturn, and Mars three years before, but within less than a generation after its first appearance in the West the physicians of Ragusa suspected that the ships from overseas carrying sick passengers or crew might have had something to do with it. The physicians of Marseilles came to the same conclusion shortly after this, and they were soon followed by those of Venice, and the practice of quarantine for all sick or suspected persons on incoming ships was inaugurated at both ports.

# The Rebirth of the Medical Profession

Thorndike, Sarton, and Singer have all remarked on the fact that no notable contributions were made to medical literature for more than a century after the Black Death. Thorndike blames this failure to advance on the influence of humanists like Petrarch and his followers. My own conviction is that the profession had made about as much progress as it could with the means they had at hand. Books were written by hand and copies were expensive. Time and time again an advance had been made in medical knowledge only to be lost, or to be known only to a few who did not pass on the information. The chief books of ancient medicine were nearly all written in classical Greek, those of the Arab and Jewish physicians in Arabic and Hebrew, and none of these languages was widely known in western Europe. Such translations as existed were very imperfect. Furthermore, medical knowledge, like all scientific and technological knowledge, cannot be effectively transmitted by words alone. Observation and didactic illustration are essential.

Fortunately these needs were being provided for by the developments in Humanism and art which culminated in the fifteenth century. The humanists, having recovered the ancient Latin literature, then turned to recover the Greek. Competent Greek scholars were brought to Italy and more were driven to migrate there by the advance of the Ottoman Turks. These refugees brought their books with them. Bessarion alone accumulated a library of nine hundred works, mostly Greek, which he bequeathed to Venice. By the end of the fifteenth century hundreds of humanists had a fairly perfect knowledge of both Greek and Latin and knew how to edit copies of ancient manuscripts. Some of these humanists also possessed a knowledge of medicine: for instance, Fracastoro, who alternated his lectures on medicine with lectures on classical literature; and Ermalao Barbaro, the scholarly Venetian noble who produced a complete edition and translation of Dioscorides; and Thomas Linacre, physician to King Henry VIII and a founder of the Royal College of Physicians, who lectured on ancient literature and translated a number of the writings of Galen. Now for the first time all the writings of Galen were available to the West, and it is well to remember that Fallopius, the most brilliant pupil of Vesalius at Padua, excused his teacher for having omitted a certain item of anatomy from his famous treatise because "the work of Galenus describing it had not yet been published." Vesalius had published his book in 1543.

While the humanists were perfecting their knowledge of ancient Greek as well as Latin, the artists were developing techniques of drawing and defining them so well that any student could master them. Leonardo da Vinci (d. 1519) marks the culmination of this technical development. What it meant for the advance of the medical profession is best told in his own words:

"And you who say that it is better to see the dissection than such drawings, you would speak well if it were possible to see all these things which are demonstrated in such drawings in a single specimen, in which you, with all your genius, will not see and will not obtain knowledge for which I have dissected more than ten human bodies, destroying all other organs, consuming with very minutest particles all the flesh which surrounded these veins, without making them bloody except with insensible sanguinification of the capillary veins; and one body did not suffice for so long a time, so that it was necessary to proceed by degrees with so many bodies that the complete knowledge might be fulfilled, which I twice repeated in order to see the difference.

"And if you do have love for such matters, you will perhaps be impeded by the stomach, and if that does not impede you, you will perhaps be impeded by the fear of living in the night hours in the company of such quartered and flayed corpses fearful to look at; and if this does not impede you, you will perhaps lack the good draughtsmanship which belongs to such demonstration; and if you have the draughtmanship it will not be accompanied by the perspective; and if it is accompanied, you will lack the order of the geometrical demonstrations, and the order of the calculation of the forces and power of the muscles; and perhaps you will lack the patience, so that you will not be diligent.

"As to whether all these things have been in me or not, the hundred and twenty books composed by me will answer yes or no." [8]

# The Rebirth of the Medical Profession

Fortunately the possibilities of the recently invented printing press had become fully realized. The artists contributed the device of engraving their drawings on wooden or metal blocks so that writings on medical subjects, fully illustrated, could be published in editions of thousands, and scholarly publishers like Aldus Manutius in Venice and Froben in Basle saw to it that these works were correctly and well printed and bound. There could be little danger henceforth that important discoveries in medicine would be lost or that the medical profession would operate on a treadmill basis. There were now many universities, hundreds of teachers, and thousands of pupils to seize eagerly upon every published new advance and add it to their libraries.

But this is telling the story too fast. To go back a bit, what was the best medical practice like at the end of the fifteenth century? We have one interesting piece of description in a letter written by Martin Luther:

"The hospitals of the Italians are built like palaces supplied with the best food and drink and tended by diligent servants and skillful physicians. The painted bedsteads are covered with clean linen. When a patient is brought in, his clothes are taken off and given to a notary to keep honestly. Then they put a white bed-gown on him and lay him between the clean sheets of the beautifully painted beds and two physicians are brought at once. Servants fetch food and drink in clean glass vessels, and do not touch the food even with a finger but offer it to the patient on a tray. Honorable matrons, veiled, serve the poor all day long without making their names known and at evening return home. These carefully tended hospitals I saw at Florence." [9]

And we have Armstrong's account of the medical treatment in the last illness of the most glamorous figure of fifteenth-century Italy, Lorenzo the Magnificent of Florence:

"A few days yet passed before the end—hope for the moment was revived by the arrival of Ludovico il Moro's doctor, Lazaro, who prepared an elixir from pulverized pearls and jewels. The remedy was in full accord with the Platonic philosophy of the day, but it had as little efficacy as the heliotrope stone worn next to the skin which had been pressed on the sufferer as an infallible specific—Lorenzo's physician, Pier Leone, had never believed that Lorenzo would die. The Milanese doctor on his arrival declared that the previous treatment was mistaken, that whereas the patient needed refrigeratives, the remedies had been calorific. On his master's death Pier Leone lost his reason. Taken to the Martelli Villa and kindly treated he would neither speak nor answer. On the following morning begging for a towel he went to the well to wash. He asked a peasant what was the depth of the water and then stayed leaning against the parapet of the well. Shortly afterwards a woman who went to draw water saw him head down." [10]

Such was the best medical practice about the year 1500. It was almost fifty years later that Vesalius escorted a cartload of engraved blocks across the Alps to Basle, where his epoch-making book was published. As Fallopius has told us, not all of Galen had been translated but it was all available in Greek and most of it in Latin translation, the rest appearing not long after Vesalius' work was issued.

Thus shortly after the middle of the sixteenth century an educated medical profession in western Europe had access to nearly all the accumulated medical and scientific literature that was then available. Doubtless some of that earlier literature had been lost, and my knowledge of technical medicine does not permit me to judge whether the contributions of the Arab-Jewish physicians represented by such scholars as Avicenna, Maimonides, and Averrhoës were sufficient to make up for what had been lost. I can assert, however, that western Europe was again in full command of that ancient medicine as it had been passed down, that the medical profession had rejoined the full stream of knowledge and progress in its field, and that in this sense it was fully reborn. But it had taken European society a full one thousand years of fumbling effort to recover the medical knowledge it had so unwittingly abandoned in the sixth century.

If the actual gains of the new Western medicine over the ancient were not impressive, the promise for the future certainly was. There were now probably more medical schools than there had been in antiquity, at least in western Europe, and more students of medicine. Thanks to the printing press and to the contributions of the artists, it was now possible to transmit medical learning and any advance in it to thousands of interested students in permanent form. It was no longer necessary for each school or professor to do over what had already been done. All could move forward to the next step.

Furthermore the profession no longer was hidebound by tradition. They had discovered that even the ancient authorities might be wrong and thus had developed a critical as well as experimental attitude. After the appearance of Vesalius' book Fallopius thought at first there was nothing more to be done in this field. As he said, "Carpi in his revision of Mondino was the founder of modern anatomy and Vesalius had perfected it." [11] But then he reflected that if Hippocrates, Galen, and all the other earlier authorities had erred, even Vesalius might be in error, and so he resumed his study of anatomy, with important results for medical knowledge. The same spirit led Fabricius, probably Fallopius' pupil, to continue the search, and he made such significant contributions that Dr. Richard Scammon called him "the father of embryology." And the same critical attitude led William Harvey, pupil of Fabricius, to discover the circulation of the blood. Such was the spirit of the medical school at Padua throughout the sixteenth century and of many another medical school too.

You will recall the observation of Isidore of Seville about medicine in ancient times being "a second philosophy" embracing all the liberal arts. The inquiring spirit, so marked in the medical faculty at Padua and echoed at other centers, led its professors and students into many new areas. It was an M.D. from Padua, Copernicus, who turned his attention to the stars and published his great work on the movement of the heavenly bodies in the same year that Vesalius published his on anatomy. It was another M.D. from Padua, Georgius Agricola, who wrote an equally epochal work on mining, metallurgy, and geology. It was still another M.D. of Padua, Jerome Cardan, who made important contributions to mathematics. And it was a professor of medicine at Padua, Galileo, who made

The Long Road Back

important contributions not only to medicine but also to physics and astronomy. Paracelsus, who may have studied medicine at nearby Ferrara, is treated with respect by students of chemistry and pharmacology if not always by those of medicine and surgery, and Conrad Gesner, also an M.D. in Switzerland, became the first professor of biology, making important contributions to botany and zoology as well as to library science.

Yes, Isidore's observation had become once more fully justified in the sixteenth century. The medical faculty felt it must know all the liberal arts and add to them. But the road back to this point of departure had been long and rocky.

NOTES

[1] E. Brehaut, *An Encyclopedist of the Middle Ages, Isidore of Seville* (New York: Columbia University Press, 1912), p. 163.

[2] D. C. Munro and G. C. Sellery, *A Syllabus of Medieval History* (New York: Longmans, Green & Co., Inc., 1909), pp. 74–76.

[3] J. B. Ross and M. M. McLaughlin, *Medieval Reader* (New York: The Viking Press, Inc., 1950), pp. 448–49.

[4] E. A. Babcock and A. C. Krey, *A History of Deeds Done Beyond the Sea, by William, Archbishop of Tyre*, vol. 2 (New York: Columbia University Press, 1943), pp. 292–93 and 395.

[5] F. H Garrison, *Introduction to the History of Medicine*, 4th ed. (Philadelphia: W. B. Saunders Co., 1929), p. 173.

[6] A. Castiglione, *A History of Medicine*, 2nd ed. (New York: Alfred A. Knopf, Inc., 1947), p. 358.

[7] *Ibid.*, pp. 398–99.

[8] David Riesman, *Medicine in the Middle Ages* (New York: Paul B. Hoeber, Inc., 1935), pp. 182–83.

[9] Preserved Smith, *The Life and Letters of Martin Luther* (London: John Murray, 1911), pp. 17–18.

[10] E. Armstrong, *Lorenzo de Medici* (New York: G. P. Putnam's Sons, 1896), pp. 309–14.

[11] L. Thorndike, *A History of Magic and Experimental Science*, vol. 5 (New York: Columbia University Press, 1941), p. 529.

# 4

# Urban's Crusade: Success or Failure?

T HE success of the First Crusade in its capture of Jerusalem and in the foundation of the Latin states in Syria was so unprecedented and so stirring that historians generally have overlooked the possibility that from the point of view of Urban II, who inspired the crusade, it may have fallen far short of the goal which he hoped to attain when he set it in motion. It is this possibility which the present paper seeks to explore.

In recent years, it is true, there has been an ever widening awareness of the fact that Pope Urban may have sought by way of that crusade to bring about a union between the Greek and Latin churches. La Monte, for example, in commenting upon an early copy of the present paper, which was then unpublished, found support for its thesis in the writings of Norden, Munro, Leib, Duncalf, and Baldwin.[1] Some thirty years earlier, Munro also referred, in considering the possibility, to Köhler and Fuller as exponents of the same idea;[2] and a number of others, especially Brehier, might be added to the list.[3] These references will serve, perhaps, to indicate the growing conviction among historians that the union of the Latin and Greek churches was one of the impelling motives in the call for the First Crusade.

A number of the scholars named above have reached this con-

NOTE: This paper was first published in *The American Historical Review*, January 1948.

clusion through a variety of shrewd conjectures that, since the material considerations in the agreement with Alexius were so heavily in his favor, there must have been certain less tangible considerations, such as the union of the two churches perhaps, to establish the balance. Others, including Leib, Brehier, and Norden, have arrived at a similar inference through a systematic examination of the previous relations of the churches. Both these approaches have served to throw new light on the whole discussion. But in striving to weigh and canvass the full extent of the problem more thoroughly, one must also take into account a number of other factors which are to be found in the intricate interplay during the crusade of all the separate elements which these researches imply.

Some inkling, for instance, of Pope Urban's desire to bring about the union of Greek and Latin Christendom is furnished by the reports of his speech at Clermont.[4] Yet, since none of these was written at the time and since all of them were naturally influenced by later events, Urban's ambition to achieve this result is much more clearly indicated in the letters which he addressed to the assembling crusaders. In these he assigned great prominence to the plight of "ecclesias Dei in Orientis partibus"; and since he chose, in addition, to single out the liberation of "orientalium ecclesiarum" as the major objective of the expedition,[5] one may reasonably assume that his identification of the "oriental churches" as "churches of God" was no mere casual statement. Rather, it may quite well have been deliberate and, as such, intended to stress the fact that he proposed to make no distinction between Greek and Latin Christians but instead to regard them all as common members of one fold, of which the pope at Rome was the proper shepherd.

Additional evidence to this effect is the fact that Urban had established a record of friendly relations with Emperor Alexius long before Clermont. Furthermore, part of the correspondence of the emperor with the abbot of Monte Cassino has survived, and its tone is also one of friendly cooperation.[6] But more significant, perhaps, was the action of Urban in sending military aid, however meager, in response to the emperor's request, in 1092.[7] This action, as well as the presence of the envoys of Alexius at the Council of Piacenza, about which we know too little, must be counted as important evidence in establishing the probability of some friendly understanding between Urban and Alexius before the First Crusade.[8]

More convincing, though still inferential, are the deductions to be drawn from the conduct of the pope's personal representative or representatives on the expedition itself. These were, first, Bishop Adhemar of Puy, and second, Count Raymond of Toulouse, who was present at Clermont; and it may be safely assumed that Urban discussed his hopes and plans with Adhemar[9] and possibly also with Count Raymond. In any case, since Adhemar accompanied the count's forces on the long journey to the Holy Land, Raymond must have become acquainted with the pope's plans from the bishop, if not from the pope himself.

The first important occasion for the revelation of any previous understanding between pope and emperor was in connection with the treaty which the several leaders of the expedition were required to make with Alexius. This included the agreement between them that all cities and territories which had been previously held by the Empire were to be returned to Alexius; and, though no definite date for the earlier boundaries of the Empire was specified, Antioch and its environs were apparently included.[10] This fact in itself is enough to make one wonder whether so substantial a concession did not depend on other considerations, which may in turn have rested upon some previous understanding with the real leader of the crusade, Pope Urban. For over a year and a half, at any rate, this agreement was faithfully respected by the crusaders.

In further support of this general thesis let us return, for the moment, to Urban in Italy, where continued effort on his part was required to persuade the Italians to respond to his call for a crusade. Finally, however, he was successful, enlisting not only southern Normans but many from the maritime cities, Genoa, Pisa, and Venice, and, last of all, the Lombard region, whose largest contingents started after his death. More significant for our immediate argument, however, is the fact that he carefully planned a Church council at Bari to consider the union of Greek and Latin Churches. This council, in which the momentarily exiled Anselm, archbishop of Canterbury, played such an important part, met in October 1098; and though it is not certain that any of the prelates from Constantinople were present, it adjourned to meet again in Rome the following spring for further consideration of the union of the two Churches.[11]

Turning again to the crusading army, and especially to its protracted siege of Antioch, it is clear that, since much of the territory which had been recovered from the Moslems was garrisoned by crusaders, the policy adopted in filling Church offices in these regions required careful consideration, and the decisions bear on our problem. This becomes evident as soon as one recalls that whenever a former Greek prelate was available he was reinstated. In no instance up to the death of Adhemar were the two churches provided with separate leadership in the same area. So harmonious, indeed, was the relationship at that time between the Greek and Latin Churches that Simeon, the Greek patriarch of Jerusalem, who was then a refugee in Cyprus, joined Adhemar in a letter to the West asking for reinforcements.[12]

Again, when Antioch was finally secured by the crusaders, Adhemar, who seems to have assumed that the two churches were to be united, arranged for the ceremonial restoration of the Greek patriarch there;[13] and there is little reason to doubt that in following this policy he was faithfully carrying out the instructions of Pope Urban. In fact, the entire consistency of his actions with both the words and the deeds of the pope would seem to indicate that their common understanding must have been based upon something more definite than a vague hope that the union of the two churches might result from the crusade.

Assuming for the moment, then, that some such agreement between pope and emperor did exist, or at least that the union of the Greek and Latin churches was a definite part of Urban's plan for the crusade, why do we not hear more about it later?

## Urban's Crusade: Success or Failure?

The answer to this question must be sought first of all, the evidence suggests, in the events around and about Antioch, and particularly in those which occurred after the death of Adhemar. To go very far along this line of inquiry, it is important to remember that Bohemond's desire to keep Antioch for himself was already plain, even before the bishop's death. Moreover, it is Bohemond's own chronicler who assures us most clearly of all that the other leaders, presumably Adhemar among them, did not agree with Bohemond's ambition but, on the contrary, considered Antioch as part of the territory to be returned to Alexius. This disposition on their part is clearly confirmed by the anonymous author of the *Gesta francorum*, who reports that after the final capture of Antioch the council of leaders sent an embassy, of which Hugh the Great [14] was chief, to Alexius inviting him "ad recipiendam civitatem" and to the fulfillment of his treaty obligations.

So specific a statement can hardly be disregarded, and it is clear from it that, to acquire legal title to Antioch, Bohemond would have to bolster his claim by some more persuasive argument than mere possession.[15] To do so, of course, his most obvious strategy was to discredit the emperor's fulfillment of his treaty obligations; and, if we are to believe Anna, the wily Bohemond was already engaged upon this policy even before Antioch was first entered. No doubt he was, as is further suggested not only by his treatment of Taticius, the military representative of Alexius, but also by his insinuations as to the motives for the latter's departure from the siege of Antioch.[16]

Nevertheless, it would be difficult to maintain the thesis that Alexius had failed to live up to his obligations at this time, for he was personally leading an army to aid in the capture of Antioch in 1098 and was well across Asia Minor when he was dissuaded from his purpose by the panic-stricken Stephen of Blois, who assured him that the crusading army had already been destroyed. After hearing that report, the energies of the emperor's expedition were turned to applying the "parched earth" treatment to cover its retreat; and when Hugh finally arrived at the imperial court it was too late for Alexius to launch a new expedition immediately. But he did prepare another for the next year, and his envoys announcing the coming of this expedition reached Antioch as early as February and the main army of the crusaders at Arka by April.[17] In addition, Alexius must also be given credit for the supplies which came by ship from Cyprus and even from Constantinople throughout this period.

How soon Alexius became convinced that the agreement concerning Antioch was to be repudiated is uncertain, for, though Bohemond's intentions in the matter must have become clear before the year 1098 had run its course, the letter in which they are stated specifically, along with a report of Adhemar's death, was not sent before September 11. This letter from the crusading chieftains to Urban was edited or supplemented by Bohemond when most of the other leaders were absent from Antioch; and in it the pope was urged "now that his vicar was dead, to come in person and establish his See at Antioch 'the original See of Peter himself'—'urbem principalem et capitalem Christiani nominis.'" Writing in the first person, Bohemond assures the pope that he feels quite competent to cope with the Infidel but that the heretics (Greeks, Armenians, Syrians, and Jacobites are specified) are beyond him. To deal with them, he needs the pope's help "omnes haereses, cuiuscumque generis sint, tua auctoritate et nostra virtute eradicas et destruas."[18]

There in those few words Bohemond announces not only his determination to hold Antioch, even though it may mean war with the Greeks to do so, but his not too subtle purpose of gaining sanction for his usurpation, at least in the eyes of the Latins, by having the pope establish his See in that city. By 1098, therefore, Bohemond was embarked upon a course that was certain to lead to a war with Alexius for the possession of Antioch, a struggle which was to engage his energies for the rest of his life.

Bohemond's intentions and policy now being clear, it becomes necessary to discover their effect on (1) the pope, (2) Alexius, and (3) the crusading leaders.

To begin, then, with Urban: How startled he must have been,

if our conjecture about his hopes and his plans is correct, to receive the letter of September 11, which, though written ostensibly by all the crusading leaders, ended so clearly as a personal appeal from Bohemond alone. And indeed Urban had reason to be surprised by its whole general tenor, for he was not accustomed to thinking of Greek Christians as "heretics" nor had his representative, Adhemar, ever treated the Greek clergy as such. As he pondered over the letter, it must very soon have been clear to him that Bohemond was at least contemplating, if not already set upon, a course which could only lead, if carried out, to a complete reversal of the policies which had hitherto been followed.

Just when Urban received this portentous communication we do not know. Ships and fleets traveled with so little speed in those years that there are instances during the early twelfth century when certain important messages from Syria to Italy were as long in transit as six months. So it is doubtful that this special letter could have reached any Italian port much before the end of the year, and after its arrival in port it had still to be carried to its final destination in Rome.[19]

As uncertain, therefore, as we must remain about the date of the letter's arrival, we are no more sure as to what its immediate effect was upon Urban. From the nature of its contents, however, one might suppose that no hasty reply was likely to be sent. For, as the pope thought over the information which was thus conveyed to him, he could hardly have failed to understand that its import represented considerably more than a passing threat to the forthcoming council at Rome, where the question of unity with the Greek Church, which had already been debated at Bari in the previous fall, was again to receive major attention. And the fact that the reports of this council contain almost no mention of the chief question which it was supposed to consider might lead one to infer that Bohemond's letter had been so disturbing to both pope and Greeks as to render further discussion of unity momentarily impossible.[20]

Some new course of action was obviously required, but what Urban decided upon or whether he ever reached a conclusion on

65

this matter is not at all clear, for he lived little more than three months after the Council of Rome, and he may have been ill most of this time. It has usually been assumed that Daimbert or Dagobert, archbishop of Pisa, was sent by him to succeed Adhemar as the papal representative on the crusade, but this is pure assumption. All the chronological indexes that we possess indicate that Daimbert and his Pisan fleet were already at sea long before Urban could have received the official notification of Adhemar's death.[21] At most, Daimbert went as ecclesiastical leader of the Pisan contribution to the crusade, which he had done so much to enlist. True, he was the ranking Latin prelate in the East when he arrived, and he therefore assumed a position of ecclesiastical leadership, but that is another story. For our immediate purposes, it is important only to remember that he was not Urban's appointee to succeed Adhemar.

It is doubtful in fact that Urban ever nominated a successor, and there is reason to believe that Cardinal Maurice, who was appointed by Paschal II in April 1100, was the first papal vicar after Adhemar.[22] If so, every crucial event of the crusade from August 1, 1098, until the arrival of Cardinal Maurice must have occurred without the presence or the guidance of any official representative of the pope. And if we accept this view, we may conclude not only that Bohemond's letter quite probably served to paralyze the efforts of Urban II to push forward his plans for unifying the Greek and Latin churches but also that the pope himself died before he was able to go any further with that hope or expectation.

As to the effect of Bohemond's actions on Alexius, whatever disquieting rumors may have reached the emperor by the time Hugh the Great arrived at Constantinople toward the end of July 1098, they must have been more than offset by the reports of that official messenger, for Alexius immediately began preparations for another expedition and sent envoys to the crusaders to announce its coming. These envoys reached Antioch in February 1099, and only then and there did they learn for certain that Bohemond meant to keep that city. Nor did they know until they

moved on to Arka in April [23] that the crusading army meant to
go on to Jerusalem without waiting for the forces of the emperor.
As a consequence, the expedition which Alexius had prepared to
aid the crusade was diverted into an attack upon Antioch and the
region thereabout. Thus unexpectedly, at least on the part of
Alexius, was the war between him and Bohemond begun,[24] and
until that conflict was settled, the emperor was hardly in a mood
to cooperate in any plan looking toward unity between the two
churches.

We must also try to estimate the impact of Bohemond's policy
on the rest of the crusading leaders. Here it is highly important
to recall not only that the council of crusading leaders had sent
Hugh the Great to urge Alexius to come to receive Antioch and
fulfill his obligations to the crusaders but also that this action was
taken *after* the capture of that city in 1098 and likewise after
Bohemond had won, it is thought, the promise of the majority
of the leaders to give him possession of it. Furthermore, Hugh
had been sent on his mission before the death of Adhemar.

To judge from this whole series of events, one can only conclude that, on sober second thought and after the crisis at Antioch was past, the crusaders' leaders must have repented of their
earlier action in promising Bohemond the city which was so
manifestly due Alexius under the terms of their agreement with
him. Doubtless it was Adhemar's influence that thus prevailed,
but whatever may have moved them to this decision, their attitude at the end of June or early in July 1098 was based apparently, as officially voiced, on the understanding that even if any
considerable number of them had made concessions to Bohemond
about Antioch before its capture, their previous agreement with
Alexius was bound to supersede any or all such commitments to
Bohemond. Whether this general decision of the council also implied that if Alexius failed to live up to his full contract with the
crusading leaders, they would then approve Bohemond's claim to
Antioch, is not certain.

After the death of Adhemar, Count Raymond of Toulouse became the leader of the opposition to Bohemond's plans,[25] and

much of the bickering that went on among the crusading leaders during the fall and winter of 1098–99 was concerned, in general, with the disposition of Antioch. Though there were many other questions that came up during that time, this was the most persistent and far-reaching—so much so, indeed, that when the decision to march on Jerusalem was finally made, Bohemond seems to have given a somewhat equivocal promise to participate. At any rate, he apparently accompanied the rest for a short distance southward, but then returned to Antioch in a withdrawal which Raymond, who felt himself too far committed to abandon the march, vigorously resented.[26]

The next test of the opinion of the crusading leaders came in April 1099 at Arka, near Tripoli, where the envoys of Alexius, after their fruitless stay in Antioch, reached the main army and urged the crusaders to await the coming of Alexius and his expedition, which was promised to arrive on St. John's Day. Count Raymond strongly urged that course also,[27] and the decision of the leaders to reject this advice was compounded of so many diverse interests that it can scarcely be regarded as a clear indication of their attitude toward either Bohemond or Alexius. The rank and file were impatient and eager to complete their vows, and since Raymond had indicated a deep interest, which aroused no enthusiasm among the other leaders, in capturing Tripoli for himself, his motives in counseling delay were questioned even by his own followers. Having thus lost the position of leadership which he had held since Bohemond abandoned the march toward Jerusalem, Raymond never regained it, either during or after the capture of Jerusalem. His wishes, and possibly his hopes, regarding the disposition of the Holy City were thwarted by the other leaders, of whom Robert of Normandy was his leading opponent at Jerusalem as he had been at Arka earlier.[28]

In the light of these developments, the incidents at Laodicea, where the homebound crusaders encountered Bohemond, may seem strange, for there both Robert of Normandy and Robert of Flanders[29] sided with Raymond when he took an active stand against Bohemond, who was energetically engaged in the siege of that Greek town. Since in this effort Bohemond had won the aid of Archbishop Daimbert and his recently arrived Pisan fleet, the capture of the city was assured, and it is hardly surprising that his old rival, Raymond of Toulouse, expressed strong opposition to Bohemond's plans.

Yet even if Raymond's position can be thus accounted for, that of the two Roberts is far from clear, for there is every reason to believe that they personally preferred Bohemond. That they joined Raymond in the threat to take up arms against Bohemond unless he desisted from the siege can only be explained on much higher grounds than personal antagonism; it can best be accounted for on the assumption that Raymond's opposition reflected not only his own interests but also the original plan of Urban as executed by Adhemar up to the latter's death. In such a situation, of course, the two Roberts could do no less than acknowledge, as they had done in the council of leaders in Antioch after Karbuqa's defeat, the justice of Raymond's contention; for Bohemond's action at Laodicea, which was included in the environs of Antioch, had again brought into sharp focus the whole question of the return of that city to Alexius.

As a result of so many combined protests, Archbishop Daimbert called off his Pisan fleet and devoted his energies to reconciling the Latin leaders,[30] and Bohemond was forced to give up the siege. In spite of that, however, and even though the two Roberts returned to the West with their troops, Raymond and a considerable portion of his troops remained in or near Laodicea to assure protection of the Greek city, and when he himself finally sailed to Constantinople to confer with Alexius, he left his family and his troops behind.[31]

Looking closely at this whole episode, one is led to conclude that Raymond and the two Roberts must have regarded Bohemond's conduct at Laodicea as a violation not only of their common agreement with Alexius but also of the plans of Pope Urban. The circumstances would seem also to imply that Daimbert could hardly have been Urban's appointee to succeed Adhemar.

And now to go a step further in the thesis which is here being advanced, let us turn our attention more directly on the war between Bohemond and Alexius. The emperor's troops had been operating about the periphery of Antioch in the summer and early fall of 1099, but military operations had ceased at the approach of winter. The respite which the unfavorable season afforded made it possible for Bohemond to fulfill his crusader's vow by going to Jerusalem for Christmas, and on this pious excursion he was joined by Archbishop Daimbert, who had spent the better part of the fall in flitting between Raymond's troops at Laodicea and Bohemond's at Antioch. These two ambitious men, Bohemond and Daimbert, were thus able to perfect their plans, and when they arrived at Jerusalem Bohemond engineered the project for the deposition of Arnulf as patriarch of Jerusalem and the elevation of Daimbert to that office.[32] Bohemond also, when this had been accomplished, arranged for the joint submission of Godfrey and himself as vassals for their respective principalities to Patriarch Daimbert.[33]

This was no boon to Godfrey, but it was to Bohemond, who hoped thereby to commit the Latin Church to the full support of his claim to Antioch, which neither the crusading leaders nor Alexius had recognized. The fact that this ambition on his part was involved in his dealings with Daimbert is amply confirmed by the much disputed letter of Daimbert to Bohemond, which Raymond's troops intercepted and William of Tyre published.[34] Neither of the schemers profited too much, it is true, from this transaction, for Bohemond was captured by the Turks in 1101,[35] and the new papal legate, Robert, who arrived at Jerusalem in 1102, deposed Daimbert, who then sought refuge in Antioch, where he remained until Bohemond was released from captivity and decided to return to the West for reinforcements.[36]

It was doubtless before or on that westward journey that the further plans of these two were perfected. Embracing both Bohemond's plans for a new crusade and Daimbert's desire to recover the patriarchate of Jerusalem, they may also have decided to spread abroad a much edited revision of the anonymous *Gesta francorum* as propaganda for Bohemond's primary design.[37] The conspirators were very favorably received in Rome in 1105 at the hands of Paschal II, who had succeeded Urban as pope, and the end result of their efforts was that Daimbert was reinstated [38] and Bohemond was given the help of a papal legate in his appeal for a new crusade, especially in France.[39] This change in papal attitude need not concern us at the moment, however, for the war between Alexius and Bohemond had altered any prospect of a union between the Greek and Latin churches until the question of Antioch was settled.

Turning once more to Alexius, then, we find that monarch intent, from the year 1099, upon the recovery of Antioch, and in this private war Bohemond's enemies were his friends—a circumstance which must have caused him no little embarrassment in dealing with the crusade of 1101, for Bohemond's enemies included the Turks who lived near Antioch. Thus Alexius was asked to help the crusaders (many of whom would doubtless turn against him when they discovered that he was at war with the Latins of Antioch) against the Turks who were his allies in that war. It was a difficult spot to be in, so difficult in fact that the disasters which befell the crusade of 1101 in its march across Asia Minor were in part blamed upon Alexius.

When Bohemond was released from captivity and resumed active leadership of the war against Alexius, he found the alliance of the latter with the Turks too strong for his limited forces, and it was this fact that led him to seek additional aid from the West. Alexius suspected his design and began recruiting a strong army with which to meet Bohemond in the West, and Arabic chroniclers inform us that he had no difficulty in enlisting Moslem troops for this purpose.[40]

Alexius correctly surmised that Bohemond would land his "crusade" of 1107 in the neighborhood of Durazzo and had concentrated there his greatest efforts toward meeting the threat. To defeat the Latin leader he used persuasion, bribery, and force, and Bohemond was compelled at last to accept an ignominious peace.[41]

What interests us most about the terms which were then drawn up between him and Alexius is the fact that he, Bohemond, was

# The Long Road Back

required not only to recognize the previous agreement of 1097 but also to reinstate in Antioch a single Greek patriarch, who was to be nominated by Alexius. This provision, which implies that Alexius too had accepted the idea of a unified Church, recalls the action of Urban's representative, Adhemar, in setting up a former Greek patriarch in Antioch as the sole ecclesiastical head of that city.

That nothing came of this treaty is beside the point, for the great efforts of Alexius against Bohemond in the West had made it impossible for him to exert anything like an equal amount of pressure in the East, and Tancred was therefore able to hold out so successfully that Antioch remained an independent principality of the Latins until the time of Manuel, grandson of Alexius. But when it became at last a fief of Manuel, the discussions of the union of Greek and Latin churches were again resumed with some prospect of success.

We are concerned here, however, only with the fact that when the treaty had been signed and Bohemond's hostile forces had left the Balkan peninsula, Alexius seems to have felt a sense of great relief—as well he might, since Bohemond's career was virtually ended. Though the Latin leader returned to Italy and started to raise another army, he had made little progress in that endeavor when illness and death overtook him on March 7, 1111.[42] No doubt the news of his death afforded Alexius even greater assurance, and we soon find him reopening negotiations with the pope that involved specific reference to the reunion of Greek and Latin churches. As evidence that the initiative came from the emperor, one has only to read the letter of Paschal II to Alexius in 1112,[43] and the longer one meditates on that letter the more one is tempted to think that the overtures Alexius put forward at that time may have been but a repetition of those that his envoys had conveyed to Urban II at Piacenza in 1094 or even earlier and that may have constituted the basis of Urban's great hopes and plans for the First Crusade.

If the pope's instructions had been more fully carried out, it is easy to see now, the prospect of union between the Greek and

72

Latin churches would have come much nearer fulfillment, but the great opportunity was lost, or rather destroyed, by the unbridled ambition of one man, Bohemond.

Poets and novelists might find an interesting theme in the remarkable similarity of the roles which Bohemond and his father, Robert Guiscard, played in two papal efforts to unify the two great branches of the Christian Church. Such unity had been one of the dearest wishes of Gregory VII, and though circumstances prevented his launching a crusade, the prospect of the union apparently never left his mind. Guiscard was canny enough to recognize this fact and make use of it in furthering his own attempts to gain support for his attack on the Greek Empire.[44] And so, as events turned out, Gregory was forced into a position where he seemed to be trying to attain by force what could have been achieved only through persuasion and cooperation. In the same way, Bohemond strove to commit Urban to a program of force and virtually succeeded in winning support for it from Urban's successor.[45] As an end result of this double scheming of father and son, the two popes who might otherwise have succeeded in bringing about the much sought union between the two churches were both thwarted in their purposes.

Taking into consideration, then, all the factors which bear on the question, it would seem that, however much Urban desired the other objectives of the crusade, his chief aim was to bring about the union of the Greek and Latin churches under the headship of the bishop of Rome; and this conclusion, which forms the thesis of this paper, is not inconsistent with the course of Church history. Too much has been made of the so-called "definitive break" between the Greek and Latin churches in 1054, and too little of the efforts that were made during the great reform movement of the eleventh century to achieve uniformity of Christian doctrine and practice.

As a matter of fact, there was nothing definite about the affair of 1054, for negotiations for union and for the elimination of variant practices in the two churches were resumed from time to time after that date, and such negotiations were initiated by

Greeks as well as Latins. And such negotiations have recurred through the centuries right down to the present.

The most remarkable feature of the affair of 1054, it seems in retrospect, was the uncompromising insistence of the Latin Church that the union, or reunion, of Greek and Latin churches must be under the headship of the pope at Rome; and this change of emphasis must have developed as a logical consequence of the great Western Church reform program. This movement, which nearly all textbooks on medieval history describe as devoted to the elimination of simony, marriage of the clergy, and lay investiture, also supplied, as is seldom recognized, the over-all drive to re-establish uniformity of church service and practice, and even of dogma, which had seriously disintegrated under the effects of early feudalism.

That the drive for so much reform came from north of the Alps, not from Italy, and that its core was consistently monastic, seems—again in the long view—important, for the north, unlike Italy, was scarcely conscious of any Greek influence and did not share any tradition of occasional submission to Constantinople; the people of that region were conscious only of the fact that their religion had come from Rome. The monastic core of the reformers' drive explains its uncompromising attitude on the fundamentals of ecclesiastical uniformity. The Congregation of Cluny, which in a sense epitomizes the whole movement, supplied a sustained nucleus for its propagation, and whether we date the beginning of the reform drive in 910 or at some later time in eastern France or southern and western Germany, it had gained such momentum that its force was felt in nearly every portion of Western Christendom before it captured Rome in 1046.[46]

After that time the identification of the popes with the leadership of the reform movement inspired them with a consciousness of strength and a confidence born of a long succession of victories over many obstinate difficulties. Confronted with the practical problem of dealing with Greek churches in southern Italy, they could proceed with assurance, knowing they had already met and overcome a variety of other troublesome differences. So Leo IX

# Urban's Crusade: Success or Failure?

was able to address himself to that specific problem in the very same spirit that had served to iron out other such difficulties in the north and west.

Viewed in this light, the affair of 1054 meant merely that Constantinople was at that time gaining its first acquaintance with this great revival in the Latin Church, and that the experience proved momentarily to be nothing less than breath-taking.

In general, this confident attitude continued in the papacy, and men of Cluny were there to sustain it throughout the rest of the eleventh century. Abbot Hugh, who became head of Cluny in 1048, was still abbot in 1109, having lived to see at least two of the monks he had trained become popes. He was abbot when Leo IX took up the Greek problem, was with Gregory at Canossa, and counseled Urban before the memorable meeting at Clermont; and doubtless he was fired on all these occasions by Urban's dream that all Christendom might be united. Doubtless, also, he shared Urban's disappointment that the crusade had failed to realize that dream, for from Urban's point of view the crusade he had planned could hardly have been counted a complete success.

## NOTES

[1] John L. La Monte, "La Papauté et les croisades," *Renaissance*, II and III (New York, 1945), pp. 156–58.

[2] Dana C. Munro, "The Popes and the Crusades," *Proceedings of the American Philosophical Society*, LV, 5 (1916), 1–2.

[3] Louis Brehier, *L'église et l'Orient au moyen age: Les Croisades* (5th ed.; Paris, 1928), pp. 57–62. See also his two chapters, ix and xix, in the *Cambridge Medieval History*, IV (London, 1927).

[4] Dana C. Munro, "The Speech of Pope Urban II," *American Historical Review*, XI (1905–6), 231–42.

[5] The letter of Pope Urban II to the crusaders in Flanders in Heinrich Hagenmeyer, ed., *Epistulae et chartae* (Innsbruck, 1901), pp. 136–37. (Hereafter abbreviated H. Ep.)

[6] Two letters to Oderisius, abbot of Monte Cassino, H. Ep., pp. 140–41, 152–53. See also Bernard Leib, *Rome, Kiev et Byzance* (Paris, 1924), pp. 103–5.

[7] Anna Comnena, *Alexiad*, VIII, 5. Unless otherwise specified the edition of chronicles of the Crusades cited in this article is that of the *Recueil des historiens des croisades*, 16 vols. published by the Academy of Inscriptions and Belles-Lettres, Paris, 1841–1906. References to Latin chronicles are abbreviated H. Oc. References to the works of Anna Comnena (abbreviated *Alexiad*), of William of Tyre (abbreviated *W.T.*), and of the anonymous *Gesta Francorum* (abbreviated *Gesta*), are made in terms of book

and chapter to permit use of convenient editions. See also Brehier, pp. 61–62, and Leib, pp. 20–26.

[8] Dana C. Munro, "Did the Emperor Alexius Ask for Aid at the Council of Piacenza?" *American Historical Review*, XXVII (1922), 731.

[9] The letter to the crusaders in Flanders, *H. Ep.*, p. 136.

[10] A. C. Krey, "A Neglected Passage in the *Gesta*," *The Crusades and Other Historical Essays Presented to D. C. Munro* (New York, 1928), pp. 57–78.

[11] J. D. Mansi, *Sacrorum conciliorum nova et amplissima collectio* (Florence and Venice, 1759–98), XX, cols. 947–52.

[12] Letter of Simeon and Adhemar to the faithful of the northern regions, *H. Ep.*, pp. 141–42. It is noteworthy that Adhemar gives precedence to Simeon as befitted the latter's superior dignity, a further reflection of Adhemar's assumption that there was to be but one church.

[13] *W.T.*, VI, 23.

[14] Hugh of Vermandois, brother of the king of France.

[15] *Anonymi gesta francorum et aliorum hierosolymitanorum*, ca. XXX. See also Ralph B. Yewdale, *Bohemond I, Prince of Antioch* (Princeton, 1924), pp. 72–73. Hagenmeyer dates Hugh's arrival at Constantinople July 21, 1098. Heinrich Hagenmeyer, *Chronologie de la première croisade* (Paris, 1902), no. 304. (Hereafter abbreviated *H. Chron.*)

[16] *Alexiad*, XI, 6.

[17] Yewdale, pp. 77–78. See also *W.T.*, VII, 20.

[18] The letter of Bohemond and the other leaders to Pope Urban II, *H. Ep.*, pp. 161–65.

[19] The best basis for calculation on this point is afforded by two voyages which are fairly definitely dated, first that of the Bruno of Lucca who left Antioch July 20, 1098, and reached Lucca the first week in October 1098, an interval of nearly three months (*H. Chron.*, nos. 303, 319), and second, that of the Genoese who left Laodicea some time in September 1099, and reached Genoa December 24, 1099 (*H. Chron.*, nos. 430, 437). It is safe to assume that the letter of Bohemond and the other leaders of the crusade, dated September 11, 1098, did not reach Italy much before late December of 1098.

[20] Mansi, XX, cols. 961–70. See also Leib, pp. 296–97.

[21] The arrival of Daimbert, archbishop of Pisa, at Laodicea approximately a year after the death of Adhemar, the first important prelate from the West since Adhemar, has led most historians, even Leib (p. 269), to assume that he was the papal legate to succeed Adhemar. It is probable that the Pisan fleet left some time in the later summer of 1098 for it is known to have wintered on the islands in the eastern Mediterranean which it had captured (*H. Chron.*, no. 428). He had therefore left Italy before the news of Adhemar's death had been received. There is no letter of Urban's or Paschal's which describes him as papal legate in the Holy Land as there is of Adhemar or Maurice. Nor does he so style himself in his letter of September 1099 (*H. Ep.*, p. 161); nor does a close study of his conduct after his arrival in the East justify such assumption; indeed, there is much to the contrary.

[22] The letter of Pope Paschal II congratulating the triumphant crusaders in Asia (*H. Ep.*, pp. 178–79).

[23] *H. Chron.*, no. 361. See also Yewdale, p. 73, and *W.T.*, VII, 20.

[24] Yewdale, p. 87. Ferdinand Chalandon, *Essai sur la règne d'Alexis I^er Comnène* (Paris, 1900).

[25] *H. Chron.*, no. 352; Yewdale, pp. 73–78.

[26] Yewdale, p. 87; *H. Chron.*, no. 349.

[27] Raymond d'Aguilers, *H. Oc.*, III, 268; *Alexiad*, XI, 9; *W.T.*, VII, 20.

[28] *H. Chron.*, no. 411; Raymond d'Aguilers, *H. Oc.*, III, 301–3. It was Robert's chaplain, Arnulf of Choques, who broke Count Raymond's leadership by questioning the validity of the Holy Lance which Peter Bartholomew, a humble cleric and visionary in Raymond's army had found in Antioch. Count Raymond, wealthiest of the leaders, had granted subsidies to the four principal leaders after Bohemond's defection. This leadership by purchase he reinforced by keeping Peter Bartholomew close to himself. The latter continued to report visions and supernatural revelations so obviously in the interest of Count Raymond at Arka that Arnulf became skeptical and questioned the validity of the lance upon which Peter Bartholomew's reputation and influence rested. This led to the trial of the visionary by the ordeal of fire which he did not survive a sufficient number of days to prove a miracle. The other leaders had been restive to move on for some time. Now the rank and file, many of Count Raymond's troops among them, refused to stay at Arka any longer. Count Raymond was thus compelled to follow on to Jerusalem. See Charles Wendell David, *Robert Curthose* (Cambridge, 1920), pp. 111–15. The legend that Raymond was offered the rule of Jerusalem, which David unfortunately repeats, was started by Raymond's chaplain and can mean only that some of Raymond's immediate friends may have suggested the possibility but there is no evidence that any of the other leaders made, or would have acquiesced in, such an offer.

[29] Yewdale, pp. 88–89; *H. Chron.*, no. 430.

[30] The letter of Daimbert, Godfrey, and Raymond to the pope, *H. Ep.*, pp. 167–74.

[31] *H. Chron.*, no. 460.

[32] Godfrey, who had been left with no more than 200 knights and 1000 foot soldiers, was too helpless to resist this carefully planned conspiracy. He did not have the force to oppose Bohemond, and he so pathetically needed the fleet which Daimbert commanded to obtain a seaport to serve as a gateway to the West. Count Raymond's clergy had bitterly opposed Arnulf's election to the patriarchate, and they had filled Daimbert's ear at Laodicea with charges against Arnulf, some real as well as imaginary. This afforded Bohemond and Daimbert the opening needed to achieve their ends. Most writers, confused by later events, accepted the convenient explanation that Daimbert had been sent to occupy the patriarchate. The true story, however, is provided, oddly enough, by two writers, neither of whom favored Arnulf but much preferred Daimbert: Bartolf de Nanges (*H. Oc.*, III, 519) and William of Tyre (*W.T.*, X, 4). See also Yewdale, pp. 91–94.

[33] *W.T.*, IX, 15; Fulcher of Chartres, *Historia Hierosolymitana*, III, 34, 16.

[34] *W.T.*, X, 4.

[35] *Ibid.*, X, 26; Bartolf, *H. Oc.*, III, 538. The dismissal of Daimbert and subsequent events are reviewed in the letter of Pope Paschal II. (Reinhold Röhricht, *Regesta regni hierosolymitana*, Innsbruck, 1893, no. 49.) See also Yewdale, p. 92.

[36] Yewdale, pp. 99–102.

[37] Krey, *op. cit.*, pp. 57–78.

[38] *Röhricht*, no. 49.

[39] Yewdale, p. 108.

[40] Hamilton A. R. Gibb, *The Damascus Chronicle of the Crusades*, ex-

# The Long Road Back

*tracted and translated from the Chronicle of Ibn al-Qalanisi* (London, 1932), pp. 80, 91–92.

⁴¹ Yewdale, pp. 125–31. *Alexiad*, XIII, 8–12, inclusive.

⁴² Yewdale, p 133, n. 97.

⁴³ P. Jaffe, ed., *Regesta pontificum Romanorum*, 1, No. 6334, pp. 747–48.

⁴⁴ Brehier in *Cambridge Medieval History*, IV, 598. Both Guiscard and Bohemond used fraudulent pretenders to the Greek throne, chiefly, no doubt, to entice papal support for their ventures.

⁴⁵ The letter of Bohemond and the other leaders to Pope Urban II, *H. Ep.*, pp. 161–65.

⁴⁶ It seems strange that Brehier (*Cambridge Medieval History*, IV, 272) should have repeated the expression "definitive rupture" when so much of his writing (*Ibid.*, IV, 594, in particular, and all of chapter XIX in general) proves the contrary. Deno Geankoplis, who assisted the writer in preparing this paper for publication, assembled so much evidence from both Greek and Latin sources of continuing friendly relations and negotiations between Greeks and Latins after 1054 as to render such characterization absurd. He was especially impressed by the fact that the edict of excommunication issued by the pope's representative was directed at certain Greek officials, e.g., Patriarch Michael Cellularius, and exempted Greek Christians; by the very friendly attitude of the popes toward the Basilian monasteries in Italy, one of which, Grosso Ferrata, served almost as an unofficial embassy of the Greek Church to Rome; and by the very cordial relations between the Greek Church and Gregory VII until the latter lent his support to Robert Guiscard. Leib has traced the continuance of friendly relations during the days of Urban II until these were interrupted by the conduct of Guiscard's son, Bohemond, and virtually closes his book with the resumption of friendly relations in 1112 (pp. 310 ff.).

# 5

## William of Tyre: The Making of a
## Historian in the Middle Ages

T HIS great movement [the Crusades] found its fitting chronicler in William of Tyre, an historian who surpasses nearly all other of his Mediaeval fellows as much in the artistic symmetry of his work as he does in the inherent interest and almost epic completeness of his theme."

With this judgment, expressed by T. A. Archer,[1] nearly every scholar who has worked on the Crusades would probably agree. Nor does the reference of S. Lane-Poole in his biography of Saladin to "the incomparable Archbishop William of Tyre whose *Historia*, far transcending in vividness, grasp and learning all Latin or Arabic annals of the time"[2] strain their acquiescence, even though it be remembered that "the time" includes Ordericus Vitalis, Suger, and Otto of Freising. It would be a mistake, however, to assume that these judgments, based upon William's one extant work as a whole, apply with equal force to all parts of it. That work, despite its artistic symmetry, was not a single and sustained enterprise. It was, instead, the result of nearly twenty years of intermittent effort in the course of which the author developed his skill in historical composition from that of a literary tyro to full mastery of his art.[3]

NOTE: This paper was first published in *Speculum*, April 1941.

79

William of Tyre was not trained as a historian, at least not consciously so, by either his mentors or himself. Up until middle age his ambition, so far as can be learned, was to advance in the hierarchy of the secular church of Jerusalem. With favorable fortune, he aspired to the patriarchate of Jerusalem itself, and until he reached the age of fifty he had every reason to believe that his ambition would be fulfilled. His work as a historian was almost accidental, and it was quite incidental to the major interest of his life.

He was a native of Palestine. Who his parents were, whence they came, is not known. He who has so much to say about the genealogy of others and has included so many personal references in the account that he wrote, avoided completely any allusion to his own forebears. The theory that they were of Western origin is based upon the objective manner in which he alludes to all Eastern peoples, that they were French upon the fact that most of his references are to people who came from France. Both suppositions are conjectures. Even the date of his birth about 1130 is conjecture.[4]

His early education he obtained in Palestine. It would be difficult otherwise to account for his extraordinary knowledge of languages, which included, besides Latin and French, Arabic, Greek, and at least a smattering of Hebrew and other Eastern tongues. He mentions several persons who flourished during his youth, with a degree of affection and respect not fully explained by any acts of theirs which he recounts. It seems reasonable, therefore, to assume that he felt some sense of obligation to them for aid in his early education and advancement. These are Peter of Barcelona, Fulcher, the patriarch, and Geoffrey, abbot of the Temple of the Lord. Peter was prior of the Holy Sepulchre until William was about eighteen years old and then became archbishop of Tyre and remained in this post from 1148 to 1164. Fulcher became patriarch of Jerusalem when William was presumably sixteen years old and held that office for nearly twelve years. Geoffrey is always mentioned as expert in the knowledge of Greek. All were leading churchmen in Jerusalem, able and influential, and their friendship implied that the young man who enjoyed it was intent upon an ecclesiastical career.[5]

William's early education was rounded out by further study in the West. He meant to describe that education, but the chapter in which it was to have been told has disappeared, if indeed it was ever written. Only the caption of the chapter remains.[6] When he went to the West or how long he stayed may never be known. The only statement of his bearing upon these questions is his incidental observation in describing the coronation of Amaury in 1163. Amaury had been required to divorce his wife Agnes de Courtenay as a preliminary to the coronation because that marriage was in violation of canon law. William apologizes for his ignorance of the facts in the case because he "had not yet returned from across the seas where he was engaged in the study of the liberal arts at the schools." [7]

That statement about his study of the "liberal arts" at the age of thirty-three deserves more attention than it has hitherto received. A French translator of the early thirteenth century, assuming that such a statement implied study at Paris, so translated it,[8] and apparently no one since then has challenged his assumption. But why should a churchman be studying the liberal arts at the age of thirty-three? William evidently planned to return to Palestine, where there were no universities or higher schools in the Western sense to require a learned doctor of the liberal arts.

The only possibility that affords a reasonable answer to the question is that he had gone to the West primarily to study law, which was still commonly included among the liberal arts. Presumably he had already been ordained a priest, for he nowhere makes any special mention of the fact, and he may already have been a canon of the Cathedral of Tyre, under his old friend Peter of Barcelona, then archbishop there. If so, he would have been doing what many an archdeacon was doing in the twelfth century long after 1163, namely, interrupting his regular duties to acquire the "new" knowledge of law so much needed for the increased legal business of the Church.[9] But the place in which to acquire this knowledge was not at Paris but in the schools of Italy, and although William never mentions Paris or alludes to any of its great teachers or the distinguished fellow students whom he would have met there at that time, he does reveal an intimate knowledge of Italy, especially of the region south of the Apennines.

There is a strong preponderance of evidence, then, for the conclusion that his study of the liberal arts "across the seas" was in the schools of Italy and that his major interest was in law.[10] The "Willelmus Canonicus" who is mentioned in the document issued at Tyre late in 1163 was almost certainly our William just returned from across the seas, prepared to aid his archbishop, Peter, in the legal business of that diocese.[11]

William was still a "canonicus" at Tyre in the fall of 1167 when the marriage of King Amaury and the Greek princess, Maria, was celebrated there. Amaury had just returned from a successful campaign in Egypt. As the ally of the Egyptians against the invading Seljuks he had penetrated far up the Nile, had visited in the innermost portions of Cairo, and had succeeded in capturing Alexandria from young Saladin, just then entering upon his career. What Amaury saw there led him to indulge hopes of even greater success, the conquest of Egypt itself.[12] The marriage with Maria was in itself a step in that direction, for it offered assurance of an alliance with the emperor at Constantinople.

The prospect was a thrilling one. An eager student of history himself, Amaury must have felt on the threshold of a new chapter in sacred history second only to that of the capture of Jerusalem.[13] He needed a proper historian to record that chapter. Just how his attention was attracted to the young canon there at Tyre as the person best qualified to perform that task is not known. But there is reason to believe that his presence just a few days after his marriage at another ceremony in which Canon William was promoted to the office of archdeacon of Tyre "at the king's request" marked the binding of a contract whereby William undertook to write "a History of the Deeds of King Amaury."[14]

Both men were young enough to enter upon the joint venture (the king to perform the deeds, William to write them) with enthusiasm. William was thirty-seven, Amaury thirty-one. The king's regard for his chronicler grew with their acquaintance. Early in the next year he sent William with the Greek envoys to conclude the treaty of alliance for the Egyptian campaign with Emperor Manuel.[15] During most of the following year William was away, answering a charge which his archbishop, the successor of Peter, had made against him at Rome,[16] probably about the allotment of income which Amaury had insisted upon for him.

When he returned from Rome, he was met with another request from the king—namely, that he look after the education of the king's son, Baldwin, then nine years old. William, who had shown some reluctance about accepting the academic duties of historian, definitely demurred at this additional assignment which threatened to take him so much farther away from the main path of his ambitions. Only the assurance of further favors from the king won his acceptance. What those "further favors" might have been can only be conjectured.[17] For the next four years, 1170–74, William was closely confined to association with the young prince and his schoolmates, probably chiefly at Tyre.

Though William was confined in person, his duties as tutor allowed him considerable time for study and writing. The king visited Tyre as frequently as he could, and during these visits spent a generous portion of his time with William. The proposed history was never far from their thoughts. Amaury supplied William with information about current events and discussed plans for the work as a whole. It must have been some question about the background for Amaury's reign which drew their attention to the absence of any preceding history. There existed no chronicle of Jerusalem since 1127,[18] and the chronicles of the founding of Latin Jerusalem up to 1127 must have seemed very crude. It must have been these discoveries which led to the decision that William should write, or rewrite, a complete chronicle of the kings of Jerusalem from the beginning. So the recovery of the earlier years of Amaury's reign was laid aside until William should have brought the royal chronicle up to that point; only the report on current events in Amaury's reign was to be continued.

For the time being, then, William's chief energy was devoted to this second work, the introductory royal chronicle. Amaury followed its progress with interest, sometimes reading what William had written, more often having it read to him, presumably by William himself.

This had been going on for some time when Amaury made still another request. His Egyptian campaigns had aroused his curiosity about the history of the Moslem background. The royal library contained many Arabic books, and William may have occasionally read to him from some of them. At any rate the king now asked William also to compile, from Arabic books which Amaury supplied,[19] a history of the deeds of the princes of the Orient from the time of Mohammed. Apparently William worked simultaneously on all three of these historical enterprises, collecting notes on Amaury's current activities and at the same time studying and writing on the other two projects.[20]

The period up to 1174 marks the first stage in William's career as a historian. His status was that of a literary client serving a royal patron. He was composing history for the edification and entertainment of the king and his court. He must please both by word and voice an audience that was neither unsophisticated nor provincial. His attitude was that of a courtier.[21] Whatever restraints the experience may have imposed upon his judgment as a lawyer or his critical aloofness as an ecclesiastic, it developed his skill as a raconteur. Fortunately he had been so thoroughly trained in the two former respects that the more recently acquired skill could not have been very damaging to his integrity as a historian. During these years he must have written most of the material contained in the first twelve books of the royal chronicle, as well as a substantial portion of the history, "Princes of the Orient."[22] For the deeds of Amaury he had only his notes on current affairs from 1167 to 1174.

The year 1174 marks the beginning of the second stage in his development as a historian. King Amaury died on July 11 of that year at the premature age of thirty-eight. This tragedy was followed by another, the coronation of William's partially educated pupil, scarcely thirteen years old, as King Baldwin IV.

No one knew more clearly than William the nature of this second tragedy, for it was not merely the youth and partial education of the new king that were cause for worry, but the further sinister fact that Baldwin was afflicted with the incurable disease of leprosy, which William had been the first to discover.[23] Nor was his distress relieved by the highhanded way in which Milon de Plancy assumed control of affairs, including access to the young king's person. This source of anxiety was removed by the early murder of Milon at Acre and the substitution of the more competent Raymond of Tripoli as regent,[24] but William's relief was more than outweighed by the added responsibilities he was now called upon to assume.

First he was chosen, in 1174, to fill the vacant post of chancellor of the kingdom.[25] Then some months later, on June 8, 1175, he was also elected to fill the vacant archbishopric of Tyre.[26] Neither position was a sinecure. Furthermore, as chancellor of the kingdom he was thrown into intimate association with the young king and inevitably continued, even if informally, his former duties as a tutor. When two years later the king had reached the legal age of fifteen and Raymond of Tripoli automatically withdrew from the regency, William found himself in the position of chief adviser to the responsible ruler of the kingdom. His relations to the king were peculiarly intimate, almost paternal, pathetically so in view of the king's infirmity and his youth. During these years he was in constant attendance upon the king, even accompanying him on military campaigns, for which the archbishop had no personal liking.[27]

How all this development affected William's historical writing is difficult to determine. He had undertaken the work reluctantly, at the request of Amaury, now dead, and it would not have been strange if he had contemplated ending the projects. There is some reason to think that he actually did so, at least with reference to the history, the "Princes of the Orient." [28] The other two works, however, were not in a condition to be readily finished. For the reign of Amaury he had only notes on the events from 1167 to 1174, and work on the period from 1163 to 1167 had not actually been started. Furthermore this work required an adequate introduction and thus far he had been able to bring that introduction no nearer than 1127. There was still much work to be done before either or both could be completed. Besides, the young king, like his father, was also much interested in history, and no doubt had been present on occasion when his father was listening to William's readings. He would, therefore, wish to have William continue the histories. It must also have occurred to William that history was an excellent medium for imparting important advice on the conduct of affairs to Baldwin IV, and the king proved to be a good listener.[29] Thus William continued his work on the histories, even though his manifold responsibilities as chancellor and archbishop caused many and long interruptions.

During these years, however, he was learning much more than before about the conduct of public affairs. In order to advise the king he must make quick and accurate judgments on men and measures and he must discriminate between fact and hope, wishes and illusions in the reports of events brought to Baldwin. He must consider alternatives in the choice of policy and the selection of agents, and must be alert and ready to recommend changes in both as the progress of events dictated. The business was so vast, so complex, and so pressing that he had to rely implicitly upon the judgment of others much of the time. This meant the lending of trust to some, an attitude of scepticism toward others. It meant also the forming of friendships—and enmities.

All this could not fail to affect his writing of history. Though he was still writing primarily to entertain and edify his royal and courtly audience, he was now to an increasing degree writing also to inform and instruct. His task could no longer be irresponsible. There were policies he had to defend, courses of procedure he had to urge, friends he had to remember, enemies he could not forget.[30] The experience marked another stage in his development.

# William of Tyre

Compared with his work in the previous four years, the amount of progress he could make in the writing of his histories was small and intermittent. Much of it, no doubt, was in the form of notes on scattered topics about which circumstances happened to permit some investigation.[31] Only the observation of current events could be recorded systematically. The rest was more or less haphazard. It is doubtful that during these years he was able to do more than complete the material in the three books from the thirteenth through the fifteenth, and perhaps not all of that.

Meanwhile, his responsibilities as archbishop of Tyre continuously reminded him of his obligations as a churchman. Nor did he forget his aspiration to the patriarchate. If the death of Amaury had ended any specific promises of royal favor in that direction, intimate association with the present king and court presented opportunities no less influential. In fact, circumstances seemed to ensure the prospect of William's attaining that ambition.

Amalrich, the incumbent in the patriarchate of Jerusalem, had held the office for twenty years. He was old and becoming very feeble. He was unable to conduct the funeral services when William of Montferrat, the brother-in-law and prospective successor of the king, died, and this duty was performed in his stead by William, archbishop of Tyre.[32] Then in the fall of 1178, when the prelates of Jerusalem embarked to attend the Third Lateran Council, which had been summoned to meet the next spring, the patriarch was unable to accompany them. The Prior of the Holy Sepulchre went as his personal representative, but William of Tyre was the recognized head of the delegation and took a prominent part in the deliberations of the Council.[33] His colleagues unanimously chose him to draft a record of the statutes and personnel of the Council. When the Council was concluded, Pope Alexander asked him to carry out an important mission at the imperial court of Constantinople,[34] and there too William gained favor. The emperor kept him there for seven months and was reconciled to his departure only by the fact that William might perform a valuable service for him at Antioch. Doubtless William felt that this experience, as well as all the knowledge of international affairs he had gained and all the friendships he had formed, would be invaluable to both Church and State when he became a patriarch. After an absence of almost two years, he returned to Tyre in July 1180.

It was a different Jerusalem to which he returned. If he thought he would be all the more welcome for the added knowledge he had acquired during his absence, he was doomed to disappointment. The king's attitude toward him had not changed—there is no evidence of that—but his physical condition had greatly altered. His chronic malady had relentlessly continued its destructive progress, and to it now were added periods of acute affliction during which he was completely incapacitated. The recurrence of these acute attacks had raised questions of regency and ultimate succession, and the leading barons and prelates were divided as to the best solution of the problem.[35]

One faction, composed chiefly of the "native" nobles, those whose positions had been hereditary for two or three generations, looked upon Raymond of Tripoli as the best choice for regent. The other faction, composed chiefly of adventurous newcomers to the realm, were opposed to Raymond and turned to the new husband of the king's sister, Guy of Lusignan, as their choice. This faction had a powerful friend in Agnes de Courtenay, the king's mother, whose influence with the king was greatly enhanced by his increasing illness. The Courtenays, though an old family in Edessa, were relative newcomers in Jerusalem and therefore had much in common with the other ambitious adventurers. Chiefly through the influence of Agnes, this faction had now gained the ascendancy at court and William's known friendship with Raymond of Tripoli made his presence most unwelcome to them.

It was the irony of fate that this faction should have been in control of the court when, on October 16, 1180, Patriarch Amalrich finally died. The haste with which the Courtenay group rushed through the election of the patriarch's successor, Archbishop Heraclius of Caesarea, was almost indecent, for he took office within ten days.[36] Doubtless the king would have preferred

William, who was one of the two candidates submitted, but he was too enfeebled by illness to overcome the contrary wishes of his mother and her friends.

Those last months of 1180 must have been a period of serious psychological readjustment for William. The election of Heraclius, a younger man, closed all hope of his ever reaching the goal of his life's ambition. The control of the court by a party opposed to him made useless the knowledge of international affairs which he had been accumulating. Though he was still chancellor, his services were probably not required except on the most formal occasions. He who had been at the very center of affairs, wielding the greatest influence, if not power, he who had basked in the friendship of king and pope and emperor, must now reconcile himself to a life of retirement, as virtually an exile from public affairs.

His physical circumstances as archbishop of Tyre were comfortable enough, but his thoughts must have been quite unhappy. Under the circumstances, the fact that his histories were uncompleted must have been a providential blessing. Those tasks remained to be done, and his preoccupation with their demands enabled him to make the necessary adjustments. For the next two years his time was devoted chiefly to this work. He interspersed the intervals of writing and study with reading, much of it in the classical Latin authors, Horace and Virgil, Ovid and Cicero.[37]

This period marked the third stage in his development as a historian. His position now was that of a detached observer, more competent than ever before, but less involved. His life's ambition had been thwarted, his hopes of service shattered, it is true, but under circumstances that left him still devoted to king and country. The whole situation was merely the twist of circumstance. In his semiretirement, he could view events with a clear conscience and a judgment fortified by a full knowledge of affairs such as few men possessed. Above all, his vision was unhampered by a sense of immediate obligation to any group or individual.

Such a situation was ideal for any writer of history and it is to be regretted that William could not have written, or rewritten, his whole work at this stage of his development. His audience was no longer primarily the king and the court. It was now the whole of Latin Christendom. His story was that of a nation, his nation, brought forth in the name of the Lord as a boon to all believing mankind. That nation could be wrecked—no one saw this possibility more clearly than he—by men who failed to live up to the high purposes by which and for which it had been created.[38]

Unfortunately William could not be altogether oblivious to what was happening round about him. If he was not of it, he was yet too clearly in it. Nearly every move made by the court must have seemed to him a mistake or worse, because he realized so clearly the precarious condition of the kingdom with Saladin in the process of consolidating the Moslem states around it. For the moment, thanks to Saladin's preoccupation in the north or in Egypt, there was a lull in the warfare and the existence of a truce gave an illusion of safety which developments did not justify.

Saladin's work of consolidation was almost complete when, in 1182, the court party crowned its series of reckless blunders by provoking the king to the verge of actual warfare with Raymond of Tripoli. Civil war at that juncture would have been suicide for the kingdom. From this immediate calamity it was barely saved by the vigorous intervention of saner men on both sides, probably William among them, but the court party remained in power, its propensity to blunder undiminished.

It was at this juncture that William, in disgust, decided to end his histories. By concluding his account at the point reached, he would discharge his debt of conscience to king and country and avoid the disservice of recording a series of foolhardy mistakes which, in his opinion, must inevitably end in a great tragedy.

In this spirit he hastily joined the parts of the work. The joints are so evident that we can almost visualize him in the process.[39] The part with which he had begun, from 1167, was complete through the twenty-first book, and perhaps also some distance into the twenty-second. The second part, from 1095 to 1167, was not quite complete, the years from 1160 to 1167 needing additional material. William had been absent from the kingdom during a part of that time and therefore needed the recollection of others to help him. But there was no time for that now. He supplied what he could from his own memory and tied it to the rest. But looking at the combined work now, he was no longer satisfied with the beginning. The story, he thought, ought to reach back to the original loss of Jerusalem. He therefore hastily excerpted material from the "Deeds of the Princes of the Orient" and used it for his introductory paragraphs. He was thus able to present a continuous account from the fall of Jerusalem in 614 to about the year 1180, and in this form he sent the account [40] to some of his friends with a covering letter which is reflected in the first part of the present preface to the twenty-third book. He was through.

Or so he thought. But his friends urged him to continue the story, arguing that Livy and other great historians had chronicled the bad as well as the good, misfortune as well as success. For more than a year he refused. Then another turn of fortune's wheel, rather than his friends' solicitation, prompted him to resume his writing. [41]

The court party had conducted affairs so badly that the leprous king, managing to muster his failing strength in one last pathetic effort, dismissed the group about him at the end of 1183 and entrusted the affairs of the kingdom to Raymond of Tripoli. Raymond, William felt, could avert the impending tragedy, and buoyed up by this hope, he began to write again.

He finished the twenty-second book and started on the twenty-third. Then some stroke of illness must have warned him that he could not expect to write indefinitely. So he revised, or wrote, his final prologue and concluded the preface to his twenty-third book. "Vita comite," he would continue to add to the story as events developed. But only one chapter of the twenty-third book was ever written, presumably "vita non comite."

Just when his death occurred is uncertain. It could not have been later than 1185. [42] He did not live to see that this last ray of hope was illusory, that the great tragedy which he had foreseen happened very much as he had predicted, through the continued blunders of that very same court party.

## The Long Road Back

The philosophy that guided William in his writing became more clearly developed as the years went on. At the beginning he shared the generally accepted Augustinian concept of the two cities and the Lord's direct and constant intervention in the affairs of men. This point of view became somewhat more sharply defined when, starting upon his second assignment, he came to think of the establishment of the Kingdom of Jerusalem as another chapter of sacred history in which the original Christian drama was somehow repeated. Could not Peter the Hermit, he reasoned, be regarded as a forerunner announcing the new kingdom? And was there not a saintly founder of the kingdom, Godfrey of Bouillon, who in his brief and troubled reign represented an ideal toward which his less perfect successors might continue to strive? It is difficult otherwise to account for William's suppression of the defects of these two characters—defects so clearly recounted by contemporary writers.

As time went on, however, he became increasingly aware of man's own share in the success and failure of his enterprises. Though William never abandoned the Augustinian view, he supplemented it more and more by an analysis of the contributing responsibilities of man himself; and so, naturally, the exposition of the career of Peter the Hermit began to seem less and less satisfactory as a proper introduction to his account. Just when he decided to extend his story to include the time of Mohammed is not clear. This decision could not have been reached before 1175, and perhaps not until after 1180, or even 1182. His conception of the role of Godfrey, however, did not change. In fact it seems to have become more and more firmly fixed, so that at the very end of his writing he sought to change the accepted practice of the chancery and enroll Godfrey formally as the first king of Jerusalem.

His final concept of his work was as a unified story from the original loss of Jerusalem in 614 to his own time, with an almost prophetic vision of the circumstances under which it might again be lost. To round out his story, therefore, he drew excerpts from his history of the princes of the Orient.

His sense of form dictated some consistency in the arrangement of his work. As he states, he divided the work into books and chapters for the convenience of his readers, but the allotment of space caused him some trouble. He finally decided upon a sort of album arrangement, with two books alloted to each reign, the first opening with a pen picture of the ruler and the second closing with the account of his death. In view of this arrangement, William's allotment of two books to the reign of Baldwin IV, who was still living, assumes a pathetic significance. The second closes with the transfer of the regency from Guy to Raymond of Tripoli. To William this must have seemed the king's final act.

There were two exceptions to the general plan: Godfrey was allotted only one book and Baldwin III was allotted three. But these exceptions were sufficiently justified by the brief reign of Godfrey and by the very long one of Baldwin III, during part of which his mother was joint ruler. Since William's material for the different reigns was quite unequal in amount, his uniform allotments of space presented some difficulties, and it was probably to correct these that he inserted long excerpts from papal letters on ecclesiastical organization, as well as other documents from the archives.

William's work as a historian is distinguished by certain traits in which he excelled nearly all historical writers of his time. The first of these was his critical attitude toward his sources of information, whether written or oral, whether recent or hallowed with age. Not that he consistently maintained this attitude, but throughout his work his intention to do so is evident. In fact, there is scarcely a single book of the twenty-three in which he does not have occasion to question some source, either because it contradicts some other source or is inconsistent with observed fact or reason.[43]

Second must be cited the objectivity with which he views even contemporary affairs. This tendency is most clearly marked in his work after 1180. Corollary to it is his impartiality. He recounts not only the strength and the virtues but also the errors in policy and judgment of the high as well as the low, and especially of the former. This rigorous judgment is applied to friend as well as foe.[44]

Third, his freedom from prejudice, or rather his ability to rise above prejudice, is marked. Though he voices nearly all the conventional attitudes that characterized the period, yet he finds much to commend in Armenian, Greek, and Syrian, even in Arab and Turk. Indeed, William's favorable account of Nureddin and Saladin has done much to fix their reputation in the Western world.[45] Similarly he displays a sympathetic attitude toward the peasantry, whether Christian or pagan, and more than any other royal chronicle of the period his work recognizes the importance of commerce in the affairs of men. The allusions to merchants are numerous, frequently extended, and almost invariably sympathetic.[46] In like manner, he recognizes the influence of women in important affairs, for good as well as for ill.[47]

Fourth must be noted the wide range of activities which he regards important enough to mention. These include not only the geographical settings of events, the antiquarian information about places, as well as copious genealogical facts, but also references to architecture, art, music, and various forms of entertainment. Diplomatic dealings are emphasized and described in considerable detail.[48]

Fifth, William's ability to analyze the human elements involved in the progress of events and to point out the sequence of cause and effect in the affairs of men is unusual for his era, and striking. While sharing with his time the Augustinian view that men's failures were due to their sins, their success to the grace of God, he was less and less inclined to accept that explanation as complete. Increasingly he probed the motives of men and the circumstances surrounding events; increasingly he canvassed the possible choices of policy, leaders, and courses of action, and other controllable factors involved in any situation. In these particulars, doubtless, his experience as a responsible statesman stood him in good stead. His analytical powers are at their best in his later books, especially in the last three.[49]

Sixth, and not least, must be placed his concern about style.

94

Not only does he command a vocabulary adequate to describe his wide range of topics, but this vocabulary is remarkably pure Latin.[50] His skill is that of an accomplished raconteur, and some of his incidents have furnished good stories for all later times. His style is marked throughout, and increasingly through the years, by a quality of urbanity relatively unknown in the West at the time. Above all, he reveals a sense of form, not only in rounding out particular incidents but in shaping his whole work to give it unity, continuity, and consistency.[51] In this aspect of style Otto of Freising alone can be compared to him; but in other respects Otto's literary skill was inferior.

To sum up, in each of these six qualities William was at least equal to the best of his age, and in his combination of them he was probably superior to any historian between the Classical period and the fifteenth-century Renaissance.

William's major faults are insufficient to offset these more positive qualities, and most of them disappeared as he passed through the several stages of his development. Even at the beginning of his work his acceptance of legend and miracle was less credulous than that of most contemporary chroniclers, and toward the end it was noticeably absent.[52] Doubtless if he had had time to revise, he would have modified some of his earlier statements, allowing to Peter the Hermit, Godfrey, and Tancred, who by his time had become national heroes, some of the faults and weaknesses which the strictly contemporary accounts had noticed. It was clearly due to lack of time that certain repetitions, inconsistencies, one or two actual contradictions, and several lacunae were permitted to remain in the final text.

William's handling of chronology, however, was seriously at fault. In his regard for the sequence of events within a given topic he was scrupulous, but in his relation of concurrent minor events he was vague. He was scrupulous also in his choice of dates from written sources, even though these were at times confusing, but he was not always careful to adjust to a common standard those taken from varied sources. His chief difficulty, however, arose from his effort to include in the final organization of his book a chronological framework. This effort was made without due regard to the gaps in his material and without a standardization of chronological statements already written. As a result, the effect of the chronological framework has been to throw nearly all his statements of date into doubt.[53]

The most serious fault of William's work, however, arises from his professional bias. In this he did not change in any marked degree from the beginning to the end of his writing. Apparently he had a fixed idea of the place of the secular hierarchy of the Church in the Latin states of the East and he resented any acts which tended to diminish the authority or prestige of that hierarchy. Woe to any who contributed to such diminution! It was impossible for him to deal fairly with such persons, no matter whether they were nobles, churchmen, kings, or popes. On this account Arnulf of Choques was made to appear as an unadulterated villain, Daimbert almost a saint, Baldwin I failed to receive his full measure of glory, and Hadrian IV was definitely disparaged. Likewise the Hospitallers and Templars, who during William's lifetime gained independence from local ecclesiastical authority, received only grudging credit for their achievements but copious censure for their faults.[54] To this bias of William, in part, must also be ascribed the inclusion of so much material that is of purely technical interest to churchmen.[55]

Other faults found in William's work include the omission of matters on which he was in a position to acquire information and his references to surrounding countries primarily, if not exclusively, from the point of view of Jerusalem. By and large, however, these faults are more than matched by those of the other chroniclers of the twelfth century and leave a strong balance of credit in William's favor.

The value of William's work as a source for our knowledge of the crusading history of the twelfth century has usually been understated. Ever since Sybel published his critical study of the sources on the First Crusade, it has been customary to treat William's account of that series of events as purely secondary. Yet William added, even there, matter to be found nowhere else—

matter derived from his own great familiarity with the geography of the Holy Land, as well as from his archaeological, antiquarian, and genealogical research. Furthermore, his account is made highly valuable by his familiarity with the archives and, above all, by his unusual perspective and knowledge of the consequences of events which contemporary writers could hardly appreciate.

William's statement at the beginning of his sixteenth book that from this point onward he was writing on the basis of direct personal knowledge has usually been misinterpreted. From that statement critics have assumed that all the material before that point, 1144, was obtained from written sources and that the value of William's work as a primary source begins at that juncture. Actually, however, his written sources stopped in 1127.[56] The material for the years 1127 to 1144 was derived from interviews with people of his parents' generation, as well as from a study of the archives, and some of it from personal observation. In other words, his is our only chronicle of the Kingdom of Jerusalem from 1127 to 1184, our primary source for fifty-seven instead of forty-four years of its history. Naturally William felt more certain of events that happened after he was fourteen years old than of those occurring during the seventeen preceding years, but his record remains our chief source for the whole of that period. And his modifications and interpretations of the written sources before 1127 have something of primary value for the earlier period as well. Thus our conclusion must be that William's work cannot be disregarded at any point, and that it has some original value from beginning to end.

The advance that William made in the writing of history was not without effect upon the development of historiography in western Europe. It is a tribute to the intellectual advance of Europe by the end of the twelfth century that the quality of his writing was almost immediately appreciated. The anonymous author who probably as early as 1192 [57] began his Latin continuation of William's history paid tribute to its style as "eloquenter et eleganter"; Ernoul, supposedly the young squire of Balian of Ibelin at the battle of Hattin, who continued William's history in

French, said of him, "Li archevesque de Sur at a non Guilliaumes . . . et ne savoit on en Chrestiente mellour clerc de lui." [58] Jacques de Vitry, who came upon William's histories at Damietta, paid them the high compliment of taking over a substantial portion of them for his *History of the Orient.*[59]

The influence of William's work in England deserves more extended treatment than it can here receive. Roger Wendover was so impressed with its merit that without acknowledgement he drew from it nearly all his material on the Crusades up to 1184. Matthew Paris, who in 1235 succeeded Roger as historiographer of St. Albans, appears to have gone over this material again and made some corrections drawn from William's original.[60] He repeated this material in his briefer history, acknowledging his indebtedness to William.

It is in the margin of this work that Matthew wrote "Hunc librum tulit episcopus Wintoniensis P[etrus] de terra Sancta, quem vix, qui haec scripsi ab eo impetravi." [61] Peter des Roches, bishop of Winchester, returned from the Holy Land in 1231. The acquisition of the work by St. Albans must therefore be dated between 1231 and 1235, while Matthew was still an understudy of Roger Wendover, and it may well have been Matthew himself who prepared the summary of William's history which Roger incorporated. If so, it is interesting to speculate how much Matthew's own later writing was influenced by his careful study of William of Tyre before he entered upon his own career as historian. Certain it is that, through these two English chroniclers, William's interpretation of crusading history entered the main stream of English history, where down to the present it has continued to have some authority.

William's influence was even more widely extended through the early translation of his work into French, which in the thirteenth century had become the international language of chivalry and commerce, known from the British Isles to the Levant, from Sicily to the Scandinavian peninsulas. In its French form William's work quickly became the standard history of the Crusades to which up to 1275 various authors added accounts of later crusades.[62]

All who copied William's work were, accordingly, influenced by his conception of history. In this way he established a new norm, with which, if we may judge from the number of copies that have survived, nearly every court and castle and town in western Europe became familiar. In the process of copying and in the practice of copyists, nearly all traces of William's authorship were soon obliterated, and it is doubtful that any historian of the Middle Ages was more widely read yet less well known than William of Tyre. But his effectiveness was thereby only widened, to influence, not only Jacques de Vitry and Matthew Paris, but perhaps also Jean de Meung, Joinville, and Dante.[63] His contribution had entered the main stream of the history and literature of the Western world to exercise a lasting influence upon both.

## NOTES

[1] T. A. Archer, "On the Accession Dates of the Early Kings of Jerusalem," *English Historical Review*, 1889, 91–105.

[2] S. Lane-Poole, *Saladin*, p. viii. London and New York, 1898.

[3] This statement is the result of a cumulative impression based not only upon the statements of his reluctance to become a historiographer and tutor (Prol.: XX, 1; XX, 5; and XX, 17), but also upon the many allusions to ecclesiastical affairs and the extended discussion of matters of purely technical concern to the hierarchy.

[4] Most of the facts of his life are assembled in the comprehensive and critical study by Prutz (H. Prutz, "Studien über Wilhelm von Tyrus," *Neues Archiv der Gesellschaft für ältere Geschichtskunde*, VIII, 93–132). This work superseded the partial study which Sybel had made for Ranke's seminar (H. von Sybel, *Geschichte des Ersten Kreuzzuges*, Düsseldorf, 1841), as well as the earlier studies by Michaud (J. Michaud, *Bibliothèque des croisades*, 2nd ed., 4 vols., Paris, 1829–30) and Bongars (J. Bongars, *Gesta dei per francos*, Hanau, 1611). Additions to our knowledge of William have been made by the incidental findings of scholars working on related problems.

[5] *W.T.*, XIV, 11 (All references to the text of William's history are to the edition of the French Academy: *Recueil des historien des croisades*, 16 vols., publié par les soins de l'Académie des inscriptions et belles-lettres, Paris, 1841–1906. *Historien occidentaux*, vol. I, 1844. All citations are to the books and chapters as numbered therein.): "Fulcherius . . . modice literatus sed constans et amor disciplinae"; *W.T.*, XVI, 17: "Petrus . . . nobilis secundum carnem sed spiritu nobilier, cujus vita et conversatio, longiores et diligentiores postulant tractatus." *W.T.*, XV, 21; XVIII, 24. These and

# The Long Road Back

other references to these prelates indicate an intimacy of relationship difficult to explain on any other basis.

⁶ *W.T.*, XIX, 12.

⁷ *W.T.*, XIX, 4.

⁸ *L'Estoire de éracles et la conqueste de la terre d'outre mer.* This is published in the same volume with the text of William's history. See page 1004.

⁹ This practice of sending established clergy, usually archdeacons, to study law in the schools of Italy was quite common about the middle of the twelfth century. Stubbs mentions an instance in which two archdeacons were sent there from England in 1170 (Ralph of Diceto, *Imagines historiae,* Introd., p. xxxiv, W. Stubbs, ed.). Rashdall cites a reference to law as among the liberal arts in 1162 (H. Rashdall, *The Universities of Europe in the Middle Ages,* Oxford, 1895, Vol. I, p. 110, note 2.) The two documents, both dealing with a grant by Peter, archbishop of Tyre, in which a "Willelmus Canonicus" is mentioned, are dated by Röhricht as early in 1161 and late in 1163. Röhricht has mistakenly identified the archdeacon, William, whose name also appears in the second of these documents with our William, who did not become archdeacon until 1167, when he succeeded the other William here mentioned. There is, of course, no certainty, but a very high degree of probability, that William was the canon referred to (nos. 370 and 385 of R. Röhricht, *Regesta regni hierosolymitani,* Innsbruck, 1893; Additamentum, 1904. Hereafter referred to as *R. Reg.*).

¹⁰ *W.T.*, X, 23; XI, 13; XIII, 1; XXI, 11. In addition to these direct citations of the Code and Digest, there are numerous echoes of the Code in William's use of legal phrases, e.g., "angariis . . . parangariis." Since this suggestion that William was trained in law and was primarily interested in law is at variance with former accounts of his life, it may be proper to present somewhat more fully the evidence supporting the contention. One evidence of his interest is afforded by the detailed accounts of legal processes (e.g., Case of Hugh of Joppa, XIV, 15 and 18; impeachment of Ralph, patriarch of Antioch, XV, 13 and 16; justification of Daimbert's claim to Jerusalem, IX, 17 and 18; controversy over the jurisdiction of the archbishopric of Tyre, XIII, 23; XIV, 11–14; legal rights of Venetians in cities of the kingdom, XII, 25; income tax of the kingdom, XXII, 23). Another is afforded by his very frequent use of legal phrases. Homage and fealty are seldom mentioned without the phrases *juramentis manualiter* or *corporaliter exhibitis.* Professor Gaines Post has called my attention to the fact that the language in which William describes the procuratorship offered to Philip of Flanders or given to Raymond of Tripoli, Guy of Lusignan, or even to Eustace Granier is the language of Roman law in the procuratorship of Caesar and that William's oft-repeated quotation from Terence "quot homines, tot sententiae" was a favorite of the law schools of Europe. William shows a jurist's regard for the sanctity of treaties, taking pains to refute the claims of the Greeks to Antioch on the ground that Alexius had violated the treaty upon which those claims rested, and criticizing both Baldwin III and Amaury for breaches of treaty not only with Christians but even with Saracens. He compliments both Baldwin III and Amaury upon their expert knowledge of the customary law, XVI, 2; XIX, 2. Furthermore, his selection by the fathers at the Lateran Council of 1179 "si quis statuta . . . scire desiderat, relegat scriptum quod nos ad preces sanctorum patrum, qui eidem synodo interfuerunt, confecimus" would seem to involve some recognition

of his skill in law as well as in writing. While these instances are perhaps the most striking, there are scattered throughout his work many other allusions to law, customary, canon, and commercial, as well as a jurist's assumption that there was a definite body of law developing in the Kingdom of Jerusalem (XXI, 6; XVI, 2; and XIX, 2).

[11] R. Reg., no. 385.

[12] G. Wiet, L'Egypte arabe, Paris, 1938; R. Röhricht, Geschichte des Königreiches Jerusalem, Innsbruck, 1898 (hereafter referred to as R.G.K.J.); W. Stevenson, Crusaders in the East, Cambridge, 1907; and R. Röhricht, "Amalrich I, König von Jerusalem," Mittheilungen des Instituts für Oesterreichische Geschichtsforschung, 1891, 432–93.

[13] W.T., Prol.; XVI, 2; XIX, 2; XX, 1 and 5.

[14] W.T., XX, 17; XX,1.

[15] W.T., XX, 4.

[16] W.T., XX, 17.

[17] W.T., XXI, 1.

[18] The chronicle of Fulcher of Chartres extended through the reign of Baldwin I and nearly ten years of that of Baldwin II. None is known thereafter until the "Balduini III historiae Nicaena vel Antiochena necnon Jherosolimitana," Rec. Occid., V. 133–85, which an anonymous writer began as a chronicle of the reign of Baldwin III. It added only an item or two to the chronicle of Fulcher which it summarized. Except for good intentions, therefore, there was no royal chronicle after 1127. W.T., XX, 31.

[19] W.T., Prol.; XIX, 21. It is interesting to reflect that these books were probably from the library of Usamah which Baldwin III appropriated from the shipwreck near Acre in 1154. (P. K. Hitti, An Arab-Syrian Gentleman and Warrior in the Period of the Crusades, Memoirs of Usamah ibn-Munquidh, New York, 1929, p. 61.) If so, the Arab writer might have tempered his lament over the loss of his 4000 works somewhat with the thought that they were being put to such good use.

[20] W.T., XVI, 2; XIX, 1–3; XX, 31; XXI, 1; XXI, 5. Prutz (op. cit.) noticed the reference to the attitude of Sicily toward Jerusalem which must have been written before 1174 (W.T., XI, 29). A similar contradiction appears between the passage from the "Princes of the Orient" which he inserted (I, 4 and XIX, 21) and the statement of Saladin's overthrow of the Fatimid caliph (XX, 11). The expression "vestra dilectio," a term used in direct address and obviously intended for Amaury (I, 5), is imbedded in another passage taken from the Moslem history. Elsewhere William seems to forecast events as far as the death of Arnulf (XII, 6) and may, in fact, have written up to the point where Fulcher ends, somewhere in Book XIII. The first clear indication of his writing after the death of Amaury is the reference to the Archbishop of Tyre as his predecessor (XIII, 23).

[21] Examples of this skill, to cite only a few: Godfrey's reply to the Arabs who found him seated on the ground at Arsuf; Godfrey's prowess with the sword; the courtesy of Baldwin I to the Arab chieftain's wife; the use of the Armenian reverence for beards by Baldwin du Burg to obtain money from his father-in-law; the quarrel between Baldwin du Burg and Joscelin; the rescue of Joscelin b˞ the fifty Armenians disguised as monks; the attempted gift of a silver ᴄ ꜳparisoned white horse to Zangi by Alice of Antioch; the ruse by which Joscelin II forced Emperor John out of Antioch,

# The Long Road Back

and the subordination of the friendly Turk. *W.T.*, IX, 20; IX, 22; X, 11; X, 21; XI, 11; XI, 22; XII, 18; XIII, 27; XIV, 4; XVI, 2.

[22] See Note 20 above.

[23] *W.T.*, XXI, 1.

[24] *W.T.*, XXI, 4; XX, 9.

[25] *W.T.*, XXI, 5. The earliest extant document bearing his signature is dated Dec. 13, 1174 (*R. Reg.*, no. 518). At this time, his additional income was provided by his appointment as archdeacon of Nazareth as well as of Tyre.

[26] *W.T.*, XXI, 9; *R. Reg.*, no. 531.

[27] *W.T.*, XXI, 14–25.

[28] This impression arises from his frequent use of 570 years as the span from Mohammed to his own time, whether 1182 or 1184. The reckoning is Arabic and the year 570 A.H. corresponds to the year of Amaury's death. William knew that it was not the equivalent of 1182 for he gives the exact equivalent, 577 A.H. (XIX, 21). Nor could he have used it as the nearest round number for 580 years would have been better, especially for 1184. In the haste of his final revision, however, the number 570 recurred to him, which suggests that he had once stopped his writing at that point.

[29] *W.T.*, XXI, 1.

[30] This is best illustrated by his account of the dealings with Philip of Flanders in 1177 (*W.T.*, XXI, 14–25). He himself had conducted the negotiations and the tactics of the count led him to fear that the latter was trying to discredit the Latins of Jerusalem in the minds of western Europe. William evidently hastened to send letters describing matters to the rulers of the West for William's account of the judgment by the Lord on the matter appears in most of the chronicles of the West, even in those of William of Newburg and Robert of Torigni who could not possibly have seen William's history.

[31] The interview with Lady Stephanie in Jerusalem (*W.T.*, XIX, 4) is clearly an example. Doubtless also much of his genealogical information, which Professor John La Monte regards as extraordinarily accurate, was gained during this period.

[32] *W.T.*, XXI, 13.

[33] *W.T.*, XXI, 26. J. Dom Mansi: *Sacrorum conciliorum nova et amplissima collectio*, Paris, 1901 *et seq.*, vol. XXII, *passim*.

[34] *W.T.*, XXII, 4.

[35] The best recent discussion of the political factions is that of M. W. Baldwin, *Raymond III of Tripoli*, Princeton, 1936.

[36] *W.T.*, XXII, 4. William's account of the election is singularly brief. Ernoul, his continuator, however, is not so reticent (M. L. de Mas-Latrie, *Chronique d'Ernoul et de Bernard le Tresorier*, Paris, 1871, pp. 82–86).

[37] His quotations from these authors occur chiefly in the portions of his work which were written after 1180, e.g., Prologue, at the beginnings and endings of various books, and in book XVI *et seq.* See also Prutz, *op. cit.*, and M. Manitius, *Geschichte der Lateinischen Litteratur des Mittelalters* (3 vols.), Munich, 1911–13, vol. III, pp. 430–39.

[38] *W.T.*, Prol., XXIII preface.

[39] The statement in the Prologue, "exordium sumentes ab exitu . . . A regnis Occidentalibus, vocante Domino . . . per annos LXXXIV . . . protraximus historiam," seems to indicate his original plan for the royal chroni-

cle. That the beginning, as we now have it, was a later thought is indicated, not only by the fact that he feels it necessary to give a special reason in the next sentence of the Prologue, but also by the use of the words "paucis et succincte praemissimus." That this was his procedure is confirmed by his statements at the end of several chapters (I, 1 and I, 3) referring the reader to his other work for further information. That he was making these changes late, probably in 1182, is indicated not only by his specific mention of that date in I, 3, but by his making the same kind of changes in a book which was written after 1180 (XIX, 15; XIX, 20; XIX, 21). In other words, chapters 1 and 3 of Book I and chapters 15, 20, and 21 of Book XIX represent the same mental decision and were inserted at the same time, that is, in 1182. All were taken from his work on the history of the princes of the Orient, and in one case, at least, without change in the original wording (I, 5), another evidence of haste in finishing the work. Chapters 1 to 7 inclusive of Book I are probably all of this nature. Chapter 8 may have been part of his earlier beginning. Chapters 9 and 10 involved some dovetailing of material. IV, 11 and 24; VII, 19; VIII, 3; IX, 17-19; X, 17; XIII, 3; XVIII, 4 and 5; XIX, 15, 20, 21, also contain material derived from the "Princes of the Orient," much of which was probably inserted at the same time. The history of the princes of the Orient, as he states in the Prologue, began with Mohammed. His selection of Emperor Heraclius for the first sentence of his final beginning must, therefore, have been a matter of deliberate choice for reasons of his own. Since he felt at the time that the blunders of the court were leading the kingdom to destruction, William too may have attached some significance to the identity of the names.

[40] This action, which is so clearly implied in the preface to the twenty-third book, derives interesting confirmation from Ernoul. Balian of Ibelin, one of the partisans of Raymond of Tripoli, was a near neighbor and presumably an intimate friend of William. Ernoul had been Balian's squire as a young man in 1187 and remained in close touch with the family for the rest of his life. When Ernoul undertook the continuation of William's history he briefly summarized material up to about 1180 and began his independent writing at that point. As has already been pointed out, some of his statements were in direct contradiction to those contained in William's final three books and Prologue (see no. 42). This contradiction can be best explained on the theory that his version of William's account did not include those books. It was probably the early copy which had been given to Balian and had then passed into the possession of Ernoul.

[41] W.T., XXII, 29; XXIII, preface and 1.

[42] W.T., Prol.: XXIII, preface, "vita comite." The date and circumstances of William's death are nowhere definitely recorded. The preposterous account of Ernoul that William protested the election of Heraclius, appealed to Rome and died there of poison administered by the physician whom Heraclius had sent after him, is directly refuted by William's twenty-second book and Prologue. Prutz has dealt adequately with the mistaken identification of the archbishop of Tyre present in the West in 1188. Röhricht has offered the interval between October 17 and 21, 1186 as the time of William's death (R.G.K.J., pp. 391-92, note 5). This suggestion, though the most definite, presents difficulties. William was still chancellor in 1184 (W.T., Prol.), while Baldwin IV was yet alive and Raymond of Tripoli was regent. William's successor in the office, his own vice-chancellor, ap-

# The Long Road Back

pears as early as May 16, 1185 (*R. Reg.*, no. 643). Under those conditions, neither illness nor adverse political conditions could account for William's resignation of the office. The document (*R. Reg.*, ad. N. 652) from which Röhricht derives the date October 17, 1186, is not signed by William. He is merely mentioned as one of five judges delegate appointed by Pope Urban III sometime before. The use of his name in the document in which the judges rendered their verdict does not prove he was alive at the time. Furthermore, there is no other document since 1183 (*R. Reg.*, no. 625) in which William's name is recorded. The conclusion that he died before a chancellor was chosen to succeed him, sometime before May 16, 1185, thus offers the fewest difficulties.

[43] The most thorough study of William's use of the sources for this period is contained in the various editions published by H. Hagenmeyer: *Anonymi gesta francorum et aliorum hierosolymitanorum*, Heidelberg, 1890, p. 49 *et passim*; *Ekkehardi uraugensis abbatis hierosolymita*, pp. 34–38; *Galterii cancellarii bella Antiochena*, pp. 46–52 *et passim*; *Die Kreuzzugs-briefe aus den Jahren 1088–1100*, pp. 1–6 *et passim*; *Fulcherii carnotensis historia hierosolymitana*, pp. 85–91 *et passim*, Heidelberg, 1913; Sybel, *op. cit.*; Prutz, *op. cit.*

[44] The best examples of this attitude are his character sketches of Amaury, Baldwin IV, and Raymond III of Tripoli. (*W.T.*, XIX, 1–4; XXI, 1; XXI, 5.)

[45] *W.T.*, XVI, 7; XVIII, 34; XXI, 6–8.

[46] Perhaps the best illustration is that quoted by C. H. Haskins, *Renaissance of the Twelfth Century*, p. 270, *W.T.*, XX, 10, but the detailed account of the agreements with Italian cities (X, 14 and 18; XII, 25; XVIII, 4), and William's lament over the loss of both "principal and interest" by the merchants whom Raymond's pirates plundered (XVIII, 33) also deserve special notice.

[47] At least twenty women attain a distinct individuality in his pages. Melisenda is perhaps the one most highly appreciated, Alice of Antioch the most despised, and Agnes de Courtenay the most detested. There are numerous references to each of them.

[48] The most detailed discussion of diplomatic dealings is that with Philip of Flanders in 1177 (*W.T.*, XXI). His inclination, however, is apparent from the outset for he almost invariably expands and improves the discussion of diplomatic matters which he draws from the writers on the First Crusade. His description of Patriarch Fulcher at Rome, of King Amaury at Constantinople, of Hugh of Caesarea at Cairo or even of his own dealings with Emperor Manuel are also excellent examples.

[49] The best examples are perhaps *W.T.*, XII, 7; XXII, 10–11.

[50] Manitius (*op. cit.*) was unable to discover more than two terms which were obviously coined in medieval fashion. At least one of these terms was derived from Albert of Aix.

[51] *W.T.*, Prologue. See also p. 154, no. 3.

[52] In two instances, during the first stage of his writing, he actually went beyond the imaginative extravagances of his sources. One was in his justification of the betrayal of Antioch to Bohemond by Firuz, and the other in Godfrey's skill with the sword. He refused, however, to accept Albert's story of Godfrey's descent from the swan.

[53] T. A. Archer (*op. cit.*) and W. Stevenson (*Crusaders in the East*, Appendix) have attempted to discover a key to the systematic chronology.

The difficulties of the problem, however, are clearly illustrated by Röhricht's translation of the date of Amaury's death given by William (XX, 31), "regni vero duodecimo, mense quinto," as twelve years and five months. In another passage (XIX, 1) William states the length of Amaury's reign in noun form: "Regnavit autem annis undecim, mensibus quinque." Usually, however, William uses the adjectival form which defies precise addition.

[54] William's treatment of the Templars has been examined in detail by F. Lundgreen (*Wilhelm von Tyrus und der Templerorden*, Berlin, 1911).

[55] It is probable that William introduced some of his material, especially papal documents relating to the reorganization of the Church in the East, as a filler in those reigns for which he did not have sufficient material, e.g., the end of Baldwin II's, and that of Fulk.

[56] See note 18 above.

[57] Marianne Salloch, *Die Lateinische Fortsetzung Wilhelms von Tyrus*, Prologue, Leipzig, 1934.

[58] Mas-Latrie, *op. cit.*, p. 82.

[59] Prutz (*op. cit.*) noted these borrowings. His conclusion is supported by Zacher (Gustave Zacher, *Die Historia Orientalis des Jacob von Vitry*, Königsberg, 1885) and also by Funk (Philipp Funk, *Jakob von Vitry, Leben und Werke*, Leipzig, 1909).

[60] *Matthaei Parisiensis, monachi sancti Albani, chronica majora*, ed. H. R. Luard, II, XXXI.

[61] *Matthaei Parisiensis, monachi sancti Albani historia Anglorum sive ut vulgo dicitur historia minor*, ed. Sir Frederic Madden, I, 163.

[62] The French versions of William's chronicle are so numerous and varied that the determination of their relationship to each other and hence to William is still a major problem for scholarship. Mas-Latrie's attempt to solve this problem (*op. cit.*) remains the most serious effort. Paris (Paulin Paris, *Guillaumes de Tyr et ses continuateurs*, Paris, 1879) and Colvin (Mary Noyes Colvin, ed., *Godeffroy of Boloyne or the Siege and Conquest of Jerusalem by William, Archbishop of Tyre*, trans. from the French by William Caxton and printed by him in 1481, London, 1893) have also grappled with the problem. Miss Colvin distinguishes some eight categories among French versions and notes more than seventy manuscript copies under at least seven titles: *Roman d'Eracles; Le Livre des passages d'outre mer; Le Livre del' acquisition et de la perte de la terre sainte; Les chroniques d'outre mer; Libres des voyages à la terre sainte; Histoire du passage de Godefroy de Bouillon; Le livre du conquête.* See also Gustav Gröber, *Grundiss der Romanischen Philologie*, II, Pt. I. Strassburg, 1902, pp. 721–22.

[63] At least one Italian of the fourteenth century knew the French version. This was Francesco Pipino who translated it into Latin, unaware that it had originally been written in Latin. This affords an interesting comparison of the quality of William's Latin, which is far superior, to that of Pipino. (L. A. Muratori, *Rerum Italicarum scriptores*, 25 vols., in 28, Milan, 1723–51, IX).

# 6

# The New Learning

THE medieval historian has long been accustomed to regard the whole pattern of man's activities as his proper concern. How could he fail to do so? For in the Middle Ages politics was inextricably interwoven with religion, and with religion was associated the wide range of social, intellectual, eleemosynary, and artistic undertakings in which the organized Church engaged. The economic conditions of the period were also of great concern to both Church and State. The medievalist, therefore, came early to the conclusion that every activity of society during this period was of potential significance, and that, since the humanities interested medieval people, they also interested him.

The questions centering around the humanities are, however, of more than incidental concern to the historian of this period. As he moves on through its centuries, he finds his vision obscured in the fourteenth century by the formidable terms *Humanism* and the *Renaissance*. He is asked then to recognize Humanism as a new phenomenon and Petrarch as its creator, and he is called upon to recognize the dawn of a new era named the Renaissance.

These terms are not of the historian's own coining and the concepts they describe, or veil, are not his either. He has been

NOTE: This essay originally formed part of a paper called "History and the Humanities," which appeared in *The Meaning of the Humanities*, edited by Theodore Meyer Greene and published by Princeton University Press, 1938.

led to a reluctant acquiescence in their use only by the enthusiasm with which some of his friends have accepted them. I believe that he has never been quite happy in employing the words, which he always approaches gingerly and with some embarrassment. His mind, like Edmund Burke's, is perpetually troubled by the effort to discover "what simple ideas, things, events and circumstances are included in these pulpy aggregates" called Humanism and the Renaissance.

The main cycle of events which they represent is clear enough. With Petrarch, the historian is told, Humanism begins. Thereafter humanists continue to appear in ever increasing number. Boccaccio espouses the new learning. John of Ravenna teaches it to groups of disciples at Florence, Milan, and Venice. Coluccio Salutati and Niccolo Niccoli promote it. Within fifty years after the death of its founder, the movement numbers such persons as Leonardo Bruni, Poggio, Filelfo, Guarino, Lorenzo Valla, Vittorino da Feltre—all major luminaries among a much greater number of followers. And Humanism is but just started. In another half-century its devotees include the mighty of Italy. Two popes, practicing humanists themselves, and many princes both of state and commerce are equipped with the new education.

By this time Italy is no longer large enough to hold the swelling numbers. They burst across the Alps to Germany, France, Spain, Hungary, and England. Reuchlin and Agricola, Budaeus and Lefevre, Ximenes, Vives, Grocyn, and Linacre, not to name Erasmus, all challenge comparison with any of the distinguished humanists in Italy. Thereafter the movement widens and deepens, becoming a permanent part of the intellectual equipment of modern times.

The historian is distressed, not by the rather attractive name given to all this burgeoning of intellectual activity, but by the narrowness of its application. That is, he has much difficulty in discovering among the activities of the humanists anything he has not met before.

Much stress is laid, for example, on the fact that the humanists were collectors of manuscripts and builders of libraries. That passion, however, had existed in the earlier centuries, when the library of York, for instance, was celebrated in verse and when Fulda, St. Gall, and other monasteries likewise gained great renown for their collections. Was not Gerbert himself accused of plundering the library of Bobbio, perhaps to enrich that of Rheims? Rulers, too, are known to have accumulated libraries, even though they housed them in Church buildings. Did not Vincent of Beauvais dip freely into the capacious purse of St. Louis to build up a royal library in Paris? Indeed, it is rather surprising to note how many of the major discoveries of classical manuscripts so enthusiastically applauded by the humanists of Italy were made in libraries north of the Alps.

Or, again, much is made of the intensive study the humanists gave to the ancients, and of their success in eliminating corruptions introduced into manuscripts by copyists. But despite the decline of education during the Middle Ages, the classics had never been lost; Greek was not altogether unknown, and grammars had been written at intervals. Even books of style were not unknown, and John of Garland is certainly reckoned a distinguished scholar in this branch of what was later to be called philology, though more than a century was to pass before Petrarch began to achieve his reputation and two before Valla was to establish a new norm in such matters.

As for the errors of copyists in the corruption of texts, did not Alcuin, as early as the late eighth century, persuade the mighty Charlemagne to issue a capitulary on this subject? And did any of the Renaissance humanists urge more truculently than Roger Bacon the need for establishing correct texts by a nice study of manuscript copies?

Certainly the classical learning and interest in libraries cannot be said to have begun with the Renaissance.

Great emphasis, of course, is placed on the aesthetic appreciation of the classics by the humanists, on their interest in the style of the ancient authors, on their discriminating taste, and their modeling of their own writings on the best work of the past. Yet even in these respects the historian is troubled. Certainly Bede was not innocent of style, as is displayed both in his own volumes and in his choice of reading material. The scholars who learned from Alcuin and vied with each other in composing both poetry and prose on classical models were more than dimly aware of what Horace calls the "glory and charm" of words. Virgil and Terence, Cicero and Seneca, Livy and Sallust are all clearly recognized as superior stylists not only by Lupus Servatus, Theodulphus, Angilbert, and Eginhard, but also by later writers of the Middle Ages. Does not the nun of Gandersheim compel Terence to pious uses? And, according to Lambert of Hersfeld, does not Henry IV make his memorable journey over the Alps to Canossa in the words of Livy?

Furthermore, long before the fourteenth century appreciation of good writing was rather widespread. For example, all France seemed to shudder at the barbarous style used by the anonymous writer of the *Gesta* in presenting the story of the First Crusade. Thereupon at least three writers, all men of position, one of them Guibert de Nogent, undertook, with more ambition than success, to rewrite the chronicle. And this happened two centuries and a half before Petrarch proclaimed the new era. Ekkehard of Aura and Otto of Freising may be a bit difficult to read, but no one can deny their conscious use of classical models. John of Salisbury, William of Tyre, and after them the historians of Henry II's reign, particularly Matthew of Paris, can scarcely be impugned either for their own performance or for their choice of models. Many of the humanists of the Renaissance wrote far worse Latin than did these authors.

Nor did the writers of the pre-Renaissance times regard their efforts at style altogether as penitential labors calculated to ensure their speedier salvation. John of Salisbury's frequent repetition of Quintilian's observation that "otium sine litteris mors est vivique hominis sepultura" suggests a resigned willingness to postpone that state in favor of a longer lingering among the classical writers, and there is no reason to suppose that he was alone among the writers before the Renaissance in harboring such emotions. Nor need we join Symonds in exploring the poetic outbursts of ebullient undergraduates to understand that there was joy in letters during the centuries before Petrarch and Boccaccio. There were many past forty who felt that delight—the same delight that (as Catullus complained) still excites a reader to sleeplessness when he comes upon an unusually fine passage of prose or poetry.

Among some modern writers on Humanism there is also a tendency to identify that movement with knowledge of Greek. This, however, is a distinction which it would be difficult to maintain and one which neither the majority nor the most thoughtful of commentators would care to accept. Indeed, this measure of discrimination would eliminate many who have an enduring claim upon this title. It would eliminate, among others, Petrarch himself. Equally embarrassing would be the compulsion, on such a basis, to extend the ranks of humanists. John Scotus certainly knew Greek, as did also scattered scholars in the centuries that followed. During the twelfth and thirteenth centuries there appear to have been scholars capable of extensive and even accurate translations from the Greek. Both John of Salisbury and Roger Bacon knew at least as much Greek as Petrarch did.

Even the conflict between the devotees of the classics and the dialecticians, about which so much is said in the period of the Renaissance, is not unknown in the earlier centuries. John of Salisbury, for example, balances the variant arguments bearing on the education of a scholar, while Roger Bacon denies the efficacy of dialectics as a sound approach even to a theological career. Both denounce the hair-splitting of the dialecticians, and John at least emphasizes the greater and more lasting satisfaction to be found in the study of the classics.

Nor does the contrast between secular and clerical scholarship establish any effective demarcation between the age of Petrarch and the earlier time. That distinction falls down on both sides, for not only were many of the recognized humanists churchmen, but there were secular scholars in the previous period also.

In the face of all this it has been very difficult for the historian to be comfortable in the thought that with Petrarch a new age dawns. To be sure, Petrarch rather intimated that such was his own opinion of his importance. But so did Leonardo Bruni, more than a generation after Petrarch. Neither, however, was by profession a historian and each had something to sell. Surveying all that counts, the historian is forced to deny the novelty of that humanistic flowering in the fourteenth century commonly called the Renaissance.

To be sure, he has usually refrained from direct denial, and has sought instead to quiet his historical conscience by expanding the terms to cover some of the more prominent earlier occurrences of the phenomena. Munro and Haskins both refer to the "Renaissance of the twelfth century," and others, like C. W. C. Davis, have applied the term to the period of Charlemagne, naming it the Carolingian Renaissance. In time, doubtless, someone will thus describe the period of the Saxon emperors in Germany and the age of Alfred in England. Then we may have also the Ottonian or the Alfredian Renaissance.

This wider usage of the term indicates the reluctance of the historian to admit that there is any distinctive difference, at least in quality and on major counts, between the activities of the so-called humanists of the fourteenth, fifteenth, and sixteenth centuries and the work of scholars before that time. That is, the movement must be studied in perspective, taking into account the times it lay almost dormant, only slowly rising to the effulgence of the Renaissance. The development was not one of steady progression, and such variations as can be detected in its peak periods are rather of quantity than of quality. There is at one time and another a difference in the amount of work done in each of the activities, a difference in the number of persons engaged. In short, the Renaissance which opens in the fourteenth century is set apart from the others not intrinsically, but only measurably. That is, at this time there were more scholars producing more, but not necessarily better, work than in the preceding centuries.

And yet, having said all this, the student of this period cannot be entirely satisfied that he has done more than describe certain circumstances. He has offered no explanation of either their occurrence or their efflorescence. True, he has placed and named the leading humanists, has analyzed and described their activities. But how was it that these activities, which were a source of pleasure to them, were also vocations yielding a product that could be exchanged for material benefits willingly contributed by other members of society? If the historian has found nothing sufficiently distinctive in the activities of the humanists to justify the recognition of a new era, will he find it in the environment surrounding, encouraging, and supporting them?

Following this cue, we might examine Petrarch's career in terms of his education, his associates, his tendencies, his opportunities, and in terms also of the pressures which operated upon him. It is not my purpose, however, to trace in detail a career already familiar, but merely to emphasize certain aspects of it which call attention to the soil out of which his genius grew.

Florentine, born in exile, son of a notary whose means were insufficient to maintain him in idleness, the lad was moved about from place to place as his father's opportunities for employment dictated. The father finally found a haven at Avignon, then the seat of the papal court, and lived barely long enough to provide for his son's education. The boy gave early evidence of enough mental ability to justify the hope that he too might become a notary, or even a full-fledged lawyer.

The family income was sufficient to maintain him in comfort during his school days, but no longer, and on the death of his father the young man had to leave Bologna before completing his course. He was therefore constantly aware of the relationship of his college education to a gainful career. Though recognizing this fact by a satisfactory attention to his school subjects, he did not allow it to restrain the normal exuberance of youth. He attended carefully to his dress, and like many another young man, composed amatory lyrics which found great favor with his classmates, if not also with the objects of his fancy. He seems also to have won friends through his scholastic abilities, the rich stores of his knowledge doubtless serving his associates well upon critical occasions. These college friendships were to prove very advantageous to him later.

# The New Learning

Thus far his career was only that of hundreds before him who had shown similar tastes and similar abilities. Had he lived in another age, he might have developed into a Lupus Servatus or a Guibert de Nogent. Living when he did, he was to end up quite differently. Thanks to his college friendships, he was soon drawn into the circle of the Colonna at Avignon. The members of this proud Roman family were none too happy on French soil, away from the administration of their own estates and their customary conflicts with the Orsini and other feudal politicians. It was for them a period of exile with all the usual accompanying nostalgia, and everything connected with Rome became doubly dear.

None of them suffered from homesickness more than the head of the group, Cardinal Giovanni, whose interest in theology was slight, and in larger ecclesiastical politics only moderate. He therefore comforted himself by gathering together a variety of material regarding ancient Rome, its archaeological remains, and its literature. With this man young Petrarch found employment as a secretary. The sentimental interests of the cardinal immediately provoked a congenial response in his assistant, whose business at court necessitated the use of Latin and whose attention was drawn by his employer's hobby toward classical literature.

The kind of writing that Petrarch did as secretary, whether on more sober business or in those playful letters on classical authors which must have delighted the cardinal, soon attracted enough attention to turn the head of any young man. The circle of his correspondents grew on both sides of the Alps, and the demand for his letters increased, especially after Petrarch had himself crowned poet laureate in Rome. This was a whim of vanity in which the old cardinal may well have indulged him, and the reception of the young man by King Robert of Naples was no doubt made possible through the same influences.

Literary skill and fortunate friendships thus secured for Petrarch many favors. At first these were at the papal court and in the form of ecclesiastical benefices, the customary support for writers of Latin. But the secular demand for, and appreciation of, his writings was soon so great that he was assured of a satisfac-

113

tory living at princely courts and was able to abandon the church benefices.

The turning point in Petrarch's career arrived when he left Avignon. Had he continued to depend on his churchly connections, he might have become increasingly immersed in ecclesiastical affairs and have ended his days as an abbot or a bishop. Instead he found a secular world not only ready but eager to receive him, ready to indulge him in the continued pursuit of his intellectual inclinations and to maintain him in even more comfortable circumstances than he had thus far enjoyed.

The willingness of princely courts such as those of the Visconti at Milan to entertain a literary figure is, of course, no strikingly new phenomenon. Rulers and courts of other days had been equally hospitable to men of letters. Charlemagne, Otto, Alfred, the Capetians, Philip II, Louis IX and Philip IV, the Normans and Angevins, William the Conqueror, Henry I, Henry II and Edward I, and in Italy Roger of Sicily and Frederick II—all these are listed among the most prominent instances of such earlier secular patronage. The difference, again, lies not in the quality of such patronage but in its relative quantity. There was now not merely one such court in Italy but several and Petrarch was able to move from one to another without serious difficulty.

The most significant difference in the times, however, is that suggested by Petrarch's account of his visit to the goldsmith of Bergamo. This man, distinguished in his craft, had accumulated a comfortable fortune by middle age and had then retired from active work to devote himself to the study of Latin literature. Petrarch marveled at the evidences of taste revealed in the goldsmith's home, not merely in its appointments but in its library, which included, besides classical authors, as many of the poet's own writings as his host had been able to purchase.

I cite this instance not only because Petrarch described this individual at some length, but because one wonders if there were not many other citizens like him among the numerous anonymous admirers to whom Petrarch alludes. Such a hypothesis receives additional support in the generous and flattering invitations he received from the two mercantile cities, Florence and Venice. Indeed, the whole career of this young artist seems to suggest the emergence at this time of an enlarged leisure class interested in letters.

Possibly earlier instances could be found of this kind of concern among the burghers. Historians of the twelfth century might point to the *fabliaux*, for example, as indicative of such literary interest. Later in that century or early in the next, the satirical literature represented by the *Meier-Helmbrecht* surely reflects the same turning of attention—an attention which, increased in volume and more serious in nature, welcomed in the thirteenth century the appearance of histories in the vernacular. Perhaps, too, it is that interest which accounts for those imposing didactic poems, the *Romance of the Rose* and the *Divine Comedy*, as well as the encyclopedic *Tresor* of Brunetto Latini. Such works might well have appealed to men whose wits were keen enough to procure for them a period of leisure, even if relatively late in life. It would be difficult indeed to account for the popularity of books of this kind solely on the basis of demand by a class still chiefly devoted to horses, tournaments, battles, and romance.

If these conjectures are true, they would appear to indicate a rapidly growing participation in letters by a new group with time to spare—a group that was gaining not only in numbers but in seriousness of interest as well. If this group was content in the twelfth century to be satisfied with satirical jibes at the privileged orders, and had advanced in the next century to share in the learning of the schools, diluted as that had to be in the vernacular, it might well have become ready in the following century to study Latin in order more fully to tap the stores of learning. The uncertainties which Dante voices about the use of Latin or the vernacular in his *De vulgari eloquentia* indicates the threshold of exactly such a development. A generation after him that threshold is fully crossed and the lay world is ready for the kind of learning and writing that Petrarch promotes. If this conjecture is valid, it would seem that Boccaccio, in shifting from the vernacular to the

Latin, was not so much changing his audience as meeting its new and enlarged demands.

Behind the development of Humanism as exemplified in Petrarch's career there was, then, apparently an advance in the intellectual demands of the new leisure class.

This theory may be tested by a more extensive examination of the small nonprofessional group with whom humanism begins in Florence. Boccaccio died in 1375, but before his death Coluccio Salutati, a notary, had begun to cultivate the new interest in classical letters. Though he continued in the practice of his profession, he managed to combine with it his avocational hobby, thus setting a new style in his papers as chancellor of Florence. His understudy, Leonardo Bruni, learned both vocation and avocation from him, with emphasis upon the latter. The two other leaders in the development of Humanism, Palla Strozzi and Niccolo Niccoli, were businessmen, the first a banker and the other trained as a merchant. These were the men who promoted the humanistic studies in Florence and made that city the leader in this field for nearly a century.

Niccolo Niccoli's activities in particular will justify somewhat thorough study. One of four sons of a very prosperous Florentine merchant, trained like his brothers for a practical mercantile career, he decided not long after his father's death to leave the care of the business to his three brothers. Presumably he derived an income from his share of his father's estate and was therefore free to devote himself enthusiastically to the new learning, filling his bachelor apartments with pieces of ancient sculpture, jewelry, and other archaeological treasures.

His chief energy, however, was spent in collecting ancient manuscripts, Greek as well as Latin. Through numerous correspondents over the whole Florentine commercial network, he sought out manuscripts, purchasing them or paying for their transcription, and by the time of his death he had accumulated a total of eight hundred. By that time his enthusiasm—like that of most booklovers—had quite outrun his resources, so that he left behind him a considerable debt as well as a large library.

# The New Learning

Niccolo's career is somewhat puzzling in that he appears to have been one of the few prominent Florentines not engaged in a gainful occupation. He is found frequently in the group which was wont to gather around the learned friar Ambrogio Traversari to indulge in intellectual discussion. His bachelor quarters were a constant rendezvous for young and old who were interested in learning. It was his practice to provide each of his guests as they entered with some book fitted to their tastes, and at times as many as a dozen friends were to be found reading in his apartment. He was equally generous in lending his books, and the executors of his estate found some two hundred of them thus on loan at the time of his death.

He seems to have been on terms of easy friendship with most of the important persons in Florence. Though he lived through the transition from the oligarchical domination of Florence to the rule of Cosimo de Medici, he had warm friends on both sides of that controversy. With Palla Strozzi he went about among prominent Florentines to gather the funds with which to bring the learned Chrysolaras from Constantinople to teach Greek in Florence in 1396. He was no less persuasive in procuring the support of Cosimo for similar encouragement of learning after 1434.

He interested himself especially in the young men, giving all who displayed exceptional ability ready access to his books and using his influence in behalf of those who needed employment. Some of his protégés either became secretaries at the papal court or served wealthy patrons outside and inside Florence, Poggio Bracciolini and Carlo Arentino being among them.

He was even able to induce favored young Florentines to engage in study. According to Vespasiano, Niccolo met young Piero Pazzi on the street one day and asked him what he was doing, to which the latter replied airily, "Just giving myself a good time." Thereupon Niccolo rebuked him and urged him to better ways, saying, "As you are the son of such a father, and of such good presence, it is a shame that you should not take to the study of Latin which would make a polished man of you. If you neglect learning, you will win little esteem and when the flower of your youth has passed you will find yourself a good for nothing." The young man returned to him some days later and asked Niccolo to find him a proper instructor. The teacher Niccolo suggested taught not only young Pazzi, but also Piero de Medici, Cosimo's son, as well as the sons of several other wealthy Florentines.

In Niccolo's career, it seems to me, we have exemplified the dynamics of the humanistic development. He himself, like the goldsmith of Bergamo, took to the new learning as an adult, though apparently somewhat earlier than the latter. Perhaps he regretted that his father had not provided him with such an education in his youth. From his conversation with young Pazzi one judges that wealth had become sufficiently secure to permit anticipation of leisure and to justify education toward its enjoyment. The advantages of the new learning which Niccolo held out to Piero were, not a steady and remunerative job, but polish and a worthwhile old age—values which a number of prominent educators have asserted are too little emphasized in American colleges. For Niccolo, as for the goldsmith of Bergamo, these ends were doubtless chief and sufficient inducements.

The career of Palla Strozzi is likewise interesting. Strozzi was one of the oligarchy whom the Medici were to displace and his learning made him an especially effective ambassador for Florence on many occasions. When at the age of sixty-two he found himself an exile, he whiled away many weary hours by studying classical letters. Thus he passed more than twenty years in a foreign land, not, like Odysseus, "ever sighing and weeping for his own dear land," but enjoying his books and his new friends. The interest he felt in learning evidently became a family heritage, for cultivated Strozzi continued to appear for many generations in northern Italy.

This compensatory value of the classics is even more vividly emphasized in the letter of Machiavelli, similarly exiled on a humble rural estate, to his friend Vettori—a letter that Cicero himself might have written from his Tusculan villa.

"But when evening comes," wrote Machiavelli, "I return home

and shut myself up in my study. Before I make my appearance in it, I take off my rustic garb soiled with mud and dirt and put on a dress adapted for courts and cities. Thus fitly habited I enter the antique resorts of the ancients; where being kindly received, I feed on that food which alone is mine and for which I was born. For an interval of four hours I feel no annoyance, I forget every grief, I neither fear poverty nor death, but am totally immersed."

The group we are considering relied on classical learning for more than comfort and amusement, however. They recognized that the "polish" to be derived from the study of Latin and Greek classics was apt to prove advantageous in many fields. They were clever enough to observe that Petrarch's conversation and writing, together with his ability to cloak the acts and persons of contemporary men in classical simile and metaphor, ensured his welcome at any court and in any circle. They were aware also of an even more practical side to this polish, as is revealed in the oft-repeated comment of Gian Galeazzo Visconti that a letter written by Coluccio Salutati, then chancellor of Florence, was worth a thousand soldiers.

So secretaries trained in the new learning soon became the fashion, the demand long continuing far in excess of the supply. Even the swashbuckling condottieri found a definite value in having their abilities and achievements described by such writers, who in the fifteenth century were supported at most of the little courts of the Romagna. We can still share the chagrin of the Florentines when their ill-trained gonfalonier failed to reply in kind to the eloquent Latin address of the Neapolitan ambassador, a chagrin all the deeper because there were present cultivated Florentines able and willing to make a proper reply.

Florence was seldom caught in this plight and regularly sent on important embassies citizens who possessed humanistic learning. Such men she found of advantage even at the court of France, not then noted for its encouragement of letters. Indeed, by the end of the fifteenth century the diplomatic value of men of cultivation had become so generally appreciated that not only did nearly all Italian courts, small as well as great, employ them, but so too did the important courts outside of Italy, notably in Spain, France, and England.

But it is a serious mistake, and one which is too commonly made, to think that "polish," personal distinction, and a happier old age were the only values the new leisure class sought or found in the study of the classics. They were interested in the substance as well as the form of that literature. They were keenly on the alert for any advice the ancients might supply toward the solution of their own problems. This, I believe, was true of the humanistic movement in Italy from its so-called beginnings in the fourteenth century throughout the period of the Renaissance.

One of the first lessons they derived from such study was in the realm of education. Cicero's *Orator*, Plutarch's essay on education, and above all Quintilian's *Institutes*, which were now available in complete form, provided them with the blueprint for a new system of education. We can trace this development all the way back to Petrarch, whose copyists were really apprentices in the new learning. The progress is more clearly defined in the career of Niccolo, whose energetic efforts included the encouragement of wealthy young men for whom, as for Piero, he procured teachers. His efforts were so successful that private tutors soon began to be superseded by distinguished teachers who received a number of promising pupils at their homes.

As a result of both the increased demand for such instruction and the more careful study of Quintilian, education developed to the stage represented in the schools of Vittorino da Feltre at Mantua and of Guarino at Ferrara. These schools became institutions capable of indefinite perpetuation. Their fame attracted students and observers from a distance and they became models for similar establishments elsewhere. To them we owe, with remarkably little change in curriculum and even less in spirit, the *lycée* of France, the *Gymnasium* of Germany, and the great public schools of England, not to mention the best of the private preparatory schools in the United States. The debt of all these schools to Quintilian is obvious, but in their emphasis upon the combination of mental, physical, and moral training there is a definite accent derived from the needs of the fifteenth century. That this development was not a mere imitation of classical models is abundantly attested by the numerous treatises on education which continued to appear throughout that century and later.

These devotees of Humanism also sought and found in classical writings much that ministered to the art of living, especially to human relations. These lessons they applied all the way from the conduct of the family to the conduct of a court, indeed of a whole society. Here, as in the case of education, this dependence was not mere slavish imitation. In fact their findings were based less upon a single classical work than upon a discriminating use of many bearing directly on their own needs. Thus the *De re uxoria* of Francesco Barbaro, along with the works of Cicero and Plutarch, was esteemed a worthy guide for the management of a household. It is significant that a large share of the writings in this area of interest were not only in the vernacular, but were composed at a time when, it is commonly thought, the language of the people was completely submerged. Among them may be cited Palmieri's *Della vita civile* and Alberti's *Libri della famiglia*.

The application of classical learning to contemporary problems of human relationships is evident in the fact that the two greatest productions of Italian humanists were both written in the vernacular. I am referring, of course, to Castiglione's *Il Cortegiano* and Machiavelli's *Il Principe*. If the Greek and Latin classics, if Plato and Aristotle, Cicero, Seneca, Quintilian, and many others, can be recognized as sources of culture, so too can the conditions of life in fifteenth- and early sixteenth-century Italy and Europe. In fact, for those interested in the effects of humanistic study upon the ideals of human intercourse, there is no more revealing exercise than to compare the court of Urbino with that of King Arthur, or Castiglione with Malory.

The use of classical sources to throw light on contemporary problems is even more concretely revealed in the arts. Both literary and archaeological sources were drawn upon. Perhaps Alberti reveals most fully the conscious process by which the fine arts of the Italian Renaissance—architecture, sculpture, and even painting—were influenced by the artist's knowledge of classical studies. Very few of these products, however, can be correctly described as pure imitation. Whether our taste entirely approves of all of them or not, we must recognize in them the use of past learning in the service of contemporary artistic problems.

No less practical was the use of classical learning in connection with the art of war. The interest of the condottieri in the classics was by no means exhausted in hearing themselves compared to Caesar and Alexander, to the disparagement of the latter. They were also keen to study the tactics and strategy of the ancient generals, and they did not overlook the contributions the ancients might make to the science of fortification and siegecraft. Nor were literary scholars entirely innocent of calling to the attention of the condottieri the help that artists might supply in the conduct of military activities.

This joining of talents is mostly highly dramatized by Caesar Borgia, in whose campaigning both Machiavelli and Leonardo da Vinci shared, but it had also occurred much earlier in the fifteenth century and was to continue later. Though the armies of France and Spain had little to learn from the Italians about the wholesale destruction of the enemy, their generals could take instruction from them about the art of war, tactics and strategy, fortification and siegecraft. Vitruvius and Vegetius, as well as the classical historians, both Greek and Latin, contributed a good deal to this knowledge, but so also did the experience of fifteenth-century Italy.

If one undertook to select a single individual to illustrate the relation of the new learning to practical affairs, it would be difficult to find a better example than Cosimo de Medici. The leading banker of Europe and for thirty years master of Florence—or "pater patriae" as the devoted citizens styled him—he was as deeply involved in the affairs of this world as a man could be. Yet he found time to be the patron of scholars and artists, to cultivate their society, and somehow or other to do a great amount of reading as well. Apparently no subject was strange to him. He could discuss agriculture with farmers and actually pruned his own vines; he could talk literature with men of letters and theology with scholarly priests and monks; he was more than an amateur in law and delighted in ethics and philosophy. His conversations with Pagolo on astrology show, as do his interests in architecture, sculpture, painting, music, and landscape gardening that these were more than passing fancies with him. His judgment and taste as displayed in his choice of certain artists to do particular pieces of work, as well as his dealings in finance and foreign affairs, have brought him deserved fame.

Indeed, nearly all that Cosimo did in promoting scholarship, in building churches, in developing libraries, and in planning and equipping his own town and country homes reflects a judicious blending of learning with a practical understanding of immediate conditions and requirements. However fantastic the Platonic Academy, which he really founded, may seem to us now, even that project was not without some bearing on trade with Greece and the Levant, and the genuine interest in Plato which he displayed at the very end of his life can scarcely fail to arouse the admiration of philosophers today. Few men in any age have combined wide learning with a knowledge of practical affairs to better advantage than did Cosimo.

Were further proof needed that the humanists did not esteem the classics for their style alone, it might be found in abundance in the content of the libraries being assembled at their instigation. That of the Duke of Urbino, which Vespasiano has described in some detail, may be regarded as a model. It contained what was then regarded as a complete library of works in Latin, Greek, and Hebrew. Scripture, the Church fathers, and the medieval doctors of theology were all represented. So also were writings on civil law, including recent commentaries. All the chief writers on arithmetic, geometry, astrology, architecture, and military affairs were included, as well as books on painting, sculpture, and music. The medical section contained medieval Arabic treatises in addition to Hippocrates and Galen. And the library was enlarged by the works of "modern" Italian writers, both in Latin and in the vernacular, though of Boccaccio's writings only the Latin were included. The Italian writings were doubtless added by a less pious successor or book dealer.

There were other libraries larger than this, but, according to Vespasiano, none more complete. Apparently, as is indicated in Niccolo's will, the practice of making books available to scholars and students was becoming widespread. Even so small a town as Pistoia could boast of a public library of one hundred and fifty volumes housed in the palace of the seigniory.

The foregoing examples have revealed, I hope, that the interest in classical literature was widespread among a developing merchant group and not confined either to aesthetes or to erudite scholars. The instances are drawn, however, chiefly from those who might be called the patrons of Humanism: that is, men of affairs to whom Humanism was of incidental concern. Let us now consider those who made learning a profession.

The greater number of these, naturally, were teachers, either tutors in the homes of the wealthy or in schools like those at Ferrara and Mantua or in universities. Others were to be found at courts, where as secretaries they performed a variety of duties both useful and ornamental.

It has been customary to regard these professional humanists as chiefly intent upon the restoration of antiquity, "Die Wiederbelebung des klassischen Altherthums," as Voigt puts it. Their ideal is reputed to have been to write Latin as Cicero wrote it; to describe the activities of life as the ancients might have done; to converse in the idiom of the Augustan age; even to discuss the mysteries of religion in terms of classical paganism. To this group of scholars is rather generally ascribed the substitution of a stilted, affected, artificial Latin style, ill-adapted to the needs of contemporary life, in place of the natural, living, if less elegant, medieval Latin so suited to the ordinary demands of society.

If, however, we examine closely the careers of the professional humanists from Petrarch to Bembo and Erasmus, we shall be forced to admit that no one of them conforms exactly to this pattern. True, we recognize in most of them a very definite regard for style and a common practice of embellishing their writings with quotations from ancient authors—a practice that Montaigne was later to condemn as "filching-theft" and as "prejudicial to any trivial composer." Still, nearly all the professional humanists were definitely concerned about the substance of their writings, and a singularly large proportion of them were interested not only in religion and the Church, but also in reading the Scriptures and the early Church fathers in the original Greek and Latin. Though they read and taught the pagan classics, they also wrote on early Christian theology. Men who had this catholic interest are found throughout the period. There is a trace of it in Petrarch, much more than a trace in Erasmus, and it is pronounced in the careers of Luigi Marsigli and Fra Ambrogio, Ficino and Pico della Mirandola, and Lefevre, John Colet, and Melanchthon, not to mention many others who were high dignitaries of the Church.

It was perhaps only natural that many of the professional humanists were interested in law. Much of the early impulse toward Humanism came from the legal profession, and much of the support of the movement continued to come from that source. A man trained only in the technicalities of the law might seem quite illiterate to the humanists, if not also to a wider society, but many lawyers found some time for the cultivation of letters. And between these and the professional humanists there was a real and abiding affinity. Some of the lawyers become so deeply imbued with classical lore that they could and did teach the classics, and some of the humanists made important contributions to law. Examples like Petrarch, who was trained as a lawyer, and Coluccio Salutati, who remained a lawyer throughout his life but also taught the classics, are rather common throughout this period. Politian, usually regarded as the gay literary companion of Lorenzo the Magnificent, was also editor of the *Pandects of the Corpus Juris Civilis*.

The combination of Humanism and law continues to recur, not only in Italy but also in the more northern countries—as witness John Reuchlin in Germany and John Tiptoft and Thomas More in England. Indeed, one of the charges against the Earl of Worcester was that he had introduced some new laws which he had learned at Padua.

A surprisingly large number of professional humanists were also interested in subjects now generally termed science and technology. These found their outlet in translating from the Greek and in editing Latin works on natural history, cosmography, mathematics, and engineering of various kinds. Medicine too was included in their field of interest, not only as a subject of discussion and translation but even of practice. Pagolo, friend of Cosimo de Medici and a professor of astrology and other forms of mathematics, practiced medicine for a few friends, as did also the uncle of Savonarola at Ferrara. An even better example is the professor of philosophy, Fracastoro, who also practiced medicine and wrote his famous description of the *Galli morbus* in verse.

It seems to be the fate of every intellectual advance to suffer a trailing band of semimoronic followers who glory in belonging to a movement but are less than vaguely aware of its real purpose. Just as the achievements of modern scientists tend to lose luster under a cloud of factual tabulators and the real contributions of scholastic philosophers have been obscured by the logic-choppers who followed in their wake, so the humanists were cursed with a following incapable of doing more than imitating the classics. If instead of staring at this sophomoric fringe we follow the professors of Humanism into their studies, we shall find almost none of them whose interest is confined to form alone. Even the schoolmaster Guarino found satisfaction in translating Strabo's work on geography.

To appreciate fully the intellectual activity stimulated by the development of Humanism, however, we must turn to the universities established in connection with the movement. Omitting the many incipient schools whose careers were more or less brief, we may confine our attention to four: Padua, Pavia, Pisa, and Ferrara.

Two of these may trace their actual origin to an earlier time, but all four owed their vitality to the force of humanistic studies, and should therefore be regarded as humanistic foundations. All of them were essentially city universities, that is, universities serving the intellectual demands of the city states: Padua served Venice; Pavia, Milan; Pisa, Florence; and Ferrara, really an offshoot of Padua, owed its being to the influence of Guarino at the court of the Este family.

All these universities were in close touch with their respective city patrons and there was a great deal of intermingling and constant visiting back and forth between faculty, students, and citizens. In the case of Florence, the university was actually divided, the humanities being kept at Florence for some time while law, medicine, and theology were taught at Pisa. But this did not mean that those at Pisa were without interest in the humanities. Benvenuto Cellini, for instance, on unveiling his Perseus at Florence, received many laudatory sonnets from the professors and students at Pisa, who were then on vacation. Where there were courts, as at Milan and Ferrara and even at Florence under the Medici, leading scholars of all kinds from the universities were frequently found rubbing elbows with courtiers of varying interest in learning, humanistic or otherwise.

This mingling, at both universities and courts, of the scholars with the laity, who were employing artists, was to be extremely fruitful in the later development of learning and of art. In such association the humanistic scholars learned to appreciate the justice of the high regard which the ancients extended to artists. In addition, the joint efforts of all three groups proved valuable, whether they were enlisted, as at Venice, in improving the design of ships and the science of navigation; or, as at Florence, in the planning and construction of military defense; or, as at Ferrara, in strengthening the fortifications of land and harbor; or, as at any of these cities, in the selection and execution of mural decorations for palaces and public buildings, and of scenery for pageants and plays. No matter what the occasion, the partnership was profitable.

The service of scholarship to art which resulted from this association requires no elaboration here. Without it the frescoes of the early sixteenth century that still excite the wonder and admiration of the most cultivated would scarcely have been possible. Less clearly recognized was the service of medieval art to scholarship. There is, to be sure, a hint of this recognition in Castiglione's recommendation that the perfect courtier should also possess a knowledge of painting. His argument is buttressed, of course, with reference to the high regard in which painters were held by leaders of antiquity like Alexander, but it is also supported by some shrewd observations of his own:

"And do not marvel," he writes, "that I desire this art, which today may seem to savor of the artisan and little to befit the gentleman . . . which besides being very worthy in itself, is of great utility, and especially in war for drawing places, sites, rivers, bridges, rocks, fortresses and the like; since however well we may keep them in memory (which is very difficult) we cannot show them to others."

Though one of the first to mention this function of art, Castiglione was by no means the first to notice it or to make use of it. Mention has already been made of the fact that on his campaigns in the Romagna, Caesar Borgia enjoyed the services of both Machiavelli and Leonardo da Vinci.

It is not a mere freak of genius that at Pavia, Padua, and Florence Leonardo was so much in the company of professors of medicine, mathematics, and the humanities. That association was occurring among less famous men at all these centers, for the artists had developed their skill in the observation of visible phenomena to a point scarcely then imagined by professors of medicine or other scientists. With the help of mathematicians, the artists had been able so to extend their powers of observation and to record their results that many turned to them for instruction in precision and accuracy, and the development of printing afforded a medium through which such recorded observations could be quickly communicated to scholars in all parts of Europe.

This blending of talents undoubtedly helped to make possible a considerable advance in science and technology. The anatomical drawings of Leonardo da Vinci are now well known, and he is still accorded credit for having observed and recorded details of human anatomy not hitherto known to medical professors. Likewise the drawings of much lesser artists contributed to the epoch-making work of Vesalius, student and professor at the University of Padua. Fracastoro's important work in the diagnosis of disease was another product of learning combined with improved observation. It was at Padua from a newly printed book on the writings of ancient Greek astronomers that the young Polish scholar, Copernicus, received encouragement in formulating his heliocentric theory of the universe. It was also there and at Pisa that Galileo developed his telescope, which was so instrumental in confirming the theory of Copernicus. How much that erratic genius, Paracelsus, gained from his stay at Padua and Ferrara may never be determined, but modern medicine, chemistry, and pharmacy all acknowledge a debt to him.

This productive combination of talents is also seen in the work of that humble schoolmaster from north of the Alps whose first bid for wider fame was the composition of a Latin grammar. With the savings from several years of teaching he went to Italy, where, chiefly at Padua, he became interested in medicine and science. Circumstances brought him into contact with mining, about which he wrote a lavishly illustrated book—one that has become a landmark in the history of both mining and geology. This man was Georgius Agricola, whose *De re metallica* has been translated into English by Herbert and Lou Henry Hoover.

Still another example is Conrad Gesner, who turned from collecting words in many languages to collecting and describing plants and animals, eventually producing a work which was to remain standard almost to the time of Darwin.

All these works represent a distinct advance beyond the classical heritage. It is a temptation to dwell upon this connection of Humanism with science, all the more so since historians of science are so loath to acknowledge the relationship, but these illustrations must be sufficient.

Thus by the sixteenth century the great centers of Humanism, Pavia, Padua, and Pisa, had become the leading centers of learning in Europe, overshadowing even those great old universities,

Paris, Bologna, and Oxford. The latter had already discovered that their hope of maintaining or regaining their position was somehow dependent upon the extent to which they took over the new learning. However, by this time the interest in it had increased so greatly that neither three nor even six universities could satisfy the demand. Humanism had spread to all parts of Europe, bringing with it the establishment of new centers of learning under secular auspices. It had come, in fact, to be an accepted part of the intellectual interest of modern times.

Yet it is at this point, the sixteenth century, that the historian of Humanism finds himself most deeply perplexed. The humanities have become accepted as the best means of education. Practically all secondary education employs them and all the older universities have been forced to yield them a place. Ariosto and Tasso, Rabelais and Montaigne, Vives and Ximenes, Copernicus, Georgius Agricola, and Gesner are all products of humanistic education. Luther and Calvin are heavily indebted to it, while Melanchthon and the whole Jesuit order are even more fully influenced by it. Scholars trained in the humanities make important contributions not only in literature and philology but also in law and medicine, mathematics and astronomy, geography and geology, botany and zoology, technology of many kinds including the art and science of war, history, political science, philosophy, and even theology, Catholic as well as Protestant. There appear to be no limits to the area of humanist inquiries.

While many confine their production to fields of special aptitude, many others, like Gesner, apparently assume that all knowledge is the legitimate goal of the individual scholar. Nor is there at the end of the century much evidence of any active quarrel about vested intellectual interests. True, there are serious objections to particular discoveries and the embattled religious groups strike out harshly at what they regard as heresy, but there seems to be no longer any objection to the theologian's interest in the humanities or the humanist's interest in theology, or to the interest of either in natural phenomena.

This is all so contrary to the conventional description of either

Humanism or the intellectual interests of the period that one must try to account for it.

One obvious explanation for the failure to note this peculiar character of intellectual activity in the sixteenth century is the possibility that the historian, like the newspaper editor, drops a subject when it loses "news value." Humanism having become so widely accepted by that time, it may be taken for granted and historical attention devoted to other matters more controversial.

Another explanation may lie in the fact that the medievalist who is interested in Humanism usually closes his work about 1500 A.D., while the modern historian, who begins at that point, is so much more engrossed in the clash of religious, national, and economic groups that he dismisses Humanism as soon as possible, usually confining his remarks to its early connection with the religious controversy. As a result this widening of humanistic interest has escaped his attention.

Whatever the reason for the historian's neglect of the phenomenon, the fact that the interests of humanists or of scholars trained in the humanities should deploy over such a vast horizon of intellectual activity can be more readily explained. Instruction was based on masterpieces of Greek and Latin literature, and the brighter pupils quickly extended their reading beyond the immediate texts. By the time they reached the universities such students would be exploring a wide range of both Greek and Latin writings, young Gesner, for example, trying to explore all the writings of antiquity long before his university career was ended. The work of translating and editing had been going on for several centuries by this time and all the more obvious classics were available and familiar. There remained now only the more obscure pieces to engage the attention of the professional humanist or the advanced student profitably, and these included works of a technical nature concerned with the whole range of intellectual inquiry in antiquity.

The method of education, too, had certain marked advantages. In the first place, the necessity of translating prevented the hurried, superficial satisfaction of interest which writings in the pupil's own tongue might have permitted. The pupil was thus compelled to mull over each word, phrase, and idea in his textbook. He was forced also to seek the idea of the author in the life about him in order to discover the words in his own language which would most nearly express the author's thought. Few educators today, in appraising the value of the study of foreign languages, have taken account of this important fact: that the pupil is learning at least as much about his own times as he is about the circumstances in the work he is attempting to translate.

The use of ancient masterpieces as instructional material, therefore, had exceptional merit. They represented the greatest achievements of two unusually highly developed civilizations. It is doubtful that we have even today any more perfect laboratories for the study of human motivation than those afforded by the Acropolis and the Forum. Not that other centers, especially of modern times, do not offer as great an interplay of human motives and in even greater abundance. The advantage of those earlier centers rests in the fact that life offered fewer distractions then, and the activities were confined to smaller areas and could therefore be more accurately observed. Furthermore, the activities in each of these centers were exposed for several centuries to the cumulative gaze of unusually sensitive observers, endowed with rare powers of intuition. And these observers were able in the course of the centuries to devise words with which to express even the most delicate shades of their perceptions. Poets, orators, historians, and philosophers vied with each other in effectiveness of expression, which involved not only choice of words and form of composition but also rhythm and cadence of line and sentence.

The most nearly perfect of such achievements of observation, thought, and expression were used for instruction in the humanities. The pupil who was thus forced to find in his own world and in his own language the most nearly equivalent idea and expression of it was therefore learning to understand his own world and time much more fully than he would otherwise have done.

In scientific areas, the ancients were limited by their smaller geographical horizon but within those limits they had advanced far. Few even among the teachers of the classics have emphasized the manifold aspects of human experience which were touched upon in a curriculum such as the school of Vittorino and his followers offered. Nothing about man or nature seems to have passed unnoticed. The brighter the pupil and the more widely he read, the greater the range of human experience and thought he was able to uncover, and the process automatically promoted and cultivated his observation of his own day and age. Scholars so trained were therefore quite ready by the sixteenth century to make important additions to knowledge in a vast variety of fields.

It may be appropriate to summarize the conclusions regarding the new learning up to the end of the sixteenth century.

The first conclusion I must draw is that Humanism was no new phenomenon of the fourteenth century, and, further, that there is little justification for the designation of the next two centuries as marking a different type of life to be described by the term Renaissance. Instead, it would be more correct to say that after the days of the Roman Empire whenever any number of people were sufficiently free from immediate concern about their livelihood and lives, the more intelligent regularly began to try to satisfy their curiosity about this world.

The most efficient means for the satisfaction of this curiosity, of course, was learning, or the study of books in which, then as now, was preserved mankind's accumulated experience and thought. Those of inquiring mind therefore turned to the writings of the ancients, not through any sentimental reverence for the past, but because the more recent writings were almost exclusively concerned with matters of religion, or the relation of this life to the life hereafter. Among the ancients, on the contrary, they found persons as inquisitive about this life and this world as themselves, and persons much farther along the road to satisfying their desires in this direction.

The second conclusion which this historical survey seems to justify is that the humanists looked upon the study of the ancients, not as an end in itself, but very definitely as a means to an end. They were too deeply immersed in the affairs of their own day ever to detach themselves completely from such concerns. Had that been their wish, they could have found in the theological and scholastic writings a much more satisfactory means of psychological escape. They esteemed the ancients so highly precisely because they found in them so much that was applicable to their own affairs. Had they been able to satisfy their needs as fully and as well through more recent writings either in medieval Latin or in the vernacular, it is quite conceivable that there would have been no classical revival. The rapidity with which they turned to the translation of the ancient writings and to the composition of works in the vernacular strongly confirms this conjecture. This also suggests that the more nearly they could obtain what they wanted to know in their own language, the less inclined they would be to trouble to learn the ancient languages.

A third conclusion is that the Latin and Greek classics continued to be studied long after the demands of intellectual curiosity could be satisfied even more fully in the vernacular languages because they were believed to be a superior means of education. This position the humanists held up until our own time. Whether the humanities have advanced in the vernacular beyond the best of the ancients sufficiently to make the further study of Latin and Greek unnecessary except for those whose professions require that knowledge must be discussed by others. As a historian, I must be content with observing that many in the new world as well as the old still prefer the medium of Latin and Greek.

And a fourth and final conclusion, that the so-called Renaissance did not end with the coming of the sixteenth century or with what have usually been considered the characteristic concerns of the humanists. Its awakening influence spread into a great diversity of man's activities, roused them to new life and new discoveries, so that the "new learning" of the Renaissance, humanistic in its first stages, became the mother and the nurse of modern developments in many branches of natural and physical science. Perhaps, as many of us have long suspected, science and humanism are not mutually exclusive approaches to the problems of mankind.

# 7

# A City That Art Built

Is ART related to life? Or is it a thing apart, a gift peculiar to certain individuals in certain places and at certain times? Is its efflorescence a blessing that cannot be anticipated, its decadence a calamity that cannot be averted? Or is it something within the reach of men if they choose to strive for it? Does art represent some erratic and unpredictable burst of human energy, or is it rather a crystallization of human experience and social endeavor?

Such questions have doubtless been in the minds of men through countless ages. Homer quite simply ascribed the diverse gifts of men to the capricious favor of the gods. Both philosophers and poets after him, though using more learned words, have arrived at substantially the same conclusion. The questions, however, still remain.

The answers that have been suggested have hinged all too often upon individual opinion, but modern men ask for the evidence of fact as well as for the logic of opinion. One source of fact that may throw light upon the problem is the history of communities in which art has flourished in the past. What was the relation of art to life in those communities where art actually reached great

NOTE: This essay appeared as one of the publications of The Owatonna Art Education Project (Minneapolis: The University of Minnesota Press, 1936).

135

heights? This study explores that relationship in one such community, the city of Florence.

The place of Florence in history as a center of art is secure. Only one other community can be compared with it, the city of Athens. And Athens produced neither so many artists nor so many works of art. Histories of art recognize the high achievement of Florence in painting, sculpture, and architecture. From the time of the semilegendary Cimabue, at the end of the thirteenth century, to the death of Michelangelo, after the middle of the sixteenth, her artists were acknowledged leaders in artistic production. She claims as her own Giotto, Massaccio, Masolino, Fra Angelico, Botticelli, Ghiberti, Donatello, Brunelleschi, Michelozzo, the della Robbias, Leonardo da Vinci, Michelangelo, Benvenuto Cellini, Vasari, and hundreds of other artists. These names recall both the technical advance in painting and the final triumph of the great masters in painting, sculpture, and architecture.

In considering the relation of art to life, the historian finds the beginning of any artistic development particularly significant. But the beginnings in Florence present a strange dilemma to him. Histories of art first make mention of Florentine art about the year 1300. At that time, however, Florence was not starting upon an artistic epoch; she was already leading. Her artists were the foremost in Italy and continued to hold that position for the next two hundred and fifty years.

Can it be that Florence had no art before 1300 and then suddenly achieved the position of leadership in art? That does not seem reasonable. If art is as long as the poets say it is, there must have been a long period of antecedent development. There is, of course, the possibility that the city imported leading artists from elsewhere, but Arnolfo, Cimabue, and Giotto, with whom the list begins, were all Florentines, born in Florence or its countryside, and presumably educated and trained in Florence. Whatever early development accounts for the efflorescence of art in Florence must therefore be sought in the city itself and in activities not recognized by the histories of art.

Florence had been in existence for more than fifteen centuries before 1300 A.D. The name is mentioned incidentally during the days of Roman history and in the early Middle Ages. There is no evidence that it achieved any distinction during all these centuries, and in the Middle Ages it was rather overshadowed in importance by the castle town of Fiesole just five miles away. The size of Florence is not known, but the fact that a more important town could arise within five miles suggests that it was not a large city. It has been estimated that the population never numbered more than six thousand people before the eleventh century and presumably it had rather fewer inhabitants during most of the Middle Ages.

In other words, until the eleventh century Florence was just a country town, like hundreds of others in Italy and elsewhere, where the people of the countryside did their local marketing and where the professional people, officials, and entertainers carried on their work for the rural community. Thus our search for the origin of the artistic greatness of Florence may be limited to the period after 1000 A.D.

The lack of any distinction during all these centuries suggests that the region in which Florence is situated is not favored with an abundance of natural resources of any kind. It is not on the seacoast but inland, almost halfway across the Italian peninsula. It is located on the Arno River, which rises in the Apennine Mountains, whose crest is virtually within sight of Florence to the north, east, and southeast. The fall line of this river lies nearly halfway between Florence and the western Mediterranean, making navigation to the coast virtually impossible. During the rainy season the river is impressive enough, but during the rest of the year it will not float any craft much deeper than a rowboat. It can be crossed easily at Florence, where early in history there was a bridge that made crossing possible even in floodtime. This was probably the chief reason for the location of the town at this point.

The foothills of the Apennines here come within six miles of the river, but the valley, which widens out to the east and especially to the west, affords an excellent opportunity for agriculture. In Tuscany and southern Italy generally, the mountains are numerous and the valleys small. The double valley which lay on both sides of Florence was relatively large, and though the Po Valley north of the Apennines made this double valley insignificant as an agricultural resource, nevertheless, barring military interference, Florence was well supplied with foodstuffs. This was perhaps her greatest natural advantage over other towns in Tuscany or southern Italy.

Fiesole, the castle town in the foothills of the Apennines overlooking Florence, was, of course, a feudal town, where the barons who dominated the countryside had their residence. Ordinarily medieval communities combined castle and town, as did most Tuscan towns, notably Sienna and Pisa. At Florence, however, the hills of Fiesole offered a better site for a castle, a better point from which to keep watch on the countryside, and perhaps some advantages in climate. The nobility tended to settle there, and doubtless, too, some of the professional people who found the nobility more attractive neighbors. This left Florence, on the flats beside the river, to the ordinary folk engaged in trade and in such industry as the neighborhood required. Perhaps the bustle and cramped quarters and the smells of the various industries there pursued caused the nobles to prefer Fiesole.

Thus it happened that, unlike most medieval communities, the population of Florence did not include a full range of social classes but was composed of people who were virtually all engaged in labor of some kind, chiefly manual labor. The city, on the eve of its greater development, was thus a homogeneous community of small merchants and craftsmen. Perhaps this peculiarity is important for our problem, as it certainly is for the political history of Florence. At any rate it deserves notice.

Of natural resources other than the agriculture in the adjacent valleys, Florence had few or none. Minerals such as gold, copper, and iron were not abundant in Tuscany, and none were to be found in the vicinity of Florence. The marble and other building stones for which some parts of Tuscany are famous were quite remote from Florence. Wool, which was the material universally used for cloth, was grown to some extent on the neighboring hill-sides but was less abundant even than in most places in Italy; moreover, Florentine wool was of notoriously inferior quality. Even wood was scarce, for, though the valley was fairly fertile, most of the acreage was needed for agriculture and little was left on which to grow fuel.

The climate of Florence may be described as invigorating in comparison with that in the rest of Italy, especially in comparison with that in the lowlands along the coasts or even the sheltered valley of the Po. In the wintertime the weather might become quite severe, and the severity was felt all the more for lack of fuel. People who survived in such conditions might be expected to be fairly hardy, energetic, and possibly enterprising—more so, in fact, than in most regions of Italy.

Something of the effect of such conditions may be reflected in the story which the Florentines delighted to tell about themselves. Pisan merchants trafficking in northern Africa found their Moslem customers somewhat puzzled by the constant reference to florins and Florentines. When the Moslems inquired who these people were, the Pisans replied airily that the Florentines were "our Arabs."

There was another trait of the Florentines, even more fully attested to, which may also have developed from these conditions. Gaetano Salvemini, a graduate of the modern University of Florence and professor of Florentine history in that institution, was once asked if the Florentines might not be called the Scots of Italy. He grasped the point of the question immediately and replied, "Yes, only more so. We have a saying in Italy that a whole Florentine family can live an entire week on a single boiled egg." Thrift was early remarked as a trait in which the Florentines excelled nearly all other Italians.

Such traits as energy, enterprise, and thrift seem rather remote from matters of art, but in the absence of more direct evidence about the determining factors in the artistic development of Florence, all distinctive characteristics deserve consideration.

The period from 1000 to 1300 A.D., an important one for all of

Europe, was of special importance to Italy, both economically and politically. The cities along the coast, particularly Genoa, Venice, and Pisa, became veritable commercial empires, their interests spreading throughout the entire Mediterranean world. In their rapid expansion they invited people of the hinterland to enlist in their service. Florentines as well as others embraced the opportunities thus offered. They are mentioned as participants in the expeditions of the Genoese and Pisans in the western Mediterranean in the eleventh century. They appear also in the expedition of the Pisans to the Holy Land at the time of the First Crusade. Doubtless Florentines continued to participate in the expanded commercial activities of both Pisans and Genoese, if not also of the Venetians, which followed the capture of Jerusalem by the crusaders.

Though recruited originally to supply some of the surplus labor which these coast towns could not provide, the Florentines soon began to appear in much more dignified roles. One of these was that of service as notaries and judges in commercial agreements. The names of Florentine notaries appear in the records of Pisa and Genoa as early as the middle of the twelfth century.

Apparently the Florentines had sensed an opportunity in the situation surrounding them. While Pisa and Genoa were expanding their commercial activities, the papal city of Bologna just north of Florence was becoming renowned as a center for the study of civil law and was attracting scholars, chiefly ecclesiastics, from all over Europe. Apparently Florentines went there also, not so much for service to Church or State as did others, but rather for business reasons. Apparently, too, they had made themselves expert in the study of commercial law. Perhaps the contracts that Florentine notaries drew up stood the test of litigation unusually well, or the judgments they rendered in disputes may have seemed fairer to both parties. At any rate, they established a reputation for legal knowledge and integrity that created a demand for their services not only in Pisa and Genoa but throughout Italy. By the end of the twelfth century Florentine notaries and judges were the most highly esteemed in all Italy.

And evidently they maintained this reputation, for in the list of Florentine guilds in the fourteenth century that of the notaries and judges is accorded the place of honor above all others.

Another role in which Florentines figure prominently in the service of the maritime commercial empires is that of the money-changer. By the middle of the twelfth century it had become the habit of the Genoese, when they started their caravans of merchandise to the great wholesale markets of the fairs of Champagne, to take Florentine money-changers along with them.

Money-changing was a tricky business at that time. Every great noble had the right to coin money, and most of them did so. Nearly a thousand different mints were represented in the money used at these fairs. The coins represented different alloys of precious and baser metals and were often clipped and otherwise debased. If the merchant was to obtain his just due, the evaluation of such coins required expert knowledge of metals.

But why should the Florentines, whose region was notoriously lacking in metals, have been so expert? Perhaps for that very reason. Having no natural resources of metals, they had to make the most of the metals they bought, even to utilizing the filings. As a result they studied metals more closely than most people did, and thus built up the knowledge that made them expert. And that they should have been so generally and continuously employed by others, especially by the important commercial states, is testimony to their integrity as well as to their expert knowledge and skill. This judgment is confirmed by the fact that in 1252 the Florentines minted a gold coin called the florin, which became and remained for centuries the standard for exchange in commerce all over Europe. Its purity the Florentines guarded jealously. The guild of the money-changers was one of the important guilds of the early fourteenth century, for money-changing led naturally to banking, and the guild included banking in its operations. By 1300 the Florentines were already prominent as leading bankers of Europe.

The services of Florentine notaries and money-changers to the maritime and other commercial communities thus took them to

The Long Road Back

all parts of the Mediterranean world and to much of western
Europe. This activity undoubtedly gave them additional opportunities for the exercise of those qualities of energy, enterprise,
and thrift for which they were already noted.

Another circumstance gave the Florentines still other opportunities. Florence lay on the road to Rome. This was not a matter
of special consequence in ancient times, when there were many
roads to Rome, or during the centuries of the early Middle Ages,
when comparatively few people traveled to Rome. But times were
changing. In the eleventh century Rome was again becoming important. The papacy at Rome, regenerated by the monastic reform movement in which Cluny figured so prominently, was
becoming the real, as well as the nominal, head of the Church.
During the next century it rose to a position of leadership in the
political as well as the religious affairs of Europe. During the
thirteenth century Rome was actually the capital of Europe, secular as well as ecclesiastical.

Meanwhile the ancient roads to Rome had fallen into a state
of disrepair. The chief road from the north, along the western
coast of Italy, was infected with malaria; that which skirted the
Apennines toward the east was infested with bandits. This left
the road through Florence the main road, and at various times in
the year almost the only road, from the north to Rome. During
these three centuries from 1000 to 1300 feudal disorder had been
yielding to ecclesiastical and royal restraints, and the volume of
travel to Rome, consisting chiefly of suitors for papal justice or
favor, rose to the proportions of a steady and increasing stream.

Travel was mainly on horseback or even on foot. Progress was
slow and wearisome and required frequent periods of rest. Many
of the travelers from the north crossed the Apennines from Bologna, and frequently Florence was their stopping point. Nobles
and messengers of kings, bishops, abbots, and priests, merchants
and pilgrims, most of them well supplied with money, rested
their travel-weary bodies at Florence. Though it was not the only
one of the towns that entertained these travelers, it was one of
the most important. Some idea of the volume of this travel is sug-

gested by Villani's statement that in 1338 the number of strangers in Florence averaged fifteen hundred daily.

An enterprising people might profit greatly from this situation. In any case, of course, they must provide food and shelter, but if they were alert, they could also sell the products of their industry and learn of opportunities all over Europe from travelers who represented the upper classes of nearly all the Christian countries. That such business possibilities were not overlooked is revealed by the action of the seigniory when the old bridge was rebuilt after the disastrous flood of 1330. Shops were built along the sides of the bridge, but the demand for these shops was so great that the seigniory had to limit to forty the number of goldsmiths permitted there.

The connection of the Florentines with the maritime cities and with the great throng of visitors who passed through their city probably also affected their woolen industry. Before the end of the twelfth century the cloth of Florence was becoming famous. This seems strange at first, in view of the fact that nearly every community in Europe made its own cloth and that the wool grown around Florence was not plentiful and was notoriously of an inferior type, unlike the wool of England or Spain or even Flanders. Why, then, should Florentine cloth have been in demand?

What happened, it seems, was that the Florentines, unable to compete in quantity or cheapness, had been forced to make cloth better than others did in order to sell it even in their own countryside. They developed skill in finishing the cloth, in removing the knots to give it a finer surface, and in dyeing it with colors that were more lasting and more attractive. Apparently travelers passing through Florence liked the cloth and took bolts of it back home. And the money-changers probably took some of it along to the fairs. So famous did Florentine cloth become that by the early thirteenth century Flemish weavers were sending their cloth down to Florence to be finished and then returned for the northern markets.

Meanwhile the Florentines were constantly improving their

work, importing choice wool from England and Spain as well as woolen cloth from Flanders. In the guild list of the fourteenth century the woolen industry is represented by two guilds, the wool guild proper and the Calimala, or fine cloth guild. This was the big industry of Florence, employing great numbers of workers and doing most to swell the population.

When the official classification of Florentine guilds was made in 1293, three others were included among the great guilds, that is, in the big business of Florence. These were the physicians and apothecaries, the furriers, and silk guilds. There is no apparent reason why Florence should have developed any of these to the extent of a big business. She had no natural advantages in drugs or furs, and at that time was actually growing no silk at all.

A closer study shows, however, that the same thing occurred here as in the case of the other guilds with which we have dealt. Lacking the natural resources for developing a quantity enterprise with which to win the market through cheapness of production, the Florentine artisans devoted themselves to making their goods better—their drugs purer, their furs with a finer finish, and their silk more ornamental. The interest of the silk guild in ornamentation is demonstrated by the fact that the goldsmiths were enrolled in it, gold and silver brocade probably accounting for the connection.

Besides its seven greater guilds, Florence had the usual lesser guilds, representing the minor industries that were to be found in nearly every town, such as bakers, butchers, armorers, locksmiths, masters of stone and wood, carpenters, and tanners. No one of these was especially distinguished, either by the amount of work it did or by the prosperity it added to the city. There was no guild of sculptors, painters, or architects, not even a guild of artists as such. In fact, the term "art" as used by the Florentines at this time was a generic one for craft, applying equally to wool-weavers and stonemasons, to money-changers and armorers. Dante was enrolled in the guild of the physicians and apothecaries, and so too was Giotto, though he also belonged to one of the minor guilds.

# A City That Art Built

This brief survey of the economic development of Florence up to 1300 affords abundant evidence that its people possessed not only energy, thrift, and enterprise but certain other marked traits. Integrity of workmanship appears in all the big business of the Florentines, and they seem to have guarded their reputation most jealously, through both guild and civic action. In all their greater industry, and in their minor industries as well, there is evidence also of concern for taste, for the appearance of the product as well as for the integrity of the workmanship. Their iron grille work and their wrought iron, whether used alone or in combination with brass and bronze, as in the shields of guild arms, in tavern signs, font covers, reading desks, candelabra, gargoyles, and weather vanes; their iron fixtures, such as brackets and rings to hold torches; their fanlights, balcony railings, firebacks, locks and keys for houses, doors, cupboards, and chests; their workman's tools and toilet articles—all were celebrated not merely for their utility but as much, or more, for their perfection of workmanship and their attractive appearance.

Staley, in his history of the guilds of Florence, finds this artistic quality present in nearly all the products of Florentine craftsmanship, especially in those involving metal, stone, wood, and leather work. Nor was it characteristic only of relatively imperishable products of craftsmanship. It seems to have pervaded all Florentine activity, for Staley finds the Florentine dinner as highly and widely celebrated as the products of her craftsmen.

One might infer from the following quotation from Villani that the chief fault of some of the Florentine craftsmen was that of making their products too attractive.

In the said year i.e., 1330 on the 1st day of April, whereas the women of Florence were much addicted to excessive finery in the way of diadems and garlands of gold and silver and pearls and precious stones, and nets and plaited strings of pearls, and other costly devices for the adornment of the head, and likewise of dresses cut in divers cloths, and of drapery trimmed in various ways with silk and with pearls and brooches of pearls and of precious stones on the breast with divers emblems and letters . . .

it was thereanent provided, and laid down by certain officers in very strict ordinances, that no woman might wear any diadem or garland, either of gold or silver or pearls or stones or glass or silk, nor any semblance of a diadem or garland, even of painted paper, nor nets nor plaitings of any kind unless simple, nor any garment engraved or painted with any pattern not woven in the texture, nor any stripe or band except a simple division of two colors, nor any trimming either of gold or silver or silk, or any precious stone, or even enamel or glass; nor might they wear more than two rings on their fingers, nor any belt or girdle of more than xii bars of silver; and that from thenceforward none might dress in samite, and those who had it must mark it so that no new dresses might be made of it; and all garments of drapery trimmed with silk were banished and prohibited, and no woman might wear dresses longer than two ells at the back, nor having the bodice more than one quarter of an ell round at the neck; and in like manner were prohibited petticoats and ornate dresses for children whether boys or girls, and all trimmings even of ermine except to knights and their wives; and the men were deprived of every ornament and belt of silver and doublets of satin and of taffeta and of camlet; and order was made that no banquet should consist of more than three viands, or at weddings should have more than xx trenchers, and the bride should bring with her six women and no more, and the provisions of new knights should not exceed c trenchers of three viands, and that at the court of new knights none should dress so as to give away their clothing to the clowns, which formerly was much done (see *Statuti di S. Jacopo*, pp. 37 sqq.). In reference to the said articles, they appointed officers to search men, women, and children for the said forbidden things, with heavy penalties; also they issued orders concerning all the manufacturing arts . . . but to the great detriment of the Silk-weavers and Goldsmiths, who for their profit used to find every day new and different ornaments . . . and if the women used superfluous ornaments they were brought back to the proper limit, whereat they all complained loudly; but in spite of the strict ordinances there remained some abuses.[1]

Thus did Florentine thrift sometimes contend against Florentine taste, not always victoriously. Apparently the people of Florence exercised taste as much in what they bought as in what they made, and the conclusion that concern for taste pervaded Florentine industry before 1300 to an extraordinary degree seems more than justified.

There remains the task of examining the political and social developments of Florence during this period for any distinctive traits that might throw light on our question. The most important political development affecting Italy during these centuries was the rise of the papacy to a position of political as well as ecclesiastical power and the struggle with the emperors of the Holy Roman Empire which resulted from it. Italy naturally furnished the battleground for the struggle, and its people were forced to take sides.

In this struggle between imperial and papal forces the position of Florence was unique. It has already been said that the feudal nobles controlling the countryside of Florence had chosen to live at Fiesole, some five miles away. In nearly all the other towns of Tuscany, notably in Pisa and Sienna, the nobles dwelt within the city and tended, accordingly, to exercise political control. Everywhere in Italy, as well as elsewhere where trade and industry grew rapidly, there was natural friction between the tradesmen and the feudal nobility. In those cities in which the feudal nobles were in control, the tradesmen had to accept the situation and make the best of it.

In Florence, on the other hand, the merchants and craftsmen ruled within the city walls. As their town grew and the needs of the population required unimpeded access to an ever widening source of foodstuffs, friction with the nobles of the countryside increased. The growth of the population, however, produced a feeling of greater strength and emboldened the Florentines to settle the problem themselves. By 1125 they were ready to deal with the troublesome problem of Fiesole. Laying down their tools and picking up weapons, the burghers of Florence went out to besiege the castle town. They forced the nobles to surrender and then not only proceeded to pull down the walls and fortresses but required the nobles to agree to live in the city of Florence a certain length of time each year.

What they did to Fiesole they did also to most of the castles in the immediate countryside. This procedure is in itself note-worthy. There was little of the blood lust that characterized so much of the fighting of the period and this was to be character-istic of Florence for centuries to come. Though Florentine history is filled with disputes and quarrels, there was very little bloodshed.

The nobles forced to live within the city of Florence did so reluctantly at first, and this circumstance helped to keep the con-trol of the city in the hands of the merchants and craftsmen. Though the hatred and contempt the nobility felt for the trades-men long persisted, time tended to soften these feelings and inter-marriages between the less wealthy nobles and the wealthier mer-chants began to occur. Nevertheless, the nobles continued to constitute a minority element out of sympathy with the dominant merchant-craftsman control.

In the warfare between the Empire and the papacy the nobility of Italy were usually on the side of the Empire. Many of them were of German descent; most of them owed their positions to imperial favor and in times of difficulty had been accustomed to seek help from the emperors. The tradesmen, on the other hand, saw in the conflict an opportunity to free themselves from the annoying restrictions and exactions imposed by the nobles and joined the papal side. The tradesmen were thus as naturally sym-pathetic with the Guelf or papal party as were the nobles with the Ghibelline or imperial party. As the fortunes of war fluctu-ated, one party or the other gained the upper hand within the towns. In Florence, however, the Ghibelline faction was so much suppressed that only the presence of a victorious imperial army in the immediate neighborhood could give it control. When that army was removed, the Florentine tradition of burgher control reasserted itself. The opposite was true of Pisa and Sienna.

When these shifts occurred in the control of any of the cities, they were usually accompanied by retaliation for past sufferings. In Florence and the other cities the leaders of the opposing fac-tion were often exiled, or they fled from the city. Usually the exiles sought refuge in the nearest town controlled by the oppo-site faction, hoping for the wheels of fortune to turn again in their favor and permit them to return. As a result of these fluctuations, important merchants and craftsmen sought refuge in Florence, while the leading nobles of Florence had to retreat to Pisa or Sienna or some other Ghibelline town. How much these exiles added to the industry and prosperity of Florence can only be conjectured, for detailed records have not been preserved. The great struggle was practically ended in 1266 and Guelf Florence resumed its growth in population and prosperity. Its exiled Ghibelline nobles found such comfort as they could in Sienna, Pisa, Lucca, and Arezzo.

The highly prized banking business of the papacy, which Siennese bankers had held for so long, was now transferred permanently to Florentine bankers. In supporting the imperial cause, the Siennese, as Thompson puts it, "had bet on the wrong horse."

When the Florentine government began to extend its control over the countryside in order to ensure a food supply for its increased population and to facilitate its increased trade, both Arezzo to the east and Pisa to the west became alarmed and offered resistance, and the exiled Florentine nobles saw an opportunity to regain their position and power. From 1288 to 1292 intermittent war was waged between Florence on the one side and Pisa and Arezzo and the exiled Florentine Ghibellines on the other. The issue was really decided by the battle of Campaldino in 1289, when the citizen army of Florence overcame the allied opponents. Dante, then twenty-four years old, fought as a cavalryman in the ranks of the Florentines. Peace was finally made in 1292, and Florence proceeded to consolidate her gains and reap the fruits of victory.

The first steps taken were a series of legal enactments intended to make permanent the merchant-craftsman control of the city. These, the famous Ordinances of Justice, provided for a popular official, the Gonfaloniere of Justice, and a ruling body of twelve priors, called the Seigniory, which was changed by election every two months. The position of the guilds was definitely recognized in the conduct of common affairs, and a fixed list of seven greater and fourteen minor guilds was drawn up. Citizenship was restricted, and only regularly enrolled members of guilds were eligible to hold office. Those nobles within the city who had been incautious enough to betray their hopes for a Ghibelline victory in the recent war were exiled, and their property was confiscated and added to that already held as a result of the victory in 1266. The new constitution contained the provision that if a citizen proved obnoxious, the seigniory might declare him a noble, in effect disfranchising him.

Thus by the end of the thirteenth century Florence was an extremely homogeneous city ruled by merchants and craftsmen in the interest of industry and commerce. In this respect, too, Florence was distinctive.

The social developments in Florence that accompanied these economic and political developments during these three centuries are summarized in the remarks attributed by Dante to his great-great-grandfather:

> Florence within the ancient circling wall
>   Wherefrom she taketh still her tierce and nones,
>   Sober and chaste, abode at peace with all.
> Then necklace had she not, nor diadem,
>   Not fancy-shod fine ladies, nor yet girdles
>   Better to look at than those wearing them.
> Not yet the daughter at her birth dismayed
>   The father, for not yet did age and dower
>   Due measure on this side and that evade.
> Great houses without households had she none;
>   Nor yet had Sardanapalus arrived
>   To show what in the chamber can be done.
> Nor yet was Montemalo made look small
>   By your Uccellatoio,—which, as it hath
>   The greater height, shall have the greater fall.
> Myself have seen Bellincion Berti pass,
>   Belted with bone and leather, and his dame
>   With cheeks unpainted leave her looking-glass;
> Him of Nerli, him of Vecchio seen content
>   In unlined leather, and their womenfolk
>   With spindle and with distaff diligent.
> O fortunate! Not any feared mischance
>   Of burial in an alien land, not one

Was yet deserted in her bed for France.
One kept her vigil by the cradleside,
  And in her comforting would use the speech
  In which fathers and mothers first take pride;
Another tells the olden tales at home,
  The while she from the distaff draws the thread,
  Of Trojans, of Fiesole, of Rome.
As much in those days had seemd prodigies
  A Lapo Salterello, a Cianghella,
  As Cincinnatus or Cornelia in these.[2]

Despite Dante's implication that the city had degenerated greatly, life in it was still relatively simple. Though the prosperity of the city had much increased since 1266, there was as yet no distinct leisure class and there were no extremely wealthy families. Certain individuals had already won prominence as bankers, but their eminence was due to their investment of the savings of fellow citizens rather than to large accumulated funds of their own. The members of the greater guilds and the masters in the various crafts constituted the ruling element of the city, both politically and socially. Thrift and the simple life, though not always practiced, were still cherished as the common ideal. The people, laborers as well as merchants and master craftsmen, were still close neighbors and expressed their opinions without much reservation. In fact, criticism of each other, community self-criticism, so well exemplified by Dante, was another of the distinguishing characteristics of the Florentines.

Perhaps the best place to sense the rhythm of Florentine life was at the apothecaries' shops, already fairly numerous. Most of the workshops closed in the early afternoons, probably to enable the laborers who came in from the countryside to return to their homes at a convenient hour. Thus most of the Florentine city-dwellers had ample leisure, and the more respectable citizens spent much of this time at the apothecaries' shops. Here banker, notary, wool merchant, silk merchant, and master craftsmen of all trades were wont to gather.

Most of the shops were attractively arranged; drugs and spices were placed in ornamented containers of wood, glass, and leather;

besides chemicals and drugs, books and a great variety of miscellaneous articles were displayed and sold. Refreshments, including spiced wines, were commonly served, and there was much to attract the prosperous Florentine burgher.

Besides the merchants and craftsmen these shops also attracted the Florentine business agents returned from trips to all parts of Europe and the Mediterranean world. Writers and scholars gathered there to converse and discuss matters of mutual interest. Much of the conversation, doubtless, was merely a recounting of the day's occurrences, for newspapers did not yet exist. Much of it, too, was of ideas developed in various fields of activity—ideas that might be of value to the burgher in his own work.

It was doubtless in an apothecary's shop that Brunelleschi and Toscanelli discussed principles of mechanics and problems of mathematics. It was certainly there that Dante and Villani both acquired that informed knowledge of the achievements of their fellow citizens that led them to take so great a pride in their own city as compared with others. And out of all this interchange of news, gossip, and ideas there developed a determination that Florence should equal any other city in deserved prestige.

Civic pride ran never so high in Florence as in the decade following the Pisan peace. These were the years during which Dante conceived the idea of his *Divine Comedy* and Giovanni Villani the plan for his *Chronicle of Florence*. Dante was a member of the physicians' and apothecaries' guild, Villani of the money-changers' guild. Both probably entered wholeheartedly into the plans for the much-needed building program of the city.

None of the buildings for the common use of the city was large enough. The third wall to enclose the large additional population dwelling outside the city had already been started, though the war had interrupted the work. The Dominicans had begun their new church of Santa Maria Novella, but its progress too was lagging. The new government had no proper headquarters. Many of the guildhalls were inadequate for the needs of increased business, and the market places were cramped. Above all, Santa Reparata, the old cathedral, was altogether unsuited either to the population which it served or to the aroused civic pride whose chief material embodiment it must be.

These building needs had been voiced before, but there had been much opposition from the *grandi* and *popolo grosso*. Now many of these men had been exiled, and the sentiments of the merchants and master craftsmen were well-nigh unanimous.

The seigniory took the necessary steps. It sent for Arnolfo di Cambio, Master of Stone and Wood and a Florentine builder of some reputation, who had done some of the work on Santa Maria Novella and was then working in Rome. The immediate task for which he was summoned was work on the baptistery, the Church of San Giovanni, soon to be used as the cathedral while the new cathedral was in process of construction. Shortly afterward he was made *capo-maestro*, or city engineer and architect, a position he held to the time of his death in 1310.

Under Arnolfo's direction the building program of Florence soon took shape. Work on Santa Maria Novella was resumed, aided by a generous annual appropriation from the city treasury. The Franciscans at the other side of the city were given similar assistance in the erection of Santa Croce. The work on the third wall was resumed in earnest. A palace for the seigniory was begun. Market places were enlarged, and new halls were planned for several of the guilds.

The crown of all this building program was, of course, the cathedral. The spirit of the enterprise is indicated by the action of the seigniory: "Since the highest mark of prudence in a people of noble origin is to proceed in the management of their affairs so that their magnanimity and wisdom may be evinced in their outward acts, we order Arnolfo, head master of our commune, to make a design for the renovation of Santa Reparata in a style of magnificence which neither the industry nor the power of man can surpass, that it may harmonize with the opinion of many wise persons in this city and state, who think that this commune should not engage in any enterprise unless its intention be to make the result correspond with that noblest sort of heart which is composed of the united will of many citizens." [3]

Four years later, when the old cathedral had been torn down and the foundations laid for the new one, we find in the seigniory's proceedings this minute exempting Arnolfo from all taxes: "By reason of his industry, experience, and genius, the Commune and People of Florence from the magnificent and visible beginning of the said work of the said church commenced by the same Master Arnolfo, hope to have a more beautiful and more honorable temple than any other which there is in the regions of Tuscany." [4]

Arnolfo provided Florence with a city plan, a building program which with few changes was to be executed during the next two centuries and which was to serve the city well on into the nineteenth century. It was a community enterprise expressing the common will to a degree seldom equaled in any community. Seigniory followed seigniory and at times there were important changes in sentiment, as when Dante and his fellow Whites were exiled, but the work went on, supported by the public treasury.

The immediate costs were paid for by a tax on all products going out of or coming into the city, and though from time to time the financing of portions of the program were entrusted to certain guilds, this was virtually only a variation in the form of taxation.

The execution of this city plan continued to be a public enterprise well on into the sixteenth century, and among the *capomaestri* paid by the city to continue the work after the death of Arnolfo were Giotto, Talenti, Brunelleschi, and Michelangelo. The drawing of Florence by an unknown artist in the last decade of the fifteen century may in a sense be regarded as Arnolfo's plan achieved.

This building program afforded almost unlimited opportunity for the production of what histories of art have chosen to regard as art. Indeed, a very large part of the art they have chronicled clusters about the buildings and open areas provided for in Arnolfo's plan. To trace that work in detail would be to write a large section of the history of Renaissance art. Our concern, however, is to discover the relation of this art to the antecedent develop-

A City That Art Built

ment of Florence and to the life of its people. For this purpose a few incidents in the carrying out of Arnolfo's plan may be sufficient.

Whence did Florence obtain the artists to achieve these works of art so much admired? How were they trained? How were they selected? Who determined their tasks and how were these executed? Those are the questions of greatest moment to our problem.

One incident is especially interesting for the light it throws upon many aspects of Florentine life. It also marks one important change in Arnolfo's original plan. This incident had to do with the grain market. Florence was not a grain or milling center and the grain sold there was entirely for local consumption. The grain market was therefore comparable to a provision market in our modern cities, relatively unimportant as compared with other parts of the plan.

The market place had been enlarged by tearing down an old church of St. Michael, and it was generally referred to by the Florentines as *Or San Michele*, or Saint Michael's of the Garden. At the center of this market place Arnolfo provided a loggia to please the eye and arrest the attention of merchants and customers in their idle moments, and to afford a shelter for officials and merchants. On one of the square columns or pilasters the head of the Virgin was painted.

The people who frequented this market liked that picture, and the idea arose that the Virgin herself liked it especially well. People began to believe that if they said their prayers to her before this picture, there was a much better chance of having them answered. In vain did the clergy condemn this practice as idolatrous, pointing out that the loggia was not a church and that the picture was only a picture. The people persisted. Stories began to circulate that miraculous cures had followed the prayers of sick persons before this picture, and then thousands came there to pray and make offerings. A society of responsible persons was formed to receive these offerings and dispense them to charity.

Then about 1304 a disastrous fire swept the neighborhood.

155

Even the loggia itself was destroyed. But the column with the picture of the Virgin came through unscathed!

If there had been any doubt about that picture before, there was none now. Even the clergy had to surrender. The loggia was replaced by a building, part church and part business building, and the picture was carefully preserved and framed in a tabernacle designed by Orcagna, a goldsmith. It was placed inside the church portion of the building and continued to be visited by thousands. The humble grain market was finally removed to another part of the city, and the office or business portion of the building was assigned more or less to all the guilds. At any rate, the authorities allowed the guilds to install statues of their patron saints in tabernacles around the outside of the building, though the picture of the Virgin retained the place of honor inside. Fourteen of the guilds did so.[5]

An analysis of this incident may furnish important clues to the answers to our questions. When the opportunity to do this tabernacle came to him, Orcagna was a practicing Florentine goldsmith, trained to do the type of work that had been done by Florentine goldsmiths for centuries past. The finished work is thus described in a modern guidebook: "This magnificent work is one of the masterpieces of architecture and sculpture of the fourteenth century, built and fitted together without cement, with copper rivets set in lead so as to appear as if carved out of one block." Viewed from a distance, the work might almost seem to be a piece of jewel-setting. At close range it appears as it did to the author of the guidebook, "a masterpiece of architecture and sculpture."

The authorities in charge of the building program allotted the task to Andrea Orcagna in 1349. The high esteem in which the picture was held by the people of Florence must have served as a powerful incentive to the goldsmith. Aided by his brother, he worked on it for more than ten years and presented the completed work to the authorities in 1359.

The goldsmith who performed this triumph of architecture and sculpture is listed in histories of art as a painter. And in later years much of his talent and energy was devoted to the pictorial decoration of church walls.

Another incident in the development of the city building plan has been described in great detail by Vasari. Arnolfo had engaged Andrea Pisani, whose family had come from Pisa, to make a pair of bronze doors for the baptistery, which was being used as a temporary cathedral. Nearly a hundred years later the city authorities decided to have another set of bronze doors made for the opposite entrance. So they advertised the job and invited any who would to submit designs and plans.

A great number entered the competition, whereupon the authorities invited any Florentines who cared to do so to help them judge the relative merits of the designs submitted. The authors of the seven best designs, only three of whom were Florentines, were then asked to prepare a panel for the doors. They were all assigned the same subject for their panels, were paid to do the work, and were required to have the panels ready within a year, when the job would be finally let.

Again the authorities invited aid in judging the merits of the completed panels, but this time they were in a quandary, because one of the panels was clearly superior in design but another was equally superior in the perfection of its finish. Both, as it happened, were by Florentine goldsmiths. Though the authorities finally voted to assign the contract for the doors to one designer assisted by the other, the matter was settled by the voluntary withdrawal of one artist, so that the other might complete the task alone.

Thus it was that Ghiberti instead of Brunelleschi received the contract for the bronze doors of the baptistery, which are so celebrated in the history of art.

Ghiberti was a goldsmith who had served his apprenticeship in the shop of his stepfather, a competent but undistinguished master of the goldsmith's craft. Shortly after Ghiberti had completed his apprenticeship, he took to the road, finding such employment as he could. When the competition for the bronze doors was announced, he was helping to decorate the walls of a new palace being erected by an Italian condottiere. The competition proved to be Ghiberti's great opportunity. These and the so-called Paradise Doors which he made are, like the tabernacle of Orcagna, an example of the application of the goldsmith's craft on a large scale.

The fate of Ghiberti's nearest rival in the competition is even more interesting. The cathedral begun by Arnolfo was nearing completion, and the most important task remaining was that of covering the space where the transepts and main aisle met. The matter had been discussed by the authorities for some time, but the construction of an appropriate crown for the roof of the church presented so many difficulties that its undertaking had been delayed.

According to Vasari, Brunelleschi, having lost the competition for the bronze doors, determined to win an even greater victory. Disposing of a small piece of property which he had inherited, he used the proceeds to spend more than a year in Rome, where he browsed among the architectural ruins, measuring and sketching the remains of the ancient Roman buildings. In pursuit, probably, of this same ambition, he had cultivated the friendship of Toscanelli, the Florentine geographer, then recognized for his astronomical and mathematical knowledge. From him Brunelleschi learned much of the principles of mechanics and mathematics, especially geometry and trigonometry. And when the city authorities finally invited submission of designs for the uncompleted roof of the cathedral, Brunelleschi won the competition.

His design for this portion of the roof of the cathedral was an octagonal dome, not exactly like any construction either in Florence or anywhere else. It aroused intense interest not only among other builders but also among all the amateur architects at the apothecary shops. As the work progressed, these self-appointed critics found much fault, many of them insisting that the plan could not be executed. The city authorities, weakening under the volume of criticism, finally decided to appoint a supervising or consulting architect, and they chose Ghiberti for this position. Lacking the graciousness that Brunelleschi had shown in the competition over the bronze doors, Ghiberti accepted the position and the salary.

But Brunelleschi was equal to the situation. When the work on the dome had reached a particularly difficult and intricate stage, he professed to be ill, and when the workmen came to receive directions as to how to proceed they were instructed to go to the supervising architect. It soon became apparent to the workmen and likewise to the town authorities that Ghiberti was totally incompetent for such a task. Sensing the true situation, the authorities abrogated their arrangement with Ghiberti and permitted Brunelleschi to complete the work alone.

The result was the dome of Santa Maria del Fiore as it appears today, not only very beautiful but also structurally sound. It so enhanced the reputation of the builder that, though a goldsmith, he spent most of his time thereafter in building palaces and churches, and he is listed in histories of art as an architect.

These works of Orcagna, Ghiberti, and Brunelleschi are all described and discussed in treatises on art, though all of them were achieved by craftsmen. All three men were goldsmiths, though the first is usually classified as a painter, the second as a sculptor, and the third as an architect.

These instances in the achievement of Florentine art are not exceptional but typical. An astounding number of the works of art created in Florence or by Florentines between 1300 and 1550 and celebrated in histories of art as among the great paintings, sculpture, and architecture of the world were done by men who had served their apprenticeships in the goldsmith craft.

Donatello, famous primarily as a sculptor of figures, friezes, equestrian statues, and tombs, was a goldsmith. Michelozzo, his assistant on many of these works but famous in his own name as the architect of the Medici town house, churches, and country palaces, was likewise trained as a goldsmith. Verrocchio, almost equally famous with Donatello as a sculptor, was also a goldsmith. So too was the painter Ghirlandajo, whose numerous grand frescoes are still so much admired. These two, in turn, were the

The Long Road Back

masters in whose shops, or *botteghe*, Leonardo da Vinci and Michelangelo, respectively, served their apprenticeships. Luca della Robbia, copies of whose cantoria frieze appear in nearly every art collection in the Western world today and whose glazed earthenware began a new industry, was likewise a goldsmith. And so were Benvenuto Cellini and Vasari of the sixteenth century, both more widely known for their writings than for their sculpture and architecture, though the latter are also famous.

The list of goldsmiths who contributed to the public adornment of Florence during these centuries might be greatly extended, but these will illustrate their importance in the development of Florentine art.

A close examination of the goldsmith's craft may help to explain why so much of the art of Florence was derived from that source. The craft was prominent there in the twelfth century and even more so in the thirteenth. The goldsmiths made crucifixes of various kinds and sizes, set gems and jewels of all kinds. They made articles for use in the church service and articles of silver and gold for personal adornment. Birth plates, table service, metal clasps for chests and books, and other articles for household service came from their shops.

To contrive this variety of articles, the goldsmith worked in gold, silver, bronze, marble, wood, and clay. He cast, hammered, chiseled, filed, sawed, and carved. His work might involve a mingling of metal and textile, as in brocade, or of stone and painting, as in mosaic- and jewel-setting. Thrift compelled him to make careful drawings of what he planned to do and to make inexpensive models of anything that was to be of a large size. Commercial rivalry forced him to use the utmost ingenuity in devising original and attractive designs. He was alert to new ideas in any and all fields of human interest which he might embody in his work to please the prosperous buyer. These he drew from household needs, from recreation, from popular and classical literature, and from learning, both sacred and profane. The hours spent at the apothecary shops were, or might be, especially profitable to him. Almost every job he undertook required careful study, for it was likely always to involve some new elements, either of material, of scale, or of design.

All this was true of the goldsmith's craft before 1300 and continued to be true of it after that time. There was nothing that art required which the goldsmith was not already trained to do. Attributes of art, such as form and color, composition, perspective, harmony and proportion, taste, and beauty, were matters of concern to him in every task he undertook.

Upon reflection, therefore, it would seem that the main difference between the goldsmith's craft and art, as the historians of art have used the latter term, lay in the matter of size. Some of the other crafts, such as those of the masters of wood and stone, carpenters, workers in leather, and workers in metal, especially locksmiths, presented similar problems, made similar demands, afforded similar training, and furnished some of the creators of the works of art in Florence.

Such an inventory of the normal requirements of the artisans who regularly plied their crafts in the industry of Florence removes much of the mystery about the source of Florentine art. When the authorities of Florence decided to beautify their city and had the money with which to do so, that was all that was needed. They were not creating something that had not existed before. They were merely giving craftsmen an opportunity to do on a much larger scale the kind of work they were normally doing in industry and for commerce. That these supreme triumphs of Florentine craftsmanship should be singled out as alone deserving of the appellation "art" seems an injustice to the equally artistic work which the men were and had been doing in the pursuit of their crafts.

Having reached the conclusion that the highly developed crafts practiced all the techniques that art required, and that it was therefore natural, rather than strange, that many of the great works of Florentine art were created by Florentine craftsmen, one is tempted to examine the careers of other artists of Florence.

Such an examination, however, tends only to confirm the conclusion already reached, for nearly every one of the great artists of Florence whose career is known was first trained as a craftsman.

The works of art discussed thus far were those of men employed by the public, either directly by the city authorities or indirectly through the sponsorship of the guilds. But there were other sources of employment.

As the fifteenth century opened, Florence witnessed a widening gap in the prosperity of its citizens. A few families had acquired very great wealth, some of them, like the Medici, controlling private means of princely proportions. These families tended to adopt a standard of living proportionate to their wealth. Their modest town houses were replaced with palaces like those of the Pitti and the Medici, and their country estates were provided with attractive villas, like Careggi of the Medici. Some of them, notably the Medici, made generous gifts for the construction of churches, chapels, libraries, and hospitals and for the further adornment of buildings already erected. San Marco, the gift of the Medici to the Dominicans, is an excellent example.

These activities furnished work for Florentine craftsmen and provided incentives toward those supreme achievements that have been accorded the title of art.

There is little to indicate that the craftsmen preferred employment by private individuals. Nearly all those noted as great artists during the fifteenth century engaged in both types of employment. Even Leonardo da Vinci and Michelangelo, favorites of the Medici, were drawn by the competition for the decoration of the walls of the Palace of the Seigniory to what some regard as the highest point in art which either reached. And Michelangelo finished his career as *capo-maestro* for the city, a fitting close to the great civic enterprise so happily begun under the direction of Arnolfo. Civic pride remained throughout the period a dominant force in the lives of the Florentine craftsmen-artists.

The great increase in the amount of building, private and public, that took place during the fifteenth century offered an opportunity for specialization. And doubtless some individual workers preferred one branch or skill over the others. Michelangelo referred to himself as a sculptor, and others, like Donatello, Brunelleschi, Botticelli, did so much of their work in one field as to become regarded primarily as sculptor, architect, or painter.

Nevertheless, few if any of them did actually so specialize for any long period of time. Michelangelo, who seemed most insistent upon doing so, is known for his painting as much as for his sculpture. One of his last great works was the dome of St. Peter's in Rome, a triumph of architecture, and at the close of his career he was much concerned with the civil and military engineering problems of his native city. Brunelleschi did work in sculpture and engineering as well as in architecture, Michelozzo in both sculpture and architecture, Luca della Robbia in sculpture, painting, and architecture. And Leonardo da Vinci, in a famous letter to the duke of Milan, offered to do work in nearly all fields of art as well as in engineering. It would be difficult if not impossible to name a single famous artist of Florence, even at the close of the period, who specialized in one branch of art.

Nor, apparently, did they ever cease being craftsmen. Brunelleschi, though famous as an architect, delighted his fellow townsmen by contriving a religious drama with pulleys and weights for one of the churches in Florence. Michelangelo, whose great professional pride is illustrated by so many stories, himself designed the scaffolding from which he painted the Sistine ceiling, and he did not hesitate to make a little crucifix for Vittoria Colonna long after he had become famous both as sculptor and painter.

It is doubtful that the task Leonardo da Vinci undertook for the monks in Milan was expected to be anything more than a bit of interior decorating. The subject he painted was a strictly conventional choice for a refectory decoration, and the wall on which he painted was scarcely suitable for a great masterpiece. The central object of his artistic interest at the time was the bronze equestrian statue of the duke of Milan. This did not prevent him, however, from dabbling at various other jobs, among them anatomical drawings for some of the professors of medicine at Pavia and even so humble a task as designing a kind of wheelbarrow that is still used in northern Italy.

Almost everyone knows that Benvenuto Cellini was making salt cellars and soup tureens at the same time that he was casting bronze statues.

Instead of scorning craftsmanship, Florentine artists appear rather to have prided themselves upon their ability to do any work, great or small, which fell to their craft. Perhaps this adherence to the idea that they were craftsmen was an essential element in their achievements as great artists.

In the very persistence of the idea of craftsmanship and in the lack of specialization may, indeed, lie the secret of the many skills of Florentine artists. To us, who live in an age of high specialization, the versatility of Leonardo da Vinci and Michelangelo, who were painters, sculptors, architects, engineers, and poets, is a never ending source of amazement. But the training of Florentine craftsmen, especially of goldsmiths, was not narrowly specialized, and this was only less true of masons, carpenters, and metal- and leather-workers. All of them had to draw, design, and consider color, form, and composition. Nearly all these crafts required an acquaintance with many materials, from precious stones and metals to such baser materials as stone, wood, leather, and clay. They likewise required skill in the use of tools and a knowledge of the techniques necessary to obtain the best results with a given material. Originality in design and perfection in finish were doubtless cultivated because each task involved problems peculiar to itself. And every job was a competitive one, whether the competition lay in greater customer appeal on display counters or in the more direct competition for a public contract. This premium on originality and perfection kept the Florentine craftsmen ever young and on the alert for new ideas anywhere in life or literature.

As Florentine craftsmen frequented their favorite gathering places, they learned theology and humanism, philosophy and history, poetry and mythology, mechanics and mathematics. Since they were always learning, even at the age of seventy, is it any wonder that they displayed great versatility?

The Florentines expected their craftsmen to be versatile. Giotto, back at the beginning of the period, who chatted with Franciscan and Dominican theologians, with Dante and Villani, was just as versatile as the craftsmen-artists at the end of the period. He too was painter, architect, sculptor, engineer, and poet.

The expansion and multiplication of building operations during the fifteenth century doubtless attracted many able young Florentines into the crafts required for that work. The rivalry and the great amount of building both contributed to hasten the technical development of the arts involved. The greater achievements aroused the admiration of the Florentines themselves of course, but also of travelers, who helped to spread abroad the city's fame, so that Florence attracted young artists from all parts of western Europe who came there to study its art. The four years that Raphael spent there almost make him a Florentine.

As other communities, first in Italy, then beyond the Alps, embarked upon lavish building operations, Florentine artists were in great demand. Thus Cosimo de Medici was able to discharge a portion of his debt of hospitality to Venice by having Michelozzo erect several buildings there. Donatello's equestrian statue of Gattamelata and Verrocchio's similar statue of Colleone represented like services to the Venetians. Leonardo da Vinci served similarly at Milan. Michelangelo and many lesser artists worked much in Rome. Leonardo went finally to the court of Francis of France, and many Florentines, including Benvenuto Cellini, worked in France during the sixteenth century. Fame as well as fortune was lavished upon these Florentine artists.

It would be interesting to know whether the attitude of the Florentines toward the work of their craftsmen was changed by all these developments. In 1300 popular interest was everywhere apparent. Was the populace still a factor in the sixteenth century?

As the military cartoons of Leonardo and Michelangelo show, the more popular government established around the turn of the sixteenth century after the exile of the Medicis displayed the same interest in public adornment as had characterized the earlier period when San Marco, the gift of the Medici to the Dominican friars which was designed and built by Michelozzo, had been adorned by Fra Angelico and others.

One of the most interesting indexes to the attitude of the Florentines in the early sixteenth century is contained in a letter of a young German monk who was traveling in Italy about 1510. I have quoted this letter before,* but is worth repeating for its relevance here.

"The hospitals of the Italians are built like palaces supplied with the best food and drink and tended by diligent servants and skillful physicians. The painted bedsteads are covered with clean linen. When a patient is brought in, his clothes are taken off and given to a notary to keep honestly. They then put a white bedgown on him and lay him between the clean sheets of the beautifully painted bed, and two physicians are brought at once. Servants fetch food and drink in clean vessels and do not touch the food even with a finger but offer it to the patient on a tray. Honorable matrons, veiled, serve the poor all day long without making their names known and at evening return home. These carefully tended hospitals I saw at Florence. They also have a foundling hospital where children are well sheltered and nourished and taught; they are all dressed in uniform and most paternally cared for."

Many details in this description recall the Florentines of the twelfth and thirteenth centuries. Their integrity, represented by the notary's presence, their intelligence in summoning two physicians for the diagnosis instead of only one, their regard for sanitation, the fine courtesy of service by the noble matrons, their high regard for education in giving even the foundlings some schooling—all these qualities sound very familiar. The decoration of rooms and buildings suggests also that the spirit of Florence had changed little since the earlier period, though, to be sure, the intervening centuries had furnished additional forms of expression.

The writer of this letter was Martin Luther, and his comments

* See the paper, "The Rebirth of the Medical Profession."

indicate that there was art still in nearly everything the Florentines undertook to do.

It is entirely probable that another art which the modern tourist sees in Florence today flourished equally at that time. The writer recalls vividly a stroll he once took through the streets of Florence on a hot summer day. He passed a large open door through which could be seen a number of workmen engaged in various operations. Wheels were going around, hammers were swinging, and chisels gliding along under the blows. The temptation to linger and watch the activity was irresistible.

One of the workmen, distinguished from the rest by a white collar, was moving about from one to another of the others as a sort of foreman. As he came near the door he looked up at the curious spectator with a pleasant smile, which was returned. Thereupon he spoke in excellent English, inviting the spectator to come in and view the activity more closely. He guided the visitor from one workman to another, explaining each particular stage in the process, and before long the visitor was viewing pieces of the finished mosaic work. Large pieces were shown first, with the statement that they had been made to the order of a certain American or English visitor. Then smaller and smaller pieces were shown.

The visitor was never asked directly to purchase any of the work, but the setting was so perfectly arranged that it seemed the obvious and only proper thing to do. As a result, the visitor found himself back on the street with several small pieces of mosaic work which he had not intended to buy and lacking several dollars which he had intended to devote to other purposes.

It was a consummate example of the salesman's art—the display of activity, not of finished ware, the keen identification of the visitor's nationality without direct question, the excellent English, the courteous explanation of the process of manufacture, and the display of finished goods without direct solicitation. Luther does not mention this art in his letter. Perhaps he, in his monk's garb, was immune to its practice, but there is every reason to believe that it flourished then as much as it does now.

## The Long Road Back

After this review of Florentine development it can no longer be a matter of great surprise that it was not Rome, or Venice, or Milan, though each was larger, wealthier, and even more famous, that gave its language to Italy. Florence sold its dialect to all Italy as the modern national language, and this achievement, too, was the work of Florentine artists, especially of Dante and Boccaccio.

Nor were the literary arts altogether remote from the graphic arts. The interchange of ideas between Florentine writers and scholars and painters, sculptors, and architects is evident in nearly all the great works of art of this period. But the connection was even more direct. Not only were some of the great artists, like Giotto and Michelangelo, writers of sonnets and other poetry, but two of the Florentine artists of the sixteenth century combined the literary and plastic arts. These were Benvenuto Cellini, whose autobiography is ranked as a classic of its kind, and Giorgio Vasari, whose *Lives of Seventy Most Eminent Painters, Sculptors, and Architects* has been translated into nearly all modern languages. Both wrote in the sixteenth century, when Florentine greatness in art production was ended. Both were typical Florentine artists, trained as craftsmen and ready to undertake work large or small in sculpture, painting, architecture, or engineering, and yet their fame rests chiefly upon their literary immortalization of Italian, primarily Florentine, art and artists. It is due to them as well as to the works of art they describe that the footsteps of art lovers from all parts of the world have been turned to Florence ever since.

Confirmation of all that has been said about the relation of art to life in Florence can be found in the pages of Cellini's autobiography. The account of life in this one Florentine family may be regarded as at least indicative of the lives led by other humble Florentines in the centuries from the twelfth to the sixteenth. The description of his father's interests and abilities may be typical of those of many Florentines:

"My father in those times fashioned wonderful organs with pipes of wood, spinets the fairest and most excellent which then could be seen, viols and lutes and harps of the most beautiful and perfect construction. He was an engineer, and had marvellous skill in making instruments for lowering bridges and for working mills, and other machines of that sort. In ivory he was the first who wrought really well." [6]

The father earned his living as a musician in the band of the seigniory. The possession by this professional musician of even a few of the skills ascribed to him by his son would seem at least to indicate a wide diffusion of mechanical and artistic ability among the citizens of Florence.

Cellini's pages show that the goldsmith's craft was still the road to high artistic achievement, though a more formal pursuit of artistic proficiency is now also indicated. Art for him still means craft, for so he uses the term. He is emphatic in his assertions that there can be, and is, as much art in the smaller objects made for commerce as in the larger pieces. The whole range of materials used, of skills involved, of techniques mastered, the eternal alertness for new ideas and continual study, the sensitiveness to beauty in persons and nature, in prose and in poetry, in music and in the plastic and pictorial arts, which appeared in the careers of Arnolfo and Giotto, Orcagna and Ghiberti, Brunelleschi and Donatello, Leonardo and Michelangelo, are revealed again in the pages of Cellini.

As his reputation grew, Cellini tended to devote most of his attention to sculpture. The extent of popular interest in such matters as late as the middle of the sixteenth century may be gathered from his account of the preliminary showing and final unveiling of his Perseus, which he had done on the order of the Duke of Tuscany.

"Now it pleased God that, on the instant of its exposure to view, a shout of boundless enthusiasm went up in commendation of my work, which consoled me not a little. The folk kept on attaching sonnets to the posts of the door, which was protected with a curtain while I gave the last touches to the statue. I believe that on the same day when I opened it a few hours to the public, more than twenty were nailed up, all of them overflowing with the highest panegyrics. Afterwards, when I once more shut it off from view, every day brought sonnets, with Latin and Greek verses; for the University of Pisa was then in vacation, and all the doctors and scholars kept vying with each other who could praise it best. But what gratified me most . . . was that the artists, sculptors and painters alike, entered into the same generous competition . . .

". . . and on a certain Thursday morning I exposed it to the public gaze. Immediately, before the sun was fully in the heavens, there assembled such a multitude of people that no words could describe them. All with one voice contended which should praise it most. The Duke was stationed at a window low upon the first floor of the palace, just above the entrance; there, half hidden, he heard everything the folk were saying of my statue. After listening through several hours, he rose so proud and happy in his heart that he turned to his attendant, Messer Sforza, and exclaimed: 'Sforza, go and seek Benvenuto; tell him from me that he has delighted me far more than I expected.' " [7]

The same kind of interest, if negative, is revealed in his description of his chief rival:

". . . He [Michelangelo] had made the model for a Samson with four figures, which would have been the finest masterpiece in the whole world; but your Bandinello got out of it only two figures, both ill-executed and bungled in the worst manner; wherefore our school still exclaims against the great wrong which was done to that magnificent block. I believe that more than a thousand sonnets were put up in abuse of that detestable performance." [8]

Despite his reputation as a sculptor, which led to his selection as one of the two to represent sculpture at the funeral of Michelangelo, Cellini still continued to work as a goldsmith. Evidently he found it of advantage in pursuing his other ambitions, as the following passage implies. Having received intimations that the Duke meant to give him a commission to carve a certain piece of marble, Cellini thought it wise to have this favor confirmed by an even more important authority: "Hearing what the Duke had said, I went to the Duchess and took her some small bits of goldsmith's work, which greatly pleased her Excellency." [9]

# A City That Art Built

Cellini's autobiography closes with the year 1562. The funeral of Michelangelo occurred in 1564. Vasari issued the last edition of his famous *Lives* in 1568. These events may be regarded as closing the period of Florentine greatness in artistic production. The intimate picture which the two artist-writers, particularly Cellini, have left of this closing period is remarkable in several respects. Most noteworthy, perhaps, is the evidence of the continued existence of nearly all those factors that accounted for the artistic rise and leadership of Florence. The interest and willingness of the people, their skill and taste, even their energy, were still evident at the end of the period. Only the times had changed; the conditions of life that offered the opportunity for the supreme expression of these traits had departed.

In view of all the evidence, whether derived from the history of Florence before 1300, from the study of its artists after 1300, or from the attitude of its people throughout the period, it must be concluded that in Florence during the time of its highest artistic production art was never an activity apart from the affairs of everyday life. Instead it permeated and transfused every ordinary occupation.

The art of Florence was the work of craftsmen who were supreme in their crafts—crafts that had been developing in Florence for centuries before 1300. The object of the craftsmen was commercial; they wanted to sell the products of their skill. Every one of the Florentines who became famous as an artist after 1300, including Leonardo da Vinci and Michelangelo, Cellini and Vasari at the very end of the period, had been trained as a craftsman prepared to make small articles for sale just as their predecessors had been trained before 1300. Furthermore, each of them continued to be a craftsman to the end of his days, and most of them, despite one or two interesting exceptions, were also good businessmen. They were a part of the fabric of life in Florence and reflected the same spirit that characterized the city itself, a spirit that made little or no distinction between art and utility but sought, as it were, to unify these two aspects of reality.

## The Long Road Back

Later ages, it is true, have chosen to classify and single out some of the best of Florentine achievement as great art, but Florentine artists themselves strove only to do all work, however humble, exceptionally well. Possibly it was precisely because the Florentines were not conscious of any conflict between art and utility, between specialization and versatility, that they wrought even better than they knew.

At all events the evidence seems clear that, up to 1550, Florentine attention was concentrated upon the perfect rendering of the specific task in hand, not upon art as a mysterious vision removed from mundane affairs. During the two centuries before 1300 as well as during the two that followed, the Florentines seem to have maintained this point of view. They saw no reason, apparently, why a pictorial artist, for example, should not do house-painting, or, conversely, why a house-painter should not seek to do a thoroughly artistic job.

We must conclude that the Florentines had little interest in art as an abstract quality removed from experience but that their daily lives were ordered by a consistent impulse toward beauty in every manifest form. In Florence, at the height of the city's greatness, artist and skilled worker were not separate and somewhat antagonistic members of an indifferent community, but were one and the same person supported by the warm enthusiasm of a sympathetic group.

Such is our reading of how one community without marked natural advantages of any kind and before the age of mechanical power and mass production developed in two centuries from a country town of six thousand inhabitants into a metropolis of one hundred thousand and maintained that level for two and one-half centuries longer. Whatever other explanations may be offered for this extraordinary development, it will be difficult to deny the largest share to the sustained effort of the people of Florence to do whatever they did as well and as beautifully as possible. If that is art, then Florence of the Renaissance may well be called a city that art built.

NOTES

[1] Villani, *Croniche Fiorentine*, translated by S. J. A. Churchill in *The Goldsmiths of Italy* (London: M. Hopkinson and Company Ltd., 1926), pp. 146–47.

[2] *The Divine Comedy of Dante*, translated by J. B. Fletcher (New York: The Macmillan Company, 1931), Paradise, Canto XV.

[3] Charles C. Perkins, "Tuscan Sculptors," quoted in J. A. Symonds, *Fine Arts* (Vol. 3 of *The Renaissance in Italy*, published by John Murray, London), p. 46.

[4] Edmund G. Gardner, *The Story of Florence* (London: J. M. Dent & Co., 1924), p. 265.

[5] *Ibid.*, pp. 190–95.

[6] J. A. Symonds, *The Life of Benvenuto Cellini* (Charles Scribner's Sons, 1903), p. 7.

[7] *Ibid.*, pp. 408 and 409–10.

[8] *Ibid.*, p. 423.

[9] *Ibid.*, p. 425.

# 8

## Seeing the Renaissance Whole

It would be hard to find in any language a word more fully freighted with optimism than the term "Renaissance." Heaven alone holds more. To be born again, presumably with the opportunity to avoid all unpleasant experiences of a previous existence, to enjoy once more and to the full the springtime of youth and then as middle age creeps on to revel in the highest intellectual and aesthetic pleasures that the world has ever known—all this and more is implied in the word. And this is the term that has been applied to a period of European history variously defined but bounded roughly by the three centuries from 1300, the year when Dante made his imaginary journey through the afterworld, to the day when Shakespeare died, or, if you like, a bit later to the day of Milton's death after 1600 A.D.

This choice of name for the period is not the historian's; indeed he finds himself embarrassed by its use, for reasons that I have explained elsewhere.* But the rest of the literate world will not be dissuaded from the use of so neat and appealing a label, and the historian, not always finding it convenient to explain his objections, is forced to conform.

The historian, whose professional task it is to deal with the whole recorded past, usually works alone in restoring that record. Not so for this period. Here he finds scholars and dilettantes of

* In the paper entitled "The New Learning."

so many fields of learning and cultural interests working upon his materials that he is almost crowded out by the throng and truly has trouble gaining a hearing—or even a reading. It is, I believe, correct to say that more has been written about this period by persons who are not professional historians than by the historians themselves.

Consider the accounts of this period with which you are familiar. Most of you will readily recall the several volumes by John Addington Symonds, a literary critic. Perhaps as many of you will know the profoundly analytical work of Jacob Burckhardt, an art critic. Some of you, too, will have read the two volumes by Henry Osborn Taylor, originally a classical scholar who became something of a historian. He was so anxious to avoid the use of the term "Renaissance" that he entitled his work *Thought and Expression in 16th Century Italy*—a far worse misnomer, for his two volumes deal chiefly with the fourteenth and fifteenth centuries. And of course you will recall those beautiful essays on the Renaissance by scholars of English literature.

It is natural for workers in any field as they gain success and prosperity in their chosen occupation to develop an avocational interest in its beginnings. Thus the artist, particularly the painter, follows his interest back to Giotto, with whom, Vasari tells him, modern painting began. The classical scholar looking for the earliest traces of a secular interest in his profession is led back to Petrarch, who with no undue modesty proclaimed himself the discoverer of the secular values of classical studies and thereby won for himself the title of "Father of Humanism." And the professor of modern literature seeking the origin of his profession is carried back inevitably to Boccaccio, who as far as I can discover was probably the first to occupy a university chair in contemporary literature when Florence appointed him to lecture upon the *Divine Comedy* of Dante. The political scientist, though his traditional interests carry him back to Plato and Aristotle, finds many of his more modern ideas generated in this period by Marsilio of Padua, Machiavelli, and Grotius; the economist finds the origin of modern capitalism here; and the historian sees the birth of his critical scholarship in Lorenzo Valla.

Likewise, the scientist comes to include among his forebears Fracastoro in the study of contagious diseases, Vesalius in anatomy, Fabricius in embryology, Harvey in physiology, Copernicus in astronomy, Georgius Agricola in geology and metallurgy, Jerome Cardan in higher algebra, Gesner in botany and zoology as well as library science, Paracelsus in chemistry and pharmacy, and Paré in surgery. Technologists have come to regard Leonardo da Vinci as their patron saint, and philosophers have found the beginnings of modern lay interest in philosophy in the Platonic Academy of Florence.

I cannot possibly have enumerated all the professions and vocations that have developed a curiosity about this period of history, but I have surely named enough to indicate how thoroughly the historian finds himself crowded, if not indeed crowded out, by all this competing attention.

In passing, I should like to point out one striking feature of this listing of interests. They are all lay interests—and thus underline one essential characteristic of the Renaissance: it was the period when the laity became largely literate.

The historian's first reaction to so much competition is one of annoyance. And this annoyance is heightened by the fact that though the interest of these collateral professions is directed by their own vocational concerns, all of them have had sufficient experience of life to feel justified in interpreting the whole society of the period. But each interprets the period from his own point of reference. For Burckhardt every activity of these centuries was art-inspired; he sees art even in the way they perpetrated their murders. Symonds, of course, is at his best in the appraisal of literary developments, but he does not hesitate to include in his monumental treatment also politics and religion, fields with which he was but ill-acquainted. We could continue the roll, revealing a host of similar distortions—which leads us inevitably to recall the fable of the five blind men of India and their conclusions about the nature of the elephant.

# Seeing the Renaissance Whole

I can illustrate the reaction of the historian by a personal experience. Teaching at the University of California at Los Angeles one summer, I received an invitation to attend a two-day conference on the Renaissance at the Huntington Library, which I was most happy to accept. I looked forward to enjoying a renewal of my acquaintance with familiar characters, events, and achievements. I also hoped to hear new research and fresh points of view ably presented, and this I did. But as the conference progressed I was puzzled by the fact that I heard almost no mention of the names most familiar to me. Session followed session without a word, as far as I recall, about the many old friends whom I had grown to know in Italy in the fourteenth, fifteenth, and even sixteenth centuries.

Could this be a conference, I kept wondering, on the *Renaissance?* Reverting to the simile of the blind men and the elephant, I didn't know which part of the elephant they were fingering, but it certainly was not the whole animal. My bewilderment was allayed somewhat when I learned that this was a conference of scholars in English literature.

I described my feelings to Louis B. Wright, the director of the Huntington Library in immediate charge of the conference, insisting that even a discussion limited to the English Renaissance could not properly omit some reference to Italy. There was Thomas Linacre, court physician to Henry VII and Henry VIII, John Caius, court physician successively to Edward VI, Mary, and Elizabeth, and William Harvey at the end of the century, all of whom had taken their medical degrees at the University of Padua. These were the most distinguished physicians in England and their combined careers covered the whole of the sixteenth century. Such persistent connection between England and Italy in this vital area could only betoken a much wider cultural association.

Whether Dr. Wright was more sympathetic or amused I never knew, but he invited me to write him a letter on the subject which he published as a brief article entitled "Padua in the English Renaissance." Fortunately I was able to summon Shakespeare to my aid with this quotation from *The Taming of the Shrew*:

> To see fair Padua, nursery of the arts
> . . . for I have Pisa left
> And am to Padua come, as he that leaves
> A shallow plash to plunge him in the deep
> And with satiety seeks to quench his thirst.

A hasty search failed to reveal any other university, even Oxford or Cambridge, to which Shakespeare accorded such high praise. Apparently for him Padua was the highest center of British education in his time.

The historian's irritation at what seems to him the unwarranted presumptions of his colleagues in other fields is not without retaliation from those colleagues. When I was asked to participate in the Spencer Trask lectures on the meaning of the humanities at Princeton, I followed the natural approach of the historian in my assignment, "History and the Humanities." * Following along chronologically from antiquity to the Renaissance, I tried to point out that the interest in classical literature had never entirely ceased and that when circumstances favored there were definite outbursts of interest in the classics, notably in the eighth, tenth, eleventh, and twelfth centuries. In that perspective the humanistic activities of the Renaissance were merely wider and possibly deeper than in the earlier periods, owing primarily to the increased literacy of the laity.

This notion of a continuous flow of cultural interest, swelling at times, shrinking at other times, but always existing in some amount, proved to be most distasteful to Professor Panofsky, who had given the lecture on art. When our papers were published he added a footnote to his, protesting this notion of mine. Apparently his view was that each period developed a certain culture of its own like a beautiful globe which was broken when the period ended, leaving only a pleasant memory of its existence. The idea that the cultural urge is persistent and universal and that

* Parts of this lecture have been incorporated into two of the papers in this collection: "The New Learning" and "The Social Web."

# Seeing the Renaissance Whole

its achievements at any given period are necessarily limited by the materials and tools available at the time is not acceptable to Panofsky, for whom everything in society is subordinate or pendant to the artistic style of the period, e.g., Byzantine, Romanesque, Gothic, Renaissance.

The historian's obligation to try to comprehend society whole existed even before the psychologists invented their "gestalt" or "configuration" concept, and he must adhere to it no matter how much the amateur enthusiasts may resent it.

One summer the department of English at the University of Minnesota sponsored an institute on the Renaissance and invited me to lead one of the round-table discussions. In such company I felt privileged to indulge in a bit of literary license. I conjured up a possible scene at the dinner table of Lorenzo the Magnificent about the year 1490, add or subtract a year or two.

It was Lorenzo's regular practice when at home to dine quite informally with family, friends, and privileged visitors. The guests took their places to right and left of him in the order of their arrival. If ever the partaking of food could be characterized as accompanied by "a feast of reason and a flow of soul" it would be at those dinners. The emphasis was never on the food, which was always wholesome and tasty but seldom lavish.

The reason would be supplied on my imaginary occasion by the group who constituted the nucleus of the Platonic Academy: the saintly Ficino, the colorfully handsome and brilliant Pico, and the scholarly, if unhandsome, Poliziano. The banter would be furnished by those two arch humorists, Franco and Pulci. The company would include Lorenzo's children, then teen age—young Giovanni, later Pope Leo X, already assured a cardinal's hat, and his natural cousin Giulio, the later Clement VII—and young Michelangelo, then fifteen. It would also include Botticelli, who received the inspiration for his Neo-Platonic or Ovidian paintings here; "Arrigo the German," the leading musical composer; and Pier Leone, the family physician. Medici agents who might have happened to be in town and among the privileged guests at this time would be Thomas Linacre of England and Johann Reuchlin of Germany, possibly also John Colet of England.

Lorenzo himself, master of ceremonies, would move the conversation from grave to gay and vice versa. After a brief exchange of the day's latest news, he would probably turn to a discussion of the summum bonum or some other topic of Platonic thought; then as that became too heavy, he would give the signal to the humorous pair and Franco, the straight man, would submit to the outrageous insults of Pulci or Pulci would embark upon another episode in the career of his fancied giant, Morgante. In the latter event the others might join in the fun by suggesting supplementary adventures in this favorite satire of the feudal nobility by the bourgeoisie.

Then the conversation might again take a more serious tone, the language changing from Italian to Latin to suit the theme. Everyone was welcome to participate and certainly Linacre would, for the favorable impression he made upon young Giovanni at this time led to a lifelong friendship of great value to Linacre's friends when Giovanni had become pope.

After the feast was ended the regular guests, even Ficino, would reach for their musical instruments, and all, including the servants, would join in singing. The songs might be those which Lorenzo himself had composed, alone or in collaboration with Poliziano and which Arrigo the German had set to music. Lorenzo, despite his squeaky falsetto voice, would insist on joining in if he did not, indeed, lead the singing.

The company might then repair, as it did on special occasions, to the Church of San Lorenzo or to the cathedral, to listen to Squarcialupi playing his favorite tunes.

This scene symbolizes for me the Renaissance at its best. Represented in it were politics, business, the Church, learning, art, literature, and music, as well as gracious living. Together these representatives of the time were satisfying the cultural urge at almost its highest level. There was no pretense here but sincere enjoyment of the intellectual and artistic best. That the level was so high merely reflects the greater experience, ability, cultivation, and taste of the participants.

It is interesting to speculate as to how much of this scene the historian, left to his own devices, would have described or appreciated. He would have caught the political implications certainly, probably too the ecclesiastical, and possibly the economic, but he would most certainly have missed the rest. It is doubtful that he would have attempted to describe the scene at all. That he is now able to do so he owes largely if not entirely to his colleagues in all other fields who have become amateur historians in quest of the modern beginnings of their separate vocations. Much as he may complain about what seems to him a clutter of errors that their unwarranted interpretations of society leave in their wake for him to clean up, he owes them more thanks than blame. Without their help he could not possibly view the society of the Renaissance as nearly whole as he now does.

I must admit that the historian too has been guilty of errors. Take, for example, the commonly held notion that after Petrarch had gained prominence about 1350 Italian vernacular literature ceased, not to reappear for a hundred and fifty years. True, Boccaccio stopped writing in the vernacular then and Dante, of course, had been dead some thirty years. But Petrarch and the humanists who followed him did not kill the vernacular, even though Leonardo Bruni about 1400 thought Dante's *Divine Comedy* so good that it should be translated into Latin.

Italy in Dante's time had no literary vernacular. Its popular language consisted then of purely local dialects which varied one from the other as widely as those of Cornwall from Yorkshire or Gascon from Picard. Dante traveling through the north of Italy and Boccaccio living so much in the south of the peninsula had each broadened his native Tuscan dialect by additions from the others. So potentially these two were the parents of the Italian literary vernacular.

The historian treating of these two figures dismisses them at the time of their deaths, Dante in 1321 and Boccaccio in 1375, and does not refer to them again—as though their influence was ended with their demise!

Actually Dante had little influence in his own lifetime, earning scarcely enough to keep body and soul together. And Boccaccio did not do much better. It would be much more accurate to say that their work had only just begun when they died. But does any textbook in history mention the fact that by 1400 all the greater universities in Italy were offering courses on Dante and the Italian vernacular? Or that by 1500 virtually every literate Italian had read and many illiterate Italians had heard at least a portion of the writings of these two men? Without this education in the vernacular through a century and a half by Dante, Boccaccio, and even Petrach, the great outburst of literary production in Italian at the end of the fifteenth century and the beginning of the 16th represented by Pulci, Castiglione, Machiavelli, Guicciardini, Tasso, and Ariosto would have been impossible.

The historian has become guilty of another fault too. The body of literature for this period has become so vast and the interest in special phases so great that he has tended to specialize in certain aspects of social activity. Thus we now have specialists in economic history, in social history, in the history of science, even in the history of medicine, and more recently in intellectual history. The natural tendency of all scholarship to focus its attention upon the newest developments in its fields has led even historians to distort their treatment of the period until they are becoming guilty of the same errors for which they have hitherto blamed the enthusiastic amateurs of other fields. We are back to the blind Indians and the elephant again. In some more recent symposiums on the Renaissance the discussion has been so concentrated upon its purely intellectual aspects as to convey the impression that the period was one of sheer disembodied intellect.

Actually the period was one of full-blooded, full-bodied social activity. Let me review briefly the salient points in its development.

The birth of the Renaissance can be localized in northern Italy, north of the Papal States—in Tuscany and Lombardy with their two pendants, Venice and Genoa. This region was peculiarly ripe for unusual cultural development. It lay across the great trunk lines of luxury commerce from the eastern Mediterranean to western Europe. Venice and Genoa had been the chief carriers of this commerce for several centuries, the rest of the region having developed industrially to take over much of the luxury manufacture. Until the fourteenth century, however, their excess profits had been drained off to satisfy the needs of the two rival controlling powers, the papacy and the Empire. When the war between those two powers ended, the Empire had been rendered impotent, and by 1305 the papacy had been virtually captured by France. The Babylonian Captivity which followed removed the papacy to Avignon and minimized its influence in Italy.

The towns' profits from their trade and manufacture were now in their own control if they could find some way to maintain law and order themselves. The only organization they possessed was economic. Fortunately for them, warfare had changed and mercenary troops had superseded feudal levies. The businessmen who controlled the economic organization of the towns in this region were thus able to engage the necessary soldiery to keep order. They had to learn the art of government. Accustomed to operate by their wits instead of brawn, they turned to the study of past experience for guidance and the legal profession gained new status. Though there were innumerable separate and rival city centers aspiring to dominance in 1300, the situation in northern Italy had become fairly stabilized a century later, with Florence, Milan, and Venice, all commercial states, dominating the region.

During the same while, the condition of the rest of Europe was contributing to increase the well-being of Italy. Germany, which had been broken by the struggle with the papacy, was to remain hopelessly divided for centuries. France, the most powerful state in Europe, soon became involved in a century-long struggle with England, which had become almost as powerful. Spain was divided among several warring states. Thus there was not only no danger of invasion from outside for nearly two centuries, but, even more important, those regions, having to use their surplus energies for

# The Long Road Back

wars, became increasingly dependent upon Italy for their commercial, industrial, and financial needs. Northern Italy was thus to enjoy a degree of economic prosperity such as it had never before experienced.

The utilization of the proceeds of all this swollen prosperity became a real problem, to be solved as such problems often are, fortunately—in the satisfaction of the cultural urge. And, lacking the modern outlets for the spending of surplus wealth all over the world, these people had to spend it in their home towns.

Individual fortunes at first were not large. The surplus profits were collective rather than individual and were devoted to satisfying the cultural needs of the community as a whole. That meant civic improvements, public buildings, including of course churches and hospitals as well as city halls and gaols. Florence, for example, had embarked upon its building program by 1300. The Palazzo Vecchio, the Cathedral, the church dormitories for the two great orders of friars, Santa Maria Novella and Santa Croce, as well as the comprehensive city wall, were all projected before Dante left Florence. Other towns followed suit and the leaders of the mercenary troops, become petty despots in small territories bordering the big three, did likewise.

Large buildings were then not built in a month or a year. Santa Maria del Fiore, whose foundations were laid in Dante's time, did not receive its final touch, Verrochio's lantern, until 1475, nearly two centuries later. So northern Italy had embarked upon a building program that was to be continuous and expanding for more than two hundred years. Craftsmen builders, architects, painters, sculptors, and jewelers were to vie with each other for contracts, each generation seeking to excel its predecessors. The story of Renaissance Italian art is told in this building program.

The intellectual atmosphere in which this lay culture developed was one of extraordinary freedom. First, not only did the long absence of the papacy from Italy lead to a relaxation of papal control over that region, but because the Italians resented that absence it invited practically unlimited criticism of ecclesiastical authority and weakened the moral restraints that might otherwise

184

have prevailed. Second, the great merchant princes who ruled in northern Italy were accustomed to dealing with people of varied faiths, Greek, Hebrew, and Moslem as well as Roman, and with such tolerance did practically nothing to restrain the freedom of thought and expression, which sometimes amounted to outrageous license. One can follow this development through the writings of Dante, Petrarch, Boccaccio, Poggio, Lorenzo Valla, and Becadelli —not to mention Machiavelli.

In such an atmosphere, free of traditional restraints, self-expression and experimentation, though sometimes abused, flourished mightily. Individual initiative and enterprise were stimulated by the great rewards in both fame and fortune. As an instance, in the realm of politics it became possible for a hillbilly, Muzio Attendolo, nicknamed Sforza, to start his son on the road to establishing a ruling dynasty whose descendants have been prominent in Italian affairs down to our own time.

Even in warfare the emphasis was upon brains not brawn. Military commanders, the condottieri, were businessmen first and students of tactics and strategy next. They sold their services to the merchant princes who ruled the greater city-states. Though there were individual instances of ferocious cruelty, these seldom involved more than a few individuals and the greatest destruction recorded destroyed only one small town. The merchant rulers had no desire to kill their customers and the wars in which they engaged were primarily to safeguard their trade routes and ensure an adequate food supply, almost never for motives of power politics. They preferred diplomacy to force in achieving their ends.

Indeed it may almost be said that they invented diplomacy. Few modern states with all their advantages of speedy communication have devised a more efficient foreign intelligence than did Venice during this period. The ideal diplomats described by Machiavelli and Castiglione are still models today. Undisturbed by outside pressures the masterminds of Italy preferred their separate city-states and transformed Italy into a microcosm of international relations, an experimental laboratory of such relations from which emerged the concept both of mercantilism and of the balance of power, which the larger nations of modern Europe were to practice down to our time. Nor can one find many statesmen of modern times who have handled the problem of public relations more effectively than did Cosimo de Medici, the "pater patriae" of Florence from 1434 to 1464.

In activities other than political, individual initiative and enterprise were equally encouraged and successful. It was this invitation that led the craftsmen-artists to discover or invent one technique after another in the effort to portray on a flat surface the perfect representation of nature, human and otherwise. It was the same invitation that led the humanists to discover bit by bit the principles of literary composition which could be applied to any language, not only to Latin. And Leonardo da Vinci was only one of many who were contriving models of machines that arouse the admiration of technologists today. Indeed Leonardo's own designs were largely modifications of ideas already either in use or described.

Historians of science have not been friendly to the first two centuries of the Renaissance. Scholars, Lynn Thorndike particularly, though with some support from George Sarton, blame the period for diverting its best minds from science to humanism and art, and Thorndike goes so far as to consider humanism consciously opposed to science.

I cannot share that view, first because those two hundred years produced notable progress in some fields of science, especially in medicine, where Carpi's edition of Mondino advanced the knowledge of anatomy to the very threshold of Vesalius, and Fracastoro certainly moved the knowledge of contagious diseases to a new high plateau. But even more am I reluctant to accept Thorndike's view because both humanism and art were during these centuries fashioning the essential tools without which the striking scientific advance of the sixteenth century would have been impossible. Art contributed accurate observation and the means of precise recording of such observations. The cumulative efforts of the craftsmen-artists to portray human emotion had led them to a close study not only of the surface expression of emotion but also of the muscles beneath the skin and the bodily organs which operated those muscles. Scholarly artists like Leonardo da Vinci and Michelangelo actually performed more dissections than did 99 per cent of the medical students of the time. The humanists in their effort to recover all the writings of antiquity were editing and translating the scientific works of the ancient Greeks, thus making available to their contemporaries the Greek discoveries in mathematics, astronomy, and other sciences as well as medicine.

I have dealt with medieval developments in medicine in another paper * and so here shall say only this: It is now evident that the hoary old notion so long perpetuated in our textbooks—namely, that before Vesalius the medical profession had relied wholly upon the authority of Galen—is entirely wrong. Western Europe during the Middle Ages knew very little of Galen. It was not until the sixteenth century that the voluminous writings of this ancient authority were available to medical men.

Only a fraction of scientific knowledge can be transmitted by words alone. Illustrations are absolutely essential to understanding in science. Therefore, not until this combination of tools, the fruit of two centuries of antecedent labor by craftsmen-artists and humanists, was available could science make the strides that it did in the sixteenth century. Without that antecedent labor the achievements of Vesalius in anatomy, Copernicus in astronomy, Georgius Agricola in geology and metallurgy, Gesner in botany and zoology, even Cardan in higher algebra would have been impossible.

As we reach the sixteenth century the names I mention are no longer exclusively Italian. Times have changed. The great countries of Europe—France, England, and Spain—have all regained internal unity and peace. Thanks to the enterprise of the earlier Renaissance, new worlds and new trade routes have been discovered. The Atlantic now rivals the Mediterranean as a main artery of commerce, and the rest of Europe has ceased to be economically dependent upon Italy.

* Published in this collection under the title, "The Rebirth of the Medical Profession."

## The Long Road Back

More than that, the failure of the Italians to achieve political unity, together with the alluring achievements in nearly all branches of culture which the Italian Renaissance had accumulated, rendered Italy a most tempting field for the imperial ambitions of these power-minded neighbors. From 1494 on, Italy was a battlefield in the fierce rivalry of France and Spain, and by 1530 virtually the whole peninsula except the maritime state of Venice was politically dependent upon outside powers.

England and the Low Countries, less war-involved than France and Spain, were the first to profit from these changed circumstances. Peace and prosperity and the increased leisure they afforded enabled these regions to embark upon the fuller satisfaction of their own cultural urge. How?

So strong has been the feeling of nationalism in modern times that even scholars have been led to view their fields of learning with national bias. I have already spoken of the conference on the English Renaissance at the Huntington. Similarly Batifol has written the history of the French Renaissance as a purely sixteenth- and seventeenth-century French development, and scholars of other countries have been guilty of the same myopia. Laudable as the sentiment of national patriotism may be, it scarcely justifies such gross distortion of fact.

The Europe of the sixteenth century did not suffer from such strong nationalistic predisposition. It greatly admired the achievements of the Italian Renaissance, with many of which it was acquainted, thanks to the printing press. Business agents and cultivated refugees from now war-torn Italy were welcomed in all these countries. France and Spain, having appropriated so much of Italy, also appropriated some of its artists and scholars, carrying them back to the conquerors' homelands.

In none of these countries did people repeat the slow painful process of acquiring the various techniques of painting or the various principles of literature; they gladly accepted the full complement of both as the Italians had worked them out. Thus artists like Dürer, Holbein, and Rubens did not start where Giotto had left off but rather where Michelangelo, Titian, Tintoretto, and

188

Veronese were. Nor were Erasmus, Linacre, Vives, and Melanchthon limited as Petrarch had been, to a few Latin classics; they all had access to the whole range of recovered classical literature as Poliziano and Bembo did. Indeed, Erasmus as a schoolboy had already so thoroughly mastered the *De Elegantiis* of Lorenzo Valla with its full exposition of the principles of composition and style that his teachers asked him to prepare a compendium of it for his classmates.

No, one can only conclude that the other countries of Europe entered upon the Renaissance at the point reached by the Italians. They adopted the Italian ideal of the cultivated gentleman described by Castiglione in *The Courtier*, as witness the rapidity with which that work was translated into all the leading literary vernaculars as well as into the more universal Latin.

In addition to all this, the rest of Europe continued to go directly to Italy for vital instruction throughout the sixteenth century. Venice, now the only autonomous portion of Italy, had graciously accepted the role of residuary legatee of Italian Renaissance culture. It had two universities within its orbit, its state university of Padua and its satellite university of Ferrara, and to these it welcomed scholars not only from Italy itself but also from the rest of Europe, even Protestant Europe. Padua held a position of recognized intellectual leadership throughout the century such as few universities have ever attained. The galaxy of its students and teachers included Linacre, Fracastoro, Vesalius, Fallopius, Cardan, Copernicus, Georgius Agricola, John Caius, Fabricius, William Harvey, and Galileo.

To the artists Venice could offer Titian, Tintoretto, and Veronese, all long-lived, and the young Greek who received his training there and practiced his art in Spain under the name El Greco. In literature it had, of course, Cardinal Bembo but also some claim to Tasso and Ariosto. And the Venetian printing establishment of Aldus Manutius was the great center for the editing and translating of the Greek classics.

All Europe in the sixteenth century gladly acknowledged its indebtedness to the Italian Renaissance, past and current, as Shakespeare did for England. All shared in the advance that was made in this century, so that it may actually be wrong, as it certainly is misleading, to speak of a French, a Spanish, an English, or an Italian Renaissance, for they were all part of the same development.

This whole paper is only a summary, but if I were to list the chief points I have tried to establish in the course of it, they would be these: First, this period from 1300 to 1600, thanks to the wide interest it has aroused, is the most thoroughly studied period in all history. Second, because of the varied approaches that have been made to it, the Renaissance affords our best opportunity to view society whole, to see the interplay and interrelation of nearly all man's activities. For society, like the individual, is a complex of many interests—political, economic, social, intellectual, artistic, and religious—each affected by the others. Third, the Renaissance reveals more clearly than any other period that no activity of society can be explained in terms of itself alone, and that no one activity, be it economic, political, or religious, can safely be accepted as always the most important.

Take, for example, such an incident as the building of the Certaldo at Pavia, generally acknowledged to be one of the architectural triumphs of the Italian Renaissance. It was built at the command of Gian Galeazzo Visconti, ruler of Milan. His wife, fearful of her impending childbirth, had requested him to erect this monastery for the Carthusian monks in the event of her death. She survived, but he carried through her request anyway, as a mark of gratitude. He was by virtue of his political position able to command the financial resources to engage the best artistic talent available to construct this religious edifice.

This incident involves political, economic, social, artistic, and religious elements, and I doubt that we could all agree as to which of these elements was the most important. But need we do so? Why not just recognize that all these factors played a part in the episode?

Finally, one of the essential characteristics of the Renaissance is the appearance of a strong lay interest in the promotion of cultural activities. It is the period when the laity became literate and when they added their eager energies to that of the clergy, the traditional custodians and promoters of culture.

For all these reasons the Renaissance will long remain the model for the study of all periods. It reveals so clearly the social web that is the proper subject of history.

# PART TWO

## *The Social Web: World-Wide and Time-Deep*

# 9

# The Social Web

I WAS to have spent the year in Europe—an American scholar visiting with fellow historians abroad, shaking the dust from medieval manuscripts, and roaming among the remains of older civilizations. But the coming of war in Europe denied me this privilege and my sabbatical leave was transformed into a return to the life of a graduate student working in the library stacks at Harvard, Princeton, and North Carolina.

The illusion of a return to the days of my graduate study was heightened by the fact that I turned again to some of the problems I had to deal with then. And it has been interesting to try to analyze the difference in my approach to them a little more than thirty years later.

Let me take as an example one of these problems: a critical appraisal of William of Tyre, whose work is essential to any study of the Crusades. Nearly all that we know about him is derived from the incidental autobiographical allusions he makes in describing his own times. It seems a simple problem, therefore: just read William's history.

The diplomat-historian Bongars, who published the text of William's account in 1610, did just that and wrote a systematic account

NOTE: Parts of this essay have appeared in the paper, "History and the Humanities," in *The Meaning of the Humanities*, edited by Theodore Meyer Greene and published by Princeton University Press, 1938.

of William's life in his introduction to the text. That was sufficient for most people and remained so for three hundred years. Then Michaud, whose monumental work on the Crusades shares with that of Wilken the honor of being the first modern synthesis, found Bongars' account inadequate and set down the results of his own re-examination at much greater length in his *Bibliothèque*.[1] A decade or so later Ranke set his seminar to work upon the critical study of sources for the Crusades, and this led in 1841 to the publication of such a study on the First Crusade by Sybel, perhaps Ranke's most brilliant pupil. Forty years later Prutz, who wrote the *Kulturgeschichte*[2] of the Crusades, published a detailed series of analytical studies on William of Tyre.

That succession of appraisals should have settled this particular problem. It did for most students thereafter, and it did for me those thirty years ago. And yet as I worked upon William's history during this sabbatical year I found much to add and some statements to alter.

This raises a question. Why, when practically all that we know about William is derived from his own book, did not Bongars see and say all that was to be said about the subject? Or, if we excuse him for any shortcomings because he was merely writing an introduction to the text, what allowances can we make for Michaud or Sybel or Prutz, who looked closely and intended to put down all they saw? These scholars were among the ablest historians of the nineteenth century.

This kind of shortsightedness is a strange phenomenon but by no means an infrequent one, and so worthy of some effort to explain it.

I can now realize that as a graduate student I saw chiefly with the eyes alone and therefore caught only a fraction, and that the most obvious fraction, of what I read. I was limited by a kind of "tunnel vision" that permits people to see only a part of what they read even though they fix their attention closely upon the words.

Neither I nor any of the scholars who preceded me in a careful study of William of Tyre noticed that he wrote his history primarily to read it to king and court. William nowhere says that he did so—or, of course, it would have been noticed. What William does say is that he wrote the history at the request of King Amaury. Elsewhere he says that Amaury was especially fond of history and that he read it when circumstances permitted, but that he much preferred to hear it read. William also says that Baldwin IV, son and successor of Amaury, was likewise interested in history, to which he listened. Inasmuch as William was closely associated with both father and son and was writing his history for them, it is no long jump of the mind to realize that William was reading his history to them in installments. And once this is recognized, it helps to explain much about William's style and his selection of material.

It all seems simple enough when you finally see it, but this "seeing" involves bringing together several bits of scattered statement, and this the eye, even the studious eye, does not readily do. William's purpose to read is not obvious, and a person depending upon the eye alone is largely limited to the obvious.

Yet the use of evidence that is not patent, of indirect evidence, is a vitally important part of the historian's task. Without it the unknown facts of the world's past would be many more even than they now are.

During my stay at Princeton I was privileged to see some of the work of Dr. B. D. Meritt on Greek inscriptions. Meritt was reconstructing these inscriptions on the basis of the scattered fragments which archaeology had brought to light. One such reconstruction showed two fragments, one in the upper left-hand corner and another small bit toward the lower right. The words and letters of these fragments fitted perfectly into the reconstruction Dr. Meritt had worked out. In space the portion of the fragments amounted to less than a tenth of the whole. It was thrilling. Just as thrilling as the sight of a complete skeleton of some prehistoric animal reconstructed by biologists from a few scattered bones.

But then on reflection, is not that exactly what the historian must do constantly: reconstruct developments in society on the basis of information which is never complete? He cannot show his kind of reconstruction to visitors in the same concrete fashion and arouse the same immediate response, but for those who have the necessary background it is equally exciting.

Sometimes this essential aspect of the historian's work is lost to sight in graduate study of more recent periods, where the material is so abundant that the students are kept busy just reading the lines and have no time to read between the lines. As a rule, graduate students in either American or modern history do not receive much training in the use of indirect evidence, whereas in ancient and medieval history they cannot avoid it. And the graduate student who does not acquire some skill in this phase of historical method lacks a vital experience. For the time will probably never come when men will put down in writing the full story of what they do, much less of why they do it. Many of the major decisions of society—political, industrial, and social—are still made by word of mouth or even gesture and never get into the record. Jefferson wrote to Adams when both were old that the true story of the Declaration of Independence as they knew it would probably never be brought to light, and the same observation might be made on most of the momentous problems of society in any time. The whole truth of such matters may never be absolutely established, but by a shrewd use of all indirect evidence and a critical study of the sources it can be pretty closely approximated.

Another reason, even more important, why I failed to learn everything about William of Tyre the first time I studied him is suggested in William James' statement about a man's ability to see into a generalization only so far as his knowledge of its details extends. I did not possess a sufficiently detailed knowledge of society to grasp the real significance of many of the sentences I was reading. My knowledge of the social web was then much too sketchy, too limited to the high points, for me to comprehend or even note any but the most direct statements.

For example, William casually mentions in two words that he officiated at the funeral of Count William of Montferrat. I entirely overlooked those two words when I first read them, for the attention in that paragraph is upon the Count of Montferrat. Even later, when I caught the phrase because I was combing the work for every single personal allusion, I failed to attach any particular significance to it. It just meant that here was a clergyman doing his duty at a funeral. Only much later did it dawn on me that this funeral of the king's brother-in-law and intended successor was of major importance and therefore properly the concern of the highest clergyman in the kingdom. That clergyman was the patriarch of Jerusalem, but the patriarch was old and unable to perform the duties of his position. The choice of William for the task might therefore indicate that he was regarded as the probable successor to the patriarchate. Against a fuller knowledge of how society operates these two words, at first ignored, attain considerable significance. They do not settle the matter but they lend powerful support to several other circumstances pointing in the same direction.

That is a simple illustration of the usefulness of what is, I am convinced, a major necessity for any effective reconstruction of history: a knowledge both wide and deep of the myriad detail and intricate pattern of the social web. It was a better, broader understanding of this web, of what C. Hartley Grattan once called "the pluralistic context" of any fact, any event, any statement, that made all the difference between my first study of William of Tyre and my approach to him thirty years later—a much more significant difference than I can readily illustrate here.

This wider knowledge came from no one course or field of history—nor, indeed, from history alone. In my application of it to this specific problem of William, I can trace elements from ancient history, classical literature, and American history. And I am especially conscious of the value of my association with the group of social scientists with whom I spent nine years on the problem of social education for the next generation. Part of that time was spent in a conscious effort to describe the texture and trends of our own society today. Economist, political scientist, sociologist, modern and American historians successively contributed to the building of that description. They supplemented their own rich stores of knowledge by drawing upon the current national census and the statistical data gathered by the several national commissions sponsored by President Hoover—those on recent social trends, prohibition, housing, child welfare, and others.

The experience itself was intensely interesting, for no society in the world's history has ever been as closely inventoried as was our own at that time. But its bearing here is that from it I carried back to my study of medieval history a greatly extended and deepened understanding of the range and reach of men's actions and the closely meshing gears of the manifold phases of human affairs.

I carried away from this experience a negative conclustion too: that it is impossible to derive a rounded and satisfactory knowledge of the social web from any single source. One might think that such complete statistical investigations as those of the Hoover commissions would afford such a picture. But one soon discovers that statistics are limited to obvious material facts—the things by which man is momentarily surrounded—and do not touch the motives, urges, and forces which cause him to change those things. Even such earnestly objective efforts as those reported in the Lynds' *Middletown* and Odum's *Southern Regions of the United States* fail to penetrate much more deeply.

So one concludes, sadly, that statistics, however related and correlated, explain nothing; they merely describe, and describe only the material and obvious. They are useful as descriptions but for explanations a time-depth and sequence are necessary. It is necessary to go back through time and use such records as are available, with all the intelligence and powers of penetration we possess.

The search will take us back a long way. No age discusses in its current records much except those matters which require immediate active adjustment. These may not directly affect the lives of more than a small percentage of the population; they frequently deal with matters which are not of daily, weekly, or even monthly concern to ninety-nine per cent of the people; yet they fill the front pages of the newspapers for a whole generation. To round out the whole gamut of men's interests it is necessary to go back through the whole course of history.

For example, the church—or churches—is one of the fundamental institutions of society, yet the discussion of its place in the lives of people and the operation of society occurs fully no nearer than the sixteenth century and must be completed by recourse to the fourth century. It was in those centuries and in the period between them that churches were for any length of time front-page news. The political machine and gangsterism, which bob up from time to time as recurrent phenomena of contemporary society, are best explained in the period from 847 to about 1300, when they were constantly front-page news. The influence of the socially exclusive group that never ceases to be a factor in the operation of society can be best observed in the records of ancient Greece and Rome. These are but illustrations of what I mean. They might be multiplied indefinitely.

Just as there is no single source for adequate knowledge of the social pattern, so there is not, I now believe, any one big underlying idea that will explain all the actions of men. Many young historians, and some not so young, tend to exhaust their energies in the quest for this philosopher's stone of the social scientist, and in their zeal they have on occasion sought to give some inspired thesis or brilliant insight a universality it proved not to have: Turner's thesis of the westward movement, for example, and the economic interpretation of human activity, for another.

As a graduate student I undoubtedly shared this dream of finding the *one* thread of which the whole great web is woven, but I have become reconciled now to look for the smaller, more immediate factors in human affairs and let the big ideas take care of themselves. I have discovered that obsession with one of these ideas is likely to produce a selective perception of facts and to facilitate neglect of those that are not in accord with the theory.

Nonetheless, I do not underestimate the intensification of understanding and sharpening of vision that have come to historians from such ideas once the overemphasis upon them has passed away. The long development of history has been marked by many instances of improvement and enrichment derived from concepts and interpretations that we now consider of limited usefulness. And more often than not these ideas have come from other areas of knowledge.

It was chiefly the Church fathers who kept history alive during the early Middle Ages, even though their work consisted mostly of meager chronicles explaining events almost always as the operation of God's will on earth. It was mainly the humanist scholars of the so-called Renaissance who, through their zealous study of the ancient historians and of the classical poets, orators, and philosophers as well, gave to history a much keener appreciation of human motivation, along with more attention to the critical use of documents and a sense of the importance of style in the precise and effective recording of events.

Then, thanks to the advance in the knowledge of nature during the seventeenth and eighteenth centuries, history was able to penetrate into that area of causation which had remained veiled to the ancients under the guise of Fate, and the influence of the natural or physical environment became a recognized factor in human affairs. With the advent of humanitarianism in the eighteenth century, the part of the common man in social developments began its rise to prominence in history, and with the nineteenth century came the alluring idea of scientific evolution and the increasing importance of business with its intriguing paraphernalia of statistics. Most recently psychology has undertaken to apply scientific methods to the study of human motivation and in so doing has supplied history with yet another angle of approach to its problems.

The result of all this varied enrichment has been at times somewhat confusing, in terms both of the organization and of the content of history.

History once was the only study of man and society, but as knowledge accumulated it was forced to entrust to its offspring, the social sciences, important areas of its previous domain. This development raised important questions in academic organization.

The Social Web

What was once a single subject had become a group of subjects, even a whole division of the college curriculum. On the whole, the academic world accepted this expansion without controversy or even serious debate. But when the University of Chicago sought to set up distinct divisions of social sciences and the humanities, history found itself in an unhappy position. By implication at least, the social sciences were not regarded as humanities, and this was a conclusion which historians were not prepared to admit.

The debate raged for months and was finally stilled enough to permit action only by the compromise of having the department of history belong to both divisions. In general, those members of the department who were primarily interested in recent history were regarded as more closely identified with the social sciences, while those concerned with the earlier periods were deemed more closely associated with the humanities. Circumstances at Chicago required some sort of decision but the question still remains unsettled and is of recurrent concern to the whole academic world.

In the content, or at least the emphases, of history the influence of these modern intellectual movements has not been all gain. Overemphasis upon the determinative influence of physical environment belittled the importance of man, and many historians, fascinated by the forces of nature, completely overlooked the fact that individuals living in the same regions were behaving in widely different ways. Naturalism become ideological was quite as objectionable to Humanism as the latter was thought to have been to Scholasticism.

Likewise as the study of science led to the formulation of laws cosmic in scope, scholars in other fields were encouraged to hope that they might be able to find similar laws in their own areas of research and they sought to take over what appeared to them to be the successful methods and attitudes of scientific research. Objectivity was one of these that the historians fastened upon. To attain objectivity they ruthlessly stripped the materials of history of all subjective elements, moral or aesthetic. The quest was for bare facts, the more the better. These facts, grouped around political, social, and economic institutions, were somehow expected to "speak for themselves" and almost automatically to yield laws, or at least principles, comparable to those of science. There was little place in the vast masses of so-called fact resulting from this effort for the feelings, hopes, or wishes of man and very little for his thoughts. Any regard for style in such compilations was, of course, superfluous.

Even more naive was the attempt to adapt the theory of scientific evolution, which scarcely recognizes the development of a single new species in less than the last fifty million years, to the affairs of man, whose recorded history extends over little more than the last three thousand years. The notion that human institutions, like species, evolve from one stage inexorably toward the next, presumably ever upward, led, as Bury remarked, to an illusion of progress under whose influence everything in the present assumed all the virtues of natural selection. This conception automatically belittled the thoughts and achievements of men in the past. Under such a hypothesis, Jefferson, Hamilton, and Franklin could only be regarded as shoulder-high, Virgil and Cicero as mere pygmies, Plato and Aristotle as virtually microscopic, while poor Homer was left floundering among the amoebas.

Surely the scientist, no less than the humanist, has shuddered at this misuse of his theory. But the end of it is not yet, though surely in sight. The idea of inevitable evolutionary progress is so comforting and our society so saturated with it that we are reluctant to recognize that, no matter what help the theory of evolution may render in biology, it has no value in the understanding of society. Not so very long ago I heard a speaker cite Bury's *History of the Freedom of Thought* as one of the truly monumental works produced under the sway of the social evolution doctrine; in this speaker's mind Bury's conclusion was to the effect that society had permanently evolved in this direction so that freedom of thought and expression had become one of its immutable attributes. In light of subsequent events, we can now, unhappily, recognize this speaker's conclusion as a demonstration of the futility of applying the doctrine of evolution to social developments.

Equally unpalatable were the extreme effects of humanitarian and capitalistic influences upon writers of history. Only matters common to mankind were deemed valuable. Only facts which could be expressed quantitatively, analyzed statistically, and charted graphically seemed to matter. Both mass production and mass approval were thought to depend upon these factors and they were therefore determinative. Unusual individuals and uncommon traits of common men disappeared in the statistical hopper as of no significance. It is one of the paradoxes of life that some scholars should have sought to attain personal distinction by urging acceptance of such an interpretation of society.

As yet only a few professional historians have been swept off their feet by the contributions of scientific psychology. But there have been some, most of them amateurs, who have attempted to rewrite not only episodes but entire biographies and even to explain such phenomena as social movements and political leadership in terms of Freudian complexes. And as the contributions of the psychologists multiply, it is conceivable that the profession will become as fascinated by them as they have by the contributions of other fields of scholarship. For the momentary sway of a newly grasped concept is no less overwhelming than the lure of a single explanation for highly complex phenomena.

The very recognition of these excesses of historical scholarship is itself evidence of their transitory character. They have not all been eradicated; indeed some are still flourishing in varying measure among the several social sciences. But the trend is, I believe, definitely away from their worst effects.

Historians have come to recognize that, no matter how many persons are affected by scientific and technological devices, all such devices are made and must be operated by men. They have discovered also that, however vast the body of facts which they collect, into whatever graphic symbols these facts may be compressed, decisions regarding their use must be made by individuals. They have learned too that, however much men may have in common and however important these common characteristics may be, the dynamic quality of society is derived from the individuals who set the mass in motion or determine its direction and are therefore distinctive. They have come to understand that the three or four thousand years of documented history are too brief to assure a definite evolutionary trend, but they have gained from the experience a clear conception of development in human affairs even though the direction of that development may at times quite reverse itself. And along with this wider understanding, members of the historical profession have learned that bare facts do not speak for themselves, that if the findings of historical research are to be effectively communicated to others they must be integrated and interpreted and reported in a fitting style.

At the same time historians do not intend to sacrifice any of the gains secured by the intellectual advance of the last three centuries. They intend to include in their thinking the recognizable influence of nature on the affairs of men and of the masses on those who lead them. They will continue to use some of the convenient symbols devised by business to express large aggregates of fact briefly. And if and when psychology arrives at a more precise identification of individual and group motivation, they will doubtless make use of that advance too. They will employ all of these variant avenues to knowledge in the hope of approaching more closely to the truth of human affairs. For in the effort to record and explain the long story of man's development, the historian cannot afford to ignore any useful addition to his information and wisdom about the way men and societies behave. He must, I repeat, seek always to accumulate more knowledge of the social web.

It is because of my deep conviction on this point that I have been troubled in recent years by the number of young historians I have met who consider themselves such intensive specialists that they feel threatened with intellectual starvation if the colleges at which they are teaching do not have adequate library resources in their specialty. I wonder if our graduate training centers are not somewhat at fault either by encouraging or by not preventing too narrow specialization.

## The Social Web

With all due precautions against the human tendency to romanticize "the good old days," I believe the insistence of graduate advisers a generation ago that their students take seminar courses in a wide variety of fields was wiser than today's concentration on one or two. D. C. Munro, who was my adviser, was so concerned about this problem that he even advised members of the faculty to change the courses they taught from time to time to prevent overspecialization and encourage cross-fertilization between fields.

Many of the scholars who received their training then seem to have had little difficulty in adjusting themselves to conditions which did not favor their special interests. Men who, to judge from their thesis subjects, were trained in medieval history went on to do distinguished work in other fields. C. J. H. Hayes and W. E. Lingelbach are examples of this, and few people would suspect that Charles A. Beard and Herbert Bolton expected to become medievalists when they started upon their careers. In the same spirit, one of the most distinguished medievalists our country has produced, Charles H. Haskins, wrote his doctor's thesis on American history.

Apparently the emphasis then was on the training of historians, rather than of specialists. Today we seem to have specialized even more in example than in precept. A single century of American history now permits of nearly ten divisions of specialization. What have we gained? Chiefly technical training, a refinement of tools with which to deal with a specific problem, a specific set of conditions in a specific way. And what have we lost? Many values, of course, but chiefly, perhaps, the realization that all these specialties are derived from the great matrix of history—the whole history of society—and that the value of the work within any specialty is directly proportioned to the fidelity of its relationship to that whole.

Our plight is not unlike that of Antaeus, who, you recall, was quite invincible as long as he remained in touch with Mother Earth but was easily destroyed when kept from that contact. I believe that knowledge of the vast, intricately fashioned fabric of

207

# The Social Web

the social web, extending world-wide and time-deep, bears that same strength-giving relationship to all the specialties in social science.

## NOTES

[1] Joseph François Michaud, *Bibliothèque des croisades*, 5 vols. (Paris: A. J. Ducollet, 1829).

[2] Hans Prutz, *Kulturgeschichte der kreuzzüge* (Berlin: E. S. Mittler und sohn, 1883).

# 10

# What Is American History?

No SUBJECT in the curriculum of the social studies holds a position of greater importance than American history. There are few states or local authorities which do not require at least one course in it of all students, and many require such a course in each segment of the educational system, elementary and secondary—some too in college. It is virtually the only subject in the social studies upon whose requirement educational and lay authorities are in complete agreement. That being the case, why raise any question about it?

Yet I must insist that there is a question. In fact, there is not one but a whole host of questions involved in the query, "What is American history?" Even the layman can be jolted out of any complacent assumption that of course everyone knows what American history is, if he is asked when it begins. In 1492, in 1607, in 1620, in 1776, or in 1783? You will find advocates for each of these dates and, indeed, a variety of practice in the schools of the country. You may even find some who would begin American history in 1865, and you may suspect that some would prefer to begin it in 1898 or even 1932. In other words, there is a question at the very outset of the subject.

I recall a visit paid to us at the University of Minnesota by John

NOTE: A different version of this essay was published in the *History of Education Journal*, Winter 1952.

## The Social Web

Dhondt, royal archivist of Belgium and professor of history in the University of Ghent. He was spending several months in this country studying methods of historical research and teaching in our universities, and I asked him what impressed him most about American practice. He replied quickly and with strong feeling that he envied us our specialization, our concentration on limited periods of time and on specific phases of society, political, economic, social, or cultural. Then I asked him what was his field of teaching and research, and he replied, "The history of Ghent."

I looked at him in momentary astonishment. Ghent! A mere pinpoint on the map. His native town, in which he had grown up and received nearly all his education from the elementary grades through to the doctorate in history. Pure local history, and of his home town alone. And he was envying us our specialization!

But let us try to understand his attitude. There is no time limit to the history of Ghent; it reaches back to prehistory, a stretch of at least four thousand years without any break. And it has no topical limits; it includes all varieties of social interests: religion, art, and learning as well as political, economic, and social history. Furthermore, Ghent played a part, willing or unwilling, in most of the great events of European history. To touch only a few of the high points, this little dot on the map was involved in the careers of Vercingetorix, Julius Caesar, Clovis, Charlemagne, Otto the Great, William the Conqueror, Charles the Bold, Henry VIII, Emperor Charles V, Philip II, William of Orange, Louis XIV, Napoleon, Bismarck, Wilhelm II, Woodrow Wilson, Winston Churchill, Franklin D. Roosevelt, and Dwight D. Eisenhower. Its history includes St. Boniface, Alcuin, Thomas Aquinas, Luther, Calvin, and Simons Menno. It includes also all the developments in art, learning, and literature during that long stretch of time.

No further elaboration is needed to explain Professor Dhondt's attitude.

And is the history of our nation so much more simple? Can we understand or explain American history in terms of what happened between the two oceans in the national period, let us say, or even going back to 1492? If the function of history is to explain the past as one of the best means of understanding the present and facing the future, can we render that service to our people by confining our attention within such limits of time and space? National sentiment and the importance of the frontier in our history may, it is true, have led some of our American historians, and particularly the writers of our textbooks, to confine themselves within the national period. And the prevalence of this limited conception among so many of our adult population doubtless arises from the fact that for most of them the high school course in American history—which too often means the high school textbook alone—represents their final study of the subject.

It would be interesting, were it possible, to revive some widely traveled European who lived at the close of the Middle Ages, transport him to the present, and bring him to this country to see how much in our society would seem familiar to him. Erasmus would be an excellent choice, for his life spanned what is conventionally regarded as the dividing line between medieval and modern history.

Erasmus of Rotterdam, born about 1469 and living to 1536, was in his early twenties when Columbus discovered America. He had received his education in the schools of the Brethren of the Common Life, notably at Deventer, and was to receive his university training in Montagu College at Paris and also at both Oxford and Cambridge, where for a while he was also an instructor. He was a friend of Grocyn, Latimer, Linacre, Colet, and Sir Thomas More, the last two especially.

For a while he entertained the thought of settling permanently in England, perhaps at the court of Henry VII or his son Henry VIII, both of whom he had met. Earlier he had thought of joining the court of Philip of Burgundy, whose son Charles became the famous emperor, Charles V. He continued his friendship with members of both courts, but his restless nature led him on to Italy, where he spent the three years 1506–9 making acquaintances and friends in Bologna, Florence, Rome, and Venice. For nearly a year he was closely associated with the famous publisher

Aldus in Venice. After wandering around through France and England, the Rhineland and the Low Countries, he finally settled at Basle in Switzerland, where he became chief editor for that other famous publisher, Froben. His literary acquaintances included practically every contemporary writer of importance in England, France, Germany, Italy, and Spain, and some in other countries with whom he carried on extensive correspondence. Before his death he ranked as the dean of literary men throughout Europe and was certainly one of the most learned men of the time.

Such a man, so well-informed, so sensitive, would be almost ideal for our purpose. Let us, then, bring the revived Erasmus to America on one of the modern luxury liners. He would appreciate this for he was something of an epicure. He would thoroughly enjoy the comfort, food, and drink on such a ship after his experience with the little tubs in which he so often shuttled back and forth across the Channel. He knew there was land across the Atlantic (the Florentine Vespucci's letters or pamphlets telling of it were circulating widely) and his friends at the Spanish court had seen the people from there whom the Genoese explorer had brought back with him.

Coming into the harbor of New York and seeing the tall buildings on the skyline there, he would not be too much surprised. Nearly every city on the continent had in his time one or more such tall buildings. In Beauvais they were boastfully engaged in raising the spire of their cathedral to make it the highest building in the world, higher even than St. Peter's in Rome, which Pope Julius II had just started building. Erasmus would infer, however, that New York was a very pious city—so many churches all together there! We would have to explain to him that these were not churches but the buildings of merchants and craftsmen. If we called them guildhalls he would grasp their significance immediately, likening them to the famous guildhalls of Bruges and Ghent and Antwerp. But he would express his astonishment at the way these burghers had come up in the world to be able to raise their towers higher than those of bishops or kings.

Nor would he be too much surprised at the airplanes overhead. People were talking about their possibility in his day. He had heard that the Florentine craftsman-engineer-artist who was such a favorite of the Duke of Milan and more recently of King Francis I had even drawn a picture of an airship carrying people through space.

But Erasmus certainly would be astonished, when he landed, at the appearance of the people on the streets. According to his informants at the emperor's court, the people across the Atlantic were copper-colored and wore very little clothing. Instead, after becoming accustomed to their clothing, he would find them very like the people he had seen in his travels from England to Italy, averaging a bit larger in size but otherwise the same. The occasional dark-skinned persons among them would not surprise him, for the Portuguese had been bringing Negroes from Africa for generations, and he had seen these in many places, especially in Italy. And he had heard of the Mongols; Marco Polo's book was known to nearly everyone in his day.

As Erasmus mingled with the people he would be delighted to discover that he could understand much of what he heard. The many happy years spent in England had made him familiar with its language (his was the century of Shakespeare, whose grandparents were living when he was there) and having a quick ear he would soon overcome the difficulties of difference in accent and ordinary idiom. Philologists and experts in semantics could give us accurate figures, but we would not be far off if we estimated that he could understand more than half of the ordinary conversation about him. He would have little need of an interpreter.

Without attempting any systematic journey over the country, let us expose our visitor to some of the things we consider typically American. The national Capitol, for example, whose outlines are so often repeated in statehouses and city halls all over the country, he would recognize as quite familiar. He would even offer to name the architects, Brunelleschi and Bramante, with an added touch by the Florentine painter who was working on the ceiling of the Sistine Chapel when Erasmus was in Rome. He might have learned from talking with that painter how he would round out St. Peter's should he ever have the chance.

And those open squares so typical of the small towns scattered across the northern part of the country, which we in Minnesota think of as coming from New England, Erasmus would recognize as derived from Old England, as they actually are. Nor would he have to visit the insides of the buildings around the square to understand what activities they housed. He would be surprised to discover how large a proportion of the people were following the ideas of Luther and Calvin and even of Menno Simons, instead of those of Aquinas, which he preferred. But he would know the ideas of all of them—better, I fear, than most of us do—and as he watched the people emerge from the separate churches and mingle peaceably with each other he would wish for his friend Sir Thomas More, for he would recognize this mutual religious tolerance as one of More's dreams come true.

The courthouse would not be more strange to him than the churches, for he was thoroughly familiar with the town halls of the self-governing communes of Europe. And from his chats with his favorite English friend he was even familiar with the idea that a whole country might have representative government. But in Minnesota we should have to explain to him that the buildings so prominent on our skyline were not the fortresses he had assumed them to be, but grain elevators instead.

Erasmus would enjoy dropping in on some of our private preparatory schools, Andover and Exeter in New England, for instance, or their analogues elsewhere in the country. As he looked over their curriculums and watched the schools in operation, he would soon recognize them as essentially the same as the St. Paul's School in London which he had helped his friend Colet plan and establish. And it would flatter his vanity to see how closely his own ideas of proper secondary education were still being followed.

As for our colleges and universities, he would revel in them, though he would be surprised at first by the presence of coeds and, of course, by the huge stadiums, so reminiscent of the Roman amphitheatres he had seen in Italy. He would feel perfectly at home in the arts college. The classics department would probably urge him to stay as a member of its faculty, for he could teach almost every course it offers, and the department of philosophy would find him thoroughly familiar with nearly two thirds of its courses. He might be somewhat surprised at the prominence given to modern languages, but not too much so, for in his time Italian universities were offering courses on Dante, Petrarch, and Boccaccio, the University of Orleans permitted its students to study French as an extracurricular subject, and people in England were talking of courses on Chaucer and more recent English literature. Though Erasmus himself preferred the universal Latin, he would not be unsympathetic to modern literature.

Nor would he be altogether strange to the social sciences; he had delighted in the criticism of his own society, and with his friend More, whose *Utopia* was in a limited sense inspired by his own *Moria*, he had done his utmost to improve society both socially and politically. He would therefore be pleased to learn that these subjects were now matters of serious study in universities, but he would be distressed to learn that the unscrupulous advice which the Florentine secretary of state, Machiavelli, gave to the Medici for governing a state was being studied much more diligently than the wise book of his friend More.

Erasmus would not find it strange that history was now a major subject of study for all, not merely for princes and rulers, because his Spanish friend Vives had for years urged the importance of studying history, had even written a textbook in the subject. Erasmus would have especially enjoyed visiting with the professor of ancient history in order to learn more than was known in his day about the surroundings of the Greek and Latin authors whose works he himself had edited or translated for Froben.

The sciences would be more strange to our Renaissance visitor, yet not altogether so. Froben was forever trying to get brilliant young medical men to give him articles and books on any phase of nature. There was Vesalius, that precocious young Dutch medico who had edited one of Galen's studies for him; Froben was expecting a book on the human body from him some day. There was also Agricola, a young German physician who was serving in the mining camp of Saxony. Froben was encouraging him to send in articles on everything relating to mining—might some day get a big book from him. And Gesner, the young doctor in whose career the people of Zurich were so interested, the one who was interested in cataloguing almost everything—plants, animals, stones, even languages and books. Froben was asking him for articles, too. And of course, that fantastic doctor, Paracelsus, whom Erasmus and Froben had brought to Basle from Strasbourg to relieve them of their ailments; he had notions that minerals have therapeutic qualities. Too bad they could not keep him from getting into trouble with the medical faculty, because they thought he was the best doctor they had had. They had heard also of a Polish doctor, Copernicus, up at Frauenberg who had some unusual ideas about the stars.

So Froben was right: These were important matters for study, and the labors of these young men so persistently encouraged by the Swiss publisher had started the modern sciences of anatomy, botany, zoology, chemistry, geology, and astronomy. And young Gesner had in addition initiated another development, that of library science. Vesalius, Gesner, Paracelsus, Agricola, and Copernicus were all of them brilliant youngsters as Erasmus knew them.

Erasmus would certainly be interested in talking with members of the faculty in education, for he not only had done some teaching himself but had written on nearly every section of education, elementary, secondary, and college. As he listened to our colleagues discuss recent advances in education, he would be unable to resist pointing out how many of these newer ideas were merely names for practices in which the best schools of his time had been engaged for more than a century. Nor would he be overawed by modern educational psychology, for he had ideas on how pupils learned and he would probably engage in considerable argument on that subject.

# What Is American History?

On our way across the country we might stop off at Chicago or elsewhere to attend a meeting of one of the many Great Books discussion groups. Erasmus would enjoy this very much, as a scholar, an educator, and a publisher. It would be fun, too, for the rest of us to see how many of these books he knew even more thoroughly than do their advocates today, and it would probably surprise these gentlemen to discover how many of these great books were in the making, perhaps even with Erasmus' encouragement, during his time on earth.

Erasmus would be a discriminating visitor to the wineries of California, for he was very fond of good wine and complained bitterly of the vinegar wine he was served by Aldus. He would be delighted to learn that the Californian who translated Georgius Agricola's *De re metallica* into English had later become president of this country.

Could we share the visitor's reflections as he flew back across the continent he had just seen, I daresay we would learn that he had found as much in the experience that was familiar to him as was strange: the food we eat, the stories we tell (he would be tickled to hear so many repetitions of the adages which he himself had dug out of Greek and Latin classical literature), the superstitions we hold, even our jokes and the topics we discuss.

As he waited at LaGuardia Field for the servicing of his plane, New Yorkers made aware of their distinguished visitor would undoubtedly want to show him their newest marvel, the great flat glass tower that houses the United Nations. The building, of course, would impress him as strange, but the function of the building not at all. It was, in fact, the faculty of his own University of Paris that conceived and worked out this idea of having representatives of the nations meet to solve their common problems. The first time they met at nearby Constance little more than half a century before Erasmus was born. They remained in session there for nearly four years and accomplished much—not all of it good, Erasmus would probably think now. The next time they met in his own adopted town of Basle and it seemed they were going to stay there permanently, since their sessions continued for nearly twenty years. Froben's grandfather had lived through that time and told his grandson all about it—about the great number of distinguished delegates from all the nations of western Europe and the vast crowds of hangers-on or camp followers.

For seven years the delegates made considerable progress on their common problems, but then the more important nations withdrew their representatives and the delegates that remained made up for their lack of power by passing extremely radical resolutions. So they lost the confidence and respect of most of the people, who were happy to see King Frederick drive them out of Basle. Erasmus, who loved peace and hated war above all things, would be glad to know that the idea had been revived and he would embark upon the journey back to his final resting place happy in the thought that through this means there might be hope of ultimate peace among nations.

Having bade farewell to Erasmus, let us approach this problem of what is American history from another angle. It is one into which I was catapulted by a near accident a few years ago at Greeley, Colorado. It would be hard to find a spot on our map more remote, geographically, from any foreign entanglements, hence more thoroughly American, name and all. Whether you view it from east or west, north or south, it is certainly inland. I was conducting there a seminar on problems in the teaching of the social studies. My students, all graduates, were nearly all experienced teachers in this field.

The near accident occurred as I was walking along a sidewalk, about to cross an alley. Somewhat lost in thought, I failed to notice a truck which turned sharply into that alley across my path. Jolted out of my thoughts by the near collision, I gazed accusingly at the offending vehicle—and noticed that it was piled high with boxes all stamped with foreign labels. Where did they come from? I went back to my class and informed the students that our problem for the summer session would be "Where do the materials and the ideas used in this distinctively American town come from?" Thus are seminar topics sometimes born!

# What Is American History?

The central problem of that seminar became an inventory of the materials and ideas used by that American city in the conduct of its daily life. Each member of the seminar selected one activity as symbolized by important buildings: the courthouse, the churches, schools, libraries, stores, and workshops of all kinds, and houses, large and small. I need not report all the findings in detail; a brief summary will suggest most of them to you. The materials used in that community came from every continent of the world (those on the truck which so nearly wrecked me were from China), and the items could be traced to the remote reaches of innermost Asia, Africa, Australia. to say nothing of Europe and the Americas.

The ideas employed in Greeley's mid-twentieth-century living reflected even wider origins. The courthouse was the subject of the first report. The "Oyez Oyez" with which its sessions opened had come from Norman England, and its laws and procedures reflected ideas developed even earlier, some of them in Roman days and some, perhaps, going back all the way to the Code of Hammurabi and beyond. The churches, which we discussed next, even those of reputedly American origin, were using hymns that were written as far back as the Middle Ages, if not earlier, and were expounding morals and dogma whose origins could easily be traced back as far as ancient Judaea and Egypt, if not also to more ancient India and China.

Thus it was in every one of the reports. The material and ideas in daily use in the middle of the twentieth century in a thoroughly American community were drawn from sources world-wide and time-deep. The most astonishing revelation of that seminar was the very small part which ideas truly generated within the borders of our nation and within the span of our national life played in the total process.

Having viewed the problem from the two chronological end-points, the discovery of America and the present, let us consider briefly the period in between. Not long ago I heard a discussion of the significance of the Constitution in the teaching of American history, in the course of which reference was made to the indebtedness of that document to the ideas of John Locke. My colleagues in modern French history would claim an idea or two in that document for Montesquieu, while the classicists would undoubtedly recognize both Greek and Roman concepts in it as well.

To the same point, C. J. H. Hayes' presidential address to the American Historical Association under the title, "Frontier of What?" was based on the thesis that much of America's westward expansion was in response to the needs and desires of western Europe. And this thesis was later devastatingly confirmed by an American historian, Professor Walter Prescott Webb in his paper entitled "The Fallacy of New Frontiers," in which he recognized not only the United States but all the rest of this hemisphere and the lands beyond as the frontier whose metropolis was Europe. My colleagues in modern European history remind me that the ideas of Europe are constantly finding their way to this country and are often more avidly followed here than there. One of my associates in English history tells me that our country can usually be counted upon to repeat the experience of England thirty or twenty years afterward (though perhaps with an American accent).

It would be interesting to inventory the various aspects of American life and civilization which are not mentioned in American history textbooks. Styles of architecture: Greek, Roman, Byzantine, Romanesque, Gothic, and Renaissance. Religions: Hebrew, Greek and Roman, Catholic, Mohammedan, Lutheran, Calvinist, Baptist, and Methodist. Philosophic ideas: Platonism, Aristotelianism, Scholasticism, Humanism, Humanitarianism. Political ideas: Machiavellianism, Marxism. And all the constantly recurring problems such as Church and State relationships. The list could be expanded indefinitely for there is no problem of human relationship that has ever occurred in history which is not also a problem today. And yet how many of these that I have listed can you find mentioned in an ordinary textbook in American history.

It is not my purpose to indict the writers of textbooks on American history, many of whom I esteem highly as scholars and friends. They may be operating on the assumption that the pupils who use their books in high school will already have had a sequence of courses in ancient, medieval, and modern history before they take up American history. It was that way when my generation went to high school, and under those circumstances the textbook writers could be excused for not trying to include all these other aspects of American civilization. But many theorists have been tampering with the curriculums, with the result that now American history is for many pupils the only history they study in any systematic fashion. And since a course in American history can explain so little of our national life and civilization without the help of the antecedent courses of other days, it leaves our students figuratively provided with the coat of a suit whose vest and trousers are missing. Embarrassing? Of course!

The trouble lies in our failure to take adequate account of the invisible baggage which the immigrants to this hemisphere brought with them. Had these immigrants all been untutored infants who somehow managed to grow up, they might have developed a civilization distinctively and peculiarly American. But they came as adults heavily freighted with established ways of life, which they in turn transmitted to their children born here. These accustomed ways were in fundamental matters: the medium of communication (in our country and for its first immigrant settlers, English), the habits of food and of shelter, the ideas of man's relation to the infinite, the ideas of law and order and how to maintain them. If we were to go through the whole list of institutions which Langlois and Seignobos have so completely enumerated, we would discover that a very large portion of all of them were brought by the immigrants on their earliest arrival. And lest they might forget some of these in their preoccupation with pioneer problems, they brought or sent for books to which they could refer.

The accustomed ways of life which these first settlers brought with them, and which are still the basic ideas of our civilization, were not the achievement of one generation; they represent the accumulated lessons of social experience reaching back through

## The Social Web

Rome and Greece, Judaea, Egypt and Mesopotamia, ancient India and China, and before all these to prehistoric man.

Nowhere is this more clearly revealed than in mathematics, in which those accumulated lessons are stripped of all their social experience and transmitted dogmatically. Yet every advance in mathematical knowledge was the result of social experience and represents the satisfaction of some social need. Teachers of mathematics seldom recount the numbers of lives saved on land or sea, the disputes—yes, even wars—averted, the sufferings relieved, and the comforts won by each new addition to their subject. But mathematics is the only subject that has achieved this supreme economy in the transmission of a social heritage without repeating some of the social experience by which its successive gains were won. All other subjects do require some repetition of the social experience in order to transmit their ideas. The amount of such repetition varies with the different subjects, those involving mathematics, e.g. the sciences and technologies, requiring least; after them in rising scale come the languages and the humanities, and then the social sciences, which require most repetition of social experience. Our chief means of supplying this vicarious social experience is through the systematic study of history, the only subject, save philosophy, which treats of them all in relation to each other, for no subject can be fully explained or understood in terms of itself alone. History thus renders essential aid to all the other subjects of the curriculum—in other words, to the transmission of the accumulated social heritage.

So we return to the query, or queries, with which we started. As we saw through the eyes of Erasmus, much of American civilization had already been fashioned before ever Columbus set foot on these shores. And the social experience by which the understanding of that part of our civilization can best be imparted must be sought long ago and far away from these shores. We are thus brought face to face with the fact that our own history is by no means more simple than that of the history of Ghent by whose complexity Professor Dhondt was so staggered. Our history goes back in time at least as far as his and is derived from even wider sources. And those of us who teach medieval and ancient history are also teaching a large part of American history. No more in its beginnings than in its current phase can life in the United States be understood in terms of the American continent alone.

# 11

# Monte Cassino, Metten, and Minnesota

Mᴏɴᴛᴇ Cᴀssɪɴᴏ in Italy, Metten in Bavaria, Minnesota in the United States. What link can possibly exist between them, other than the obvious identity of initial letter?

To begin with Monte Cassino, its claim to fame for the historian at least, is that there, in 529, the Rule of St. Benedict was formulated. This Rule, better described as a constitution, came into being during the critical years when the old Roman Empire of the West was breaking down and western Europe was coming under the domination of those vigorous but untaught tribesmen from the north known as the Teutons. Among the Romans at that time there was an intense interest in the Christian religion. For some time hundreds, and even thousands, of people, persons of wealth and prominence as well as those in the humbler walks of life, had been renouncing the affairs of the world and turning their thoughts exclusively to the attainment of eternal salvation, which they hoped more certainly to deserve through a life of self-denial.

This spirit of asceticism had begun in the East and was already a century old when the West took it up, and even in the East the thought had arisen that this practice required some organization and should be made of some service to society. But it remained

NOTE: This essay, in somewhat different form, was first published in *Minnesota History*, September 1927.

for the West to realize this thought in its fullest form through the work of Benedict of Nursia, a Roman, to whom succeeding centuries have reverently paid their respect under the title of St. Benedict.

Benedict had begun his life as the scion of a family long accustomed to share in the rule of the Roman Empire, and he was being trained for the same career when as a college student (not an elementary school pupil, as legend has it) he was converted to the religious life, as were so many of the ablest Romans of his time. In his enthusiasm he adopted the ascetic life of the hermit and lived it most effectively. The problem of ruling others was not of his seeking. It was thrust upon him by the many persons who crowded around him to learn to live as he lived—a life of perfect self-denial. After several unhappy experiences with such groups, one of which nearly cost him his life, he finally accepted the responsibility for devising a form of government for such communities.

He was 49 or 50 years old when, after hard study and constant search for inspiration, he achieved the final form of the Rule. It worked so well in his community among the mountainous hills to the south of Rome, that he made an adaptation of it to meet the needs of his sister Scholastica and her community of nuns living not far from Monte Cassino.

Others have drawn up on paper regulations which, if followed, would constitute a counsel of perfection. But Benedict's Rule was not of that kind. It was instead a form of government under which men of religious zeal could live and work harmoniously together day in, day out, through the changing seasons of the year and the changing outlook of passing years, without losing their zest either for religious salvation or for service to humanity. In its provision for work as well as prayer, in its recognition of the varying needs of illness and of health, in its adjustment to changing conditions, and in its insight into human nature, the Rule laid down a form of government which men could follow, whether among the heaping snows of the Arctic Circle or under the glaring sun of the equatorial zone, whether in southern Italy in the sixth century or in midwestern America in the twentieth. And under all these conditions the ideals remained the same, personal salvation and humanitarian service.

Though complete, the Rule was not rigid. It provided for Christian asceticism without impairment of mind or body, for discipline without suppression, for obedience without despotism, and for a community which though withdrawn from the world was yet a part of it. Though members of a community, each member retained his individuality. The keystone of the Rule is provision for the religious life. All else is incidental to that main purpose, yet also essential to that purpose. Provision is made for labor of various kinds, for concern with the welfare of society round about the monastery, care of the sick and the needy, hospitality for the travel-weary, and concern for the salvation of all. Benedict's monastic order, though part of a universal church, was also distinctly regional, each community becoming fixed in and a part of the region in which it was located.

Seldom has the golden mean of moderation, moderation in all things, been so nearly attained. The Rule is indeed a monument of wisdom, one of the world's great documents for the government of men.

But Monte Cassino is as far away as southern Italy and as long ago as fourteen hundred years. It was a religious community in which Romans were striving for salvation and incidentally helping people within a radius of not more than eighty miles and usually not more than ten. It will take another chapter of history to make clear what connection that community has with Minnesota.

It was another Roman, also of the imperial administrative tradition, who, three quarters of a century later, when the times, in Italy at least, were even more out of joint than they had been in Benedict's day, discovered the supreme excellence of the Rule of St. Benedict as a guide for those who would lead a religious life. Gregory the Great had already mounted high on the ladder of Roman civil administration when he became converted to the religious life and disposed of his great inherited wealth in order to endow some seven Benedictine communities like the one at Monte Cassino, though Benedict had been dead for half a century. Gregory's genius for rule was such that when all order in Italy seemed collapsing into chaos the people turned to him and forced him to assume the position of chief bishop of Rome. To the extent that his duties would permit, he continued to follow the Rule of St. Benedict, but the widened horizon on which he as pope had to operate made him sense the dynamic possibilities of the Rule. It was he who sent St. Augustine to England to work among the still heathen Anglo-Saxons, and he who described for the world the greatness of the work Benedict had done. And so the world discovered that the Rule which St. Benedict had devised for Monte Cassino in a Christian land could function equally well in a harsher northern climate among heathen folk.

Life in these far places, however, entailed much that life in Monte Cassino had not involved. It called for, not only the conversion of the heathen to Christianity, but instruction in the very rudiments of civilized life, elementary education, the training of priests, the building of churches, the making of all the essential accessories of religious observance. Nowhere is this more clearly revealed than in the account written by one of the descendants of the Anglo-Saxons who had been converted to Christianity. He figuratively lays before our eyes the contents of the saddlebags of his abbot, Benedict Biscop, on his return from five or more successive trips to Rome and the continent: more perfect copies of the Rule, books, always books, writings of the Fathers, secular writings for elementary and preparatory instruction, vestments, vessels, cloth, pictures. Not in his saddlebags, he also brought masons and glaziers, and on one occasion he borrowed a cantor from Rome for a year to give instruction in correct church music. Seldom is the transit of civilization so concretely and clearly revealed.

During the next four centuries the conversion of northern and central Europe was almost entirely due to the Benedictines—its conversion to Christianity and to civilized life as well. The clusters of monastic buildings which the monks themselves literally built gradually became the nuclei of permanent villages and towns. In fact some of the cities of Germany today owe their origin to these early monasteries. And from these monastic centers the Benedictines taught their converts the arts of peace: agriculture and its related activities, the handicrafts, and the fine arts.

As a part of all this there developed, too, the Benedictines' interest in learning, in the accumulation of libraries, the training of teachers, and the maintenance of schools. Priests must be trained to continue the work which the missionaries had started. This required learning and the tools of learning, not only in theology but in all those other activities essential to the maintenance of the Christian religion. From the seventh century to the twelfth the best, the largest, and the most diversified libraries were to be found in the Benedictine monasteries: at Wearmouth-Jarrow, Fulda, Rheims, Bobbio, St. Gall, Gandersheim, Cluny, St. Denis, to mention only a few of the more famous. There, too, were to be found the ablest teachers and scholars: Bede, Alcuin, Rhabanus, Gerbert, for example, who are still ranked among the truly great teachers of all time. Nor can we omit either St. Benedict himself or Gregory the Great from the list of the great teachers.

One characteristic of the Benedictine Rule for which Benedict himself had provided is fully revealed by the spread of Benedictine monasteries through the north of Europe. Each new community founded by the missionaries was cut off from organic connection with the parent community almost as soon as it was self-sustaining. Sentiment and tradition often preserved the memory of the earlier connection more or less fondly, but there remained no authoritative bond. This has sometimes been called a defect of the Benedictine Rule, but it resulted in each Benedictine community's becoming essentially a part of the region in which it was located, and there were undoubtedly advantages in this fact. The people of the region did not continue to look upon the Benedictine community as foreign. The original monks were quickly replaced by others who had been born and reared in the region, and thus the feeling of community between the people and the monks facilitated both the work of conversion and more material education.

One of the monasteries established during this great missionary period was the monastery of Metten, built on the northern side of the Danube Valley some miles east of Ratisbon in the year 801. Charlemagne then ruled that territory, and the monastery was in a sense built under his auspices. The people among whom it was built were Bavarians, already Christian but still in need of civilizing influences. So the Benedictines trained priests, taught the arts of peace, and in general served as a force for improvement in the region roundabout.

About a hundred years after the founding of the Metten monastery its buildings were destroyed by the great invasion of the Hungarians, then a wild people recently come from Asia. It was rebuilt, and, when Otto the Great finally defeated the Hungarians and established the Ostmark as a protection against them, Metten embarked upon a more peaceful career.

It was never one of the largest or most important of the Benedictine monasteries, but as the centuries came and went it continued to serve its locality with more or less effectiveness. There were times when its abbots were unusually able, when its community was unusually large, and its influence radiated out over all Bavaria. At other times its community was small and its abbots neither distinguished nor important. Early in the thirteenth century its buildings were again destroyed, by fire this time, and years were required to repair the damage. Two hundred years later, in the fifteenth century, Metten was famous for its beautiful manuscripts and ornamented books, some of which are still preserved as models of calligraphy. Two hundred years after that, in the seventeenth century, the abbot of Metten stands forth as a leading figure in the religious organization of Bavaria. The great church with its two spires, which so impresses visitors today, was built in the eighteenth century.

In 1803, almost exactly a thousand years after it was founded, Metten and its properties were confiscated by the state and its twenty-three monks scattered. This was in the days of Napoleon and under his influence. Almost a generation passed before it was re-established around one of those twenty-three monks who still remained. It grew steadily though slowly and early in the twentieth century it was famous for its school, its community then consisting of seventy members, mostly priests.

Thus Monte Cassino and Metten are linked, and the sixth century has been brought into touch with the twentieth, but we are still some distance away from Minnesota.

Visitors to St. Paul are usually shown what is called "the old German church," the Church of the Assumption, as one of the most picturesque of the older sights of that picturesque city. And tourists, as they drive along the highway that leads westward out of St. Cloud, marvel at the church at St. Joseph, which seems too large for the little village that clusters about it. They are still more puzzled by the church steeples that peer out over the trees four miles beyond, at Collegeville. All three of these and many more spots in Minnesota and the Upper Midwest serve to establish the connection between Minnesota and Metten and Monte Cassino.

Not so long ago there were people still living in St. Cloud and its vicinity who remembered the little group of three priests who arrived there in the spring of 1856 and built themselves a wooden structure on a farm some two miles south of the town. Less than a year later the territorial legislature of Minnesota passed a law recognizing as a "body politic and corporate" the members of the religious order of St. Benedict—Demetrius Marogna, Cornelius Wittmann, Bruno Riss, and Alexis Roetzer being mentioned by name. The bill recognized this order "as instituted for scientific, educational, and ecclesiastical purposes" and authorized its members to establish an institution to be known as St. John's Seminary. This seminary was actually opened on November 10, 1857, with one professor and five students.

Thus began in Minnesota a community living according to the Rule of St. Benedict and dedicated like Monte Cassino to the two ideals of religious salvation and humanitarian service. The leader of this little band was originally an Italian nobleman, making the connection between Minnesota and Monte Cassino a bit more intimate. But the Very Reverend Demetrius Marogna was not an abbot. His title was that of "prior," and his community was a priory of the monastery of St. Vincent in Pennsylvania, which had been founded only a few years before by Benedictine monks from Metten in Bavaria. It was at St. Vincent's that Father Demetrius had entered the novitiate and from there he had been sent to Minnesota.

The Minnesota priory was not long kept under tutelage. In the Benedictine way the parent monastery cut it adrift in 1858. Scarcely well enough established to be recognized as a monastery, it justified the confidence of its parent by toddling along as a canonical priory until 1865, when through the efforts of the abbot of St. Vincent it was raised to the status of an abbey or monastery by the pope. Its name at that time was St. Louis on the Lake.

The coming of this little band of monk-priests to Minnesota was due indirectly to the efforts of an interesting missionary priest, Father Pierz, who had worked among the Indians and whites of the northwestern frontier for many years. Father Pierz was one of those rare individuals who thrive on hardship that would kill most people. He lived to be ninety-five years old, though he had spent many of those years in tramping the forests and fields of the region in an age when there were no roads to ease the journey of the weary traveler and very little shelter to temper the rigors of sub-zero winters.

Father Pierz came to love the Minnesota country and to see in its woods and lands, its lakes and streams, an abundance of natural resources even beyond the vivid imagination of later realtors. When settlement began in the territory Father Pierz launched an eloquent epistolary campaign urging Germans who were Catholics to migrate to the area, and it was his enthusiasm that attracted the early settlers of this race and religion.

When they arrived he sought to minister to them, but found the work too great for his declining energy; he was then already past seventy years. So he sought for others to carry on in his place. One of his assistants, a young priest, returning from an emergency service in midwinter, was frozen to death. Obviously there was need both of persons who were trained to endure hardships and of persons who understood the language and customs of these settlers. Bishop Cretin of St. Paul finally wrote to missionary societies in Bavaria asking for aid, and was by them directed to the monastery of St. Vincent in Pennsylvania, which had been established under the leadership of Father Sebastian Wimmer, himself a monk-priest from Metten in Bavaria.

With the establishment of the Benedictine foundation in Minnesota, additional members continued to come for several years, some who had entered the order at Metten, others at St. Vincent. But it was not long before the community, following the Benedictine pattern, was recruiting its new members from Minnesota and surrounding regions. Indeed, the second abbot of the institution, Father Alexius Edelbrock, was a boy in St. Cloud when the first fathers arrived. He became one of the first students of St. John's Seminary, but because his father opposed his desire to become a monk he went to St. Vincent to enter the Order. When his education was completed the abbot there sent him back to Minnesota, and he became one of the strong personalities in the history of the community and in the history of the state as well. Of pioneer stock, accustomed from earliest boyhood to pioneer life in Minnesota, he was eminently fitted to cope with the problems that arose. Under his leadership the monastery grew in membership, in material resources, and in influence. He was one of Minnesota's strong men in the iron age of James J. Hill, Archbishop Ireland, and Bishop Whipple, with all of whom he was well acquainted.

The first community had barely begun its work when it felt the need of added help from women in its educational work.[1] So a call was sent to Bavaria for women who were willing to undertake teaching under the hardships of pioneer life. The first group of Benedictine sisters responded to this call in 1857, just a year after the arrival of the fathers, and they founded the Convent of St. Benedict, which still flourishes at St. Joseph. It was their work to provide elementary education, minister to the sick, and serve as a refuge for those in need. As at Monte Cassino, so in Minnesota, the Benedictine monastery and convent grew up within a few miles of each other, and both contributed to the development of a wide locality.

The central establishment at Collegeville, with its large and growing community of priests and brothers, was not only a shelter for the priests but also a school center. Both as St. John's Seminary and later as St. John's University, it offered opportunities for higher education in communities which in themselves could not have afforded even an elementary school. The sisters looked after the primary instruction, going out to settlements large enough to maintain school buildings of their own, and receiving at their convent school the children from smaller settlements or scattered farms. The fathers also journeyed out from the monastery to conduct services in small and scattered settlements. Where the neighborhood was large enough to support a resident priest, the Benedictines remained for extended periods, sometimes years. While most of their work was among the white people, they did and still do important work also among the Indians.

The distance to which the work of these Benedictine communities was extended seems almost incredible. The monastery has helped to serve needy communities as far away as northwestern Canada and the Pacific Northwest of the United States, and the sisters have supplied elementary teachers and nurses almost as widely. The Canadian work of the men eventually reached a stage where it supported an independent monastery, one of whose first abbots had previously been in charge of the college work at St. John's.

The sisters, too, saw their work increase to such proportions as to warrant the separate establishment in 1900 of a community at Duluth, the Convent of St. Scholastica. Even so, there are more than nine hundred professed members of the community at St. Joseph, making it the largest Benedictine community of women in the world.

To the historian of early European history it is peculiarly interesting to trace the growth on Minnesota soil of an institution whose work he has so often followed in those earlier years of European civilization. It is most instructive to find repeated here and now, so to speak, so much of what occurred around Monte Cassino, or at the monastery of the Venerable Bede in Anglo-Saxon England, or at Fulda in western Germany, or at Metten in eastern Bavaria. Only the names and dates are different.

It is especially interesting to see how truly the Minnesota communities have run the course of the older monasteries in identifying themselves with the localities in which they were established. Originally the Minnesota monks came from Germany to serve the needs of the German Catholic settlers. They spoke German as their native tongue, and they conducted their work among the adults in German. But from the very opening of their seminary in 1857 they carried on instruction for their younger pupils in English. And whereas English was the acquired tongue in 1857, German has become the acquired tongue for those of the present generation. In this language matter and much besides, both monastery and convent have served a very important function in easing the transition of these settlers from their German origin to American society.

The composition of the communities reflects a similar development. Whereas their earlier membership was almost exclusively of German origin, it now embraces also Irish, Czech, Polish, French, English, and even Scandinavian names. This is even more true of the young people enrolled in the schools. And one infers from newspaper accounts of St. John's University that the students there engage in football, basketball, and baseball games, have trained coaches for the purpose, and have a very creditable record of competition with other colleges of the state. In other words, the institution has become an integral part of the characteristic life of the state.

The monks' part in the cultural life of the state is no less impressive and no less typical of Benedictine traditions. They did not rear an imposing Gothic or Romanesque or Renaissance edifice on the prairies when they arrived in 1857. Their first community dwelling and seminary was a log house measuring some twelve by twenty feet. As their needs required, this structure was enlarged and new buildings were added. The present cluster of buildings shows in some ways the influence of an education that is in touch with ideas of Europe as well as of America, but mostly they give evidence of a close connection with Minnesota and the Midwest. Architecturally, St. John's buildings are, and presumably have been since 1857, just a little in advance of the general taste of the surrounding society.

One cannot visit St. John's without becoming aware of the regard for art and science that prevails there. It is present in the care with which the grounds are kept, the trees, shrubs, and flowers planted, and in the location and character of the buildings. Within the chapel the vestments and other articles of religious service reveal this taste and interest in art. The library is a truly impressive one, and though it is dominated by the interest in theology and Church history, it includes a wide range of books in the essential fields of secular learning too. The state university, despite its much more extensive collections, has had occasion to borrow from St. John's books it did not possess. The traditional intellectual interests of the Benedictine Order have not been forgotten in the extension to Minnesota.

The St. John's faculty has included its full share of able scholars devoted to the pursuit of truth and the practice of sound science. Their horticultural experimentation has resulted in the development of several fruits specially adapted to Minnesota's severe climate. And when some years ago an attempt was made to have the state legislature arbitrarily interfere with honest research and teaching in science, the men from St. John's fought it side by side with the faculty members of the state university. In the Benedictine tradition, they were not afraid of honest efforts to advance the world's knowledge of truth.

It is not fanciful, then, to think of the Roman Benedict and the equally Roman Gregory back there in Italy of the sixth century, or the Frankish Charlemagne at the opening of the ninth, or the long line of Bavarian Benedictines at Metten as contributing to the history of Minnesota. Each of them helped to forge the chain that links Monte Cassino and Metten and Minnesota. The Benedictines of Minnesota are neither Bavarian nor Italian; they are thoroughly American and Minnesotan. But they carry on the traditions of a noble past that links them to their fellows throughout the world.

This survey is only a reminder of the fact that our civilization is composed of the achievements of the past, particularly of the European past. As our legal institutions hark back to English history, even farther back than Magna Charta, and our common language to the England of Chaucer, Wycliffe, and Shakespeare, so many of our social and economic institutions and most of our religious institutions were fashioned in the various countries of Europe anywhere from a hundred to more than two thousand years ago. The Benedictine strand from Monte Cassino to Metten to Minnesota is but one of the many strands from which the multicolored warp of American civilization is woven.

## NOTES

[1] For information about the Benedictine community the writer is indebted to a volume by Father Alexius Hoffmann entitled *St. John's University, Collegeville, Minnesota: A Sketch of Its History* (Collegeville, 1907); to a manuscript history of the monastery by the same author, which the writer was permitted to read, in the library of St. John's University; and to the kindness of the Abbot Alcuin.

236

# 12

# History in an Age of Technology

Not so long ago I thought the important questions
in history centered around such problems as whether the Battle
of Tours should be called of Tours or of Poitiers; whether Attila,
the king of the Huns, failed to make his threatened attack upon
Rome because he was ill, because he was bought off, or because
he was overawed by Pope Leo; whether Rome fell in 325, 476,
768, 1453, or has not fallen yet; whether Leif Ericson reached
Chesapeake Bay or went only as far as the Jersey coast, or perhaps Rhode Island, or Cambridge, in Massachusetts, or not any
farther south than Labrador; and whether the chroniclers used
*concilium* and *consilium* interchangeably or to represent quite
distinct ideas. To the historian these questions are not only interesting but highly important.

From the midst of such engaging problems, I was drafted to
serve on a committee to reconsider the readjustment of our school
program in social science subjects to prepare our youth to meet
the problems of modern society more adequately. With me on
that committee were economists and educators, political scientists and sociologists, as well as some who represented primarily
persons of affairs interested in the schools. That committee took
as its first problems: What are these new social forces? In what

NOTE: This essay was first published, in somewhat different form, under the
title "History in the Machine Age," in *Minnesota History*, March 1933.

direction are they moving? What kind of life are the children now in school going to face when they leave school? The attempt to answer these questions brought into sharp focus the bewildering progress of modern science and technology, the marvels it has wrought in our own day, and the hints of even greater marvels which it promises to bring forth in the near future. It brought into relief, too, the economic, social, and political changes which have followed in the wake of this technological advance.

And then, against that background of current problems and activity, came the next question of what studies we should provide to equip the pupils to cope with such a world. In the attempt to answer this question almost every possible form of social science and every conceivable arrangement of those forms was canvassed. So, too, was the question of how far back into the past this instruction should go. Would our youths be better equipped to adjust themselves to the marvels of the coming age if we did not fetter them with too much knowledge of the past, so that they would have no old ways to unlearn, would not, so to speak, be crossing arterial automobile highways in an oxcart manner? Would it be better if they learned little or no history at all?

Historians, of course, feel rudely jolted by such questions. But they have been raised in all seriousness by well-intentioned persons and so merit consideration. Does modern technology really challenge us to obliterate knowledge of the past, in whole or in part, or is the idea that it does only the superficial judgment of its self-appointed spokesmen?

There is not space here to undertake a comprehensive discussion of the cultural functions and values of history. I shall therefore confine myself to those aspects of the topic which may be of direct concern to the technologist. Let me, then, approach the question from three angles. First, the sentimental: Is knowledge of the past essential to the enjoyment of life? Second, the practical: Is knowledge of the past essential to the successful conduct of affairs? And finally, the scientific: Is knowledge of the past essential in penetrating the limitless depths of unrevealed learning?

First, the sentimental. Did you ever stroll with a child of four or five or six? If you have done so, you will have no difficulty in recalling the steady procession of questions provoked by everything in sight. What? Why? How did it happen? These questions had to be answered about each new object of interest. More likely than not you had exhausted your supply of historical fact, and unless you are a very unusual person your supply of fiction as well, long before the stroll was ended. You probably vowed then and there that you would take out a membership in the historical society and study its publications before you ventured on another stroll like that.

Or you may have made that vow when you entertained some friend or relative from a distant place. The familiar neighborhood of your routine life may not plague you with riddles, but guide some stranger around it and it at once begins to reveal its wide variety of questions—all of which you are called upon to answer. The more critical intelligence of grown-up curiosity deprives you of recourse to any reserve of fiction. You are called upon to present the facts—historical facts. And when you leave your own neighborhood, you find yourself bristling with similar questions, questions so insistent that you cannot refrain at times from asking a perfect stranger to supply the answers.

Apparently we never outgrow the tendency to ask these questions, or the urge to have them answered; nor are we satisfied with a fanciful answer, however entertaining. We insist on the truth, and that truth about most objects of interest is history. All of us, whether harassed parents, hosts to strangers, or visitors in strange places, are grateful to the local historical society for placing markers on the more significant historic sites. But we want more, and more extended, information.

Henry Johnson of Columbia University, in his book *An Introduction to the History of the Teaching of the Social Sciences* has shown how universal and persistent is the human desire to ask questions about the unusual and the strange by citing the fourth chapter of Joshua. There is told the story of the placing of the twelve stones at the crossing of the Jordan. Why were they placed there? Let me quote: ". . . that this may be a sign among you, that when your children ask in time to come, saying, What mean ye by these stones? then ye shall say unto them, Because the waters of the Jordan were cut off before the ark of the covenant of Jehovah . . ." Joshua was not only aware of this human trait, but he deliberately made important use of it.

It was something of that same thought which prompted the European statesmen of the nineteenth century to be so insistent upon teaching national history to all the children. They too erected monuments to provoke questions which that history answered.

The psychologists of at least one school would approve this wisdom of Joshua because they hold that what the individual learns affects his personality, in a sense becomes part of him. Thus persons learning the record of a common environment would to that extent become unified. Next to the consciousness of a common kinship, society knows no stronger bond than that of a common tradition. Devotion to a common ideal has held people together, but ideals have an unhappy way of crumbling in the face of reality. The knowledge of a common tradition is much more lasting, and the deeper, the truer, it is the more firmly it will bind. Ideals arising from such a foundation have a far better chance of survival. Thus the sentimental interest in the past not only contributes to the amenities of life but becomes at the same time a powerful cohesive force, the more essential the larger the society.

There is another aspect of this sentimental interest in the past. I once heard the "Skipper," as the University of Minnesota students affectionately named the conductor on the intercampus trolley line, congratulating an elderly passenger. Later the Skipper explained to me that the elderly gentleman had just discovered that his grandmother was the sister of Senator Stephen A. Douglas. Both the Skipper and the gentleman in question seemed happy at the discovery. They are not peculiar in that respect; many people are interested in finding out about their ancestors. And on the whole, the effect of this interest is good. True, most of us tend to limit our enthusiasm to those of our ancestors who achieved some distinction, but finding these, we are moved to live up to their reputations as nearly as we can. The result is that genealogical interest in this country has, on the whole, had a good influence. But, whether good or bad, the important fact here is that genealogical interest does exist on a large scale and constitutes another interest in history which will persist.

Such curiosity and its satisfaction might at first glance seem limited rather strictly to matters of local concern with a history that goes back only a few generations. A little reflection shows this to be erroneous. Once within a few months the University of Minnesota auditorium saw a celebration in honor of Björnson, the poet of Norwegian independence; there was enacted in the Minneapolis auditorium a celebration commemorating Gustavus Adolphus of Sweden, who died at Lützen in Germany three hundred years ago; and there appeared a book marshaling the evidence in support of the Kensington rune stone, which purports to be the record of a Viking expedition to western Minnesota nearly six hundred years ago. For many years St. Paul was the headquarters of a society for the commemoration of the signing of Magna Charta, which happened back in England in 1215. The state legislature has officially recognized the celebration of Leif Ericson Day in honor of his discovery of America about the year 1000. To answer questions about the Benedictine monasteries near St. Cloud one must go back to Bavaria eleven hundred years ago and to Monte Cassino in Italy three hundred years before that. And our citizens have been much interested in the Minnesota maiden of twenty thousand years ago discovered by University archaeologists and much publicized as the first American tragedy —an allusion to the fractured skull of the skeleton at the bottom of a prehistoric lake.

These are a few illustrations from Minnesota, and any state in the union could report a similar list. Apparently there are no limits in time or space from which to draw the answers to questions that purely local objects of interest may raise.

How will technological development, immediate and prospective, affect this sentimental demand for knowledge of the past?

## The Social Web

We are given increased leisure, more time to roam about the countryside, and better and cheaper transportation, ensuring that we shall thus roam about. We are provided with television to flash before our eyes scenes from all parts of the world and jet planes to carry us to far places in person. All these achievements, and many more that are promised, merely raise more questions which only history can answer and arouse more curiosity which only history can satisfy. Technological development does not obliterate our sentimental interest in the past; instead it widens the scope of that interest and provides more objects and occasions to inspire it.

Let us turn to the second interest, the practical. Thus far I have been discussing history in a way that scarcely enters the thoughts of the professional historian. He may recognize these demands for history and even admit that satisfying them is a large task, but he feels that history has a much greater function to perform in the realm of public affairs. This was stated most simply and most clearly by Carl Becker in his address as president of the American Historical Association, when he described history as serving public affairs as memory serves the individual man. Imagine, if you can, how a person would carry on his affairs if his memory of the past was gone. Consider the unhappy state of the victims of amnesia, even partial or temporary amnesia. If Professor Becker's observation is correct, then for the group history is the most practical of subjects and an indispensable adjunct of all social science and public policy. Its study must be not merely selective and sentimental, but thorough, comprehensive, precise.

The practical value of history has not always been recognized. Napoleon is said to have described history as "but a fable agreed upon." But as emperor he concerned himself much with the teachings in the schools and especially with history as a school subject. Henry Ford stated somewhat the same view in a more vigorous and American way in his famous remark that "history is bunk." But he devoted much of his energy to the history of transportation and the development of his interesting and very complete museum of the subject at Dearborn. Such testimony is rather equivocal. What these eminent men condemned with words, they approved in acts. And since their acts came after their words, we can assume that each of them really regarded history as of the utmost practical value.

But in what sense is history practical? It is true that researches in Biblical history resulted in the discovery of oil wells in the Near East and that the researches in Mexican history led to the rediscovery of some rich silver mines. But it is not in such an immediate sense, I think, that any of us would maintain that history has practical value.

A somewhat better illustration is afforded in the history of agriculture—curiously enough, a relatively recent addition to the professional historian's interests. Dr. Herbert Kellar, head of the McCormick Historical Society of Chicago and one of the pioneers in this field, observed that in American agriculture there has been a curious recurrence of mistakes every other generation. Sons seldom copied the mistakes of their fathers, but they almost invariably repeated those of their grandfathers. The reason for this, Dr. Kellar believes, is that, without any written history, American farmers have passed on their experience by word of mouth from father to son. The father was so conscious of the mistakes he had discovered that he took particular pains to teach his son to avoid them. But he forgot to emphasize the lessons which *his* father had taught him; these he took for granted. Dr. Kellar thinks this condition can be corrected by a written history of agriculture which will enable the farmer of succeeding generations to avoid not only his father's mistakes but likewise those of his grandfather and his great-grandfather. If so, that history will be eminently practical.

An illustration of even wider scope may be drawn from the field of economics. During the depression of the 1930s Alvin H. Hansen wrote a most informative and thoughtful book, *Economic Stabilization in an Unbalanced World*, which discussed the factors that played a determining part in that crisis. The book's peculiarly instructive character lay in its recognition of the many factors, some of them most remote from what we ordinarily consider economics, which determine the daily bread-and-butter existence of ordinary men. Leaving aside such cosmic matters as sunspots and weather cycles and concerning ourselves only with the man-made elements in the problem, we find these in such apparently distant reaches as moral reforms and changes in styles of beauty.

Why should the desire of a people to improve moral conditions through prohibition disturb economic affairs? Yet it did, both in Norway and in the United States. Why should the desire of both women and men to retain a youthful figure cause economic distress alike in Cuba and in Minnesota? Yet it did. Professor Hansen emphasized the fact that economic consequences flow quite as surely from peoples' ideas of art and beauty, their reactions to weather and climate, their concepts of religion and society, their development of science and technology, their political methods, as from economic factors more narrowly and traditionally construed.

Economics is pre-eminently practical in its purpose and intent, yet the work of modern economists suggests that the full understanding of our economic problems lies in the intricate interrelationships of an almost infinite variety of human activities. History, broadly grasped, can furnish us this detailed understanding of the interlocking gears of human affairs.

Politics has long been the favorite preoccupation of history and historians, and E. A. Freeman's dictum, "history is past politics, present politics future history" has become a cliché. Though historians today profess a much wider interpretation of their subject, the majority of them still cling rather closely to the political view. This may be justified by the reflection that history, like its sister social sciences, is concerned with public rather than private affairs and that sooner or later all important public affairs are registered in the realm of politics. Perhaps it will always be so.

Certainly people will always be interested in the doings of those they select to look after public affairs, and this interest can be criticized only for not being as keen and inclusive as it might be. In recent years, since the world has become so closely knit, the ordinary channels of public information have been perhaps too closely concerned with national and international affairs and too little with local needs. This has distracted the attention of the public from its immediate affairs and from its state and local officials, who still do more than one-half of the governing which directly affects us.

Voters seldom take into account a candidate's knowledge of history; they put men in office who have no such knowledge and they sometimes retire from office men who possess this important qualification to an unusual degree. Nonetheless it is remarkably true, both in national and state affairs, that leadership in the legislative branches has been provided quite consistently by the older men. In this way the oversight of the voters has been corrected. These older men may not be any more able than the younger men just entering office, they may have no loftier desires and aims, but they possess the leadership because, among other reasons, they know more of the history of the problems they must consider. They know the backgrounds of their colleagues, their preferences and prejudices; they know the conditions of each constituency; they know the problems that are apt to arise and what the ramifications of those problems are. They have learned, if not by formal study, at least through experience, a good deal of the history of state and nation. It is primarily this fact that distinguishes leaders from newcomers.

Doubtless many mistakes have been repeated in the laws enacted by Congress and the state legislatures, but the effect of the tendency to repose leadership in the older men has, I think, kept the number of such mistakes lower than it might otherwise have been. It is probable that we have suffered more from a lack of historical knowledge in the administration of law than we have in the making of it.

There is another way in which history affects the practical conduct of government. It sometimes happens that public and private affairs seem to clash. In Emily A. Babcock's excellent translation of the history of the Crusades written eight hundred years ago by William of Tyre, the scholarly archbishop says in his preface:

In the present work we seem to have fallen into manifold dangers and perplexities. For, as the series of events seemed to require, we have included in this study on which we are now engaged many details about the characters, lives, and personal traits of our subjects, regardless of whether these facts were commendable or open to criticism. Possibly descendants of these monarchs, while perusing this work, may find this treatment difficult to brook and be angry with the writer beyond his deserts. They will regard him as either mendacious or jealous, both of which charges, as God lives, we have endeavored to avoid as we would a pestilence.

It is through this devotion to truth, so clearly recognized by the archbishop as the historian's duty, that many a reputation which the passion and conflict of the day may have besmirched or neglected is finally re-established. Thus history serves to encourage the devoted public servant, despite the misunderstandings and misrepresentations to which he is momentarily subjected.

If in talking about public affairs I have seemed to devote myself largely to government, it is only by way of illustration. In business and social affairs too the application of history is of the utmost practical value. But perhaps enough has been said to indicate that, whatever the developments of technology may be, the demand for the practical aspects of history will be unimpaired.

Turning now to the third phase of our theme, the scientific, let us by way of introduction examine technology itself and the sciences upon which it rests. What is their attitude toward knowledge of the past?

The materials of technology are derived for the most part out of the earth, and the chief science of the earth is geology. How does geology make its discoveries? Where may such or such minerals be found? Will earthquakes occur again in this region or that? Will volcanoes burst forth or subside? Will changes occur in the surface of the earth, will new lands appear, old lands sink beneath the water?

These questions are about the future. And how does the geologist attempt to answer them? By delving into the past. His chief concern is to find out how the lands were formed, whether by action of fire or water or by shifting in the earth's crust, and how long each such force operated and how they interplayed in the geologic process. The more accurate his knowledge of these remote factors, the more definitely he can gauge the potential resources of the earth and the better he can forecast changes in its surface. In other words, the geologist's power to contribute to the discoveries of the future is almost directly proportionate to the accuracy and fullness of his knowledge of the past. And upon this science depend in large part all the technologies which operate in chemistry and metallurgy.

The most remote, the most objective, of all the sciences is astronomy. Concerned with the study of the universe, it contributes basic information to nearly all other sciences, physics and geology most directly. With the aid of larger, more powerful telescopes, man is peering ever farther and farther into the apparently limitless, but perhaps limited, universe. At any rate the astronomers have pushed the limits farther and farther away. Thousands of stars, hitherto invisible and hence unknown, have been brought within the range of human knowledge. Most of the astronomer's future discoveries will come in this widening and particularizing knowledge of the stars beyond the range of former instruments. And as his knowledge of these increases, he will learn more about the forces which affect the stars nearer to us.

When we examine the nature of this newer knowledge of the astronomer, we are again met with the same paradox in an even more fascinating form. The farther the stars are distant from the earth, the longer it takes the light they shed to reach us. Even the older telescopes caught glimpses of stars whose light had traveled thousands of years to reach the earth, and the newer telescopes are bringing into range the light of stars so many light-years away that figures have ceased to have meaning. It is possible, even probable, that some of the stars whose light the astronomer now sees no longer exist. The astronomer is literally looking into the past, a past more remote than any we have ever dreamed of, and he is seeing that past as it once was, though it may not now be so. Nothing could be more fantastic, and yet such seems to be the truth. And what would an astronomer not give to have detailed records of the heavens of a thousand years ago!

The relevance of all this for us at the moment is the fact that the new discoveries in astronomy promise to come from the deeper and more accurate study of the past. And from the astronomer's discoveries must come an enrichment of physics and geology and all the sciences and technologies dependent upon them.

Having considered the earth below and the stars above, we may turn to the realm of those things which exist between them. Here the biologist holds sway, and he at least is free from the fetish of the past, for his material is all of it mortal. The biological sciences are concerned with man and other living things as they relate, or may relate, to man. It is upon them that the technologies of agriculture, medicine, and psychology depend. Are these sciences less exact because they are concerned with forms so fleeting, so transitory, that they can be studied only within the limits of their own brief lifetimes? Is the future of the biological sciences less promising because, unlike geology and astronomy, they have no past to observe? Perhaps so. But the biologists have sought to correct this deficiency by creating a past; they have developed the theory of evolution. This doctrine that the higher forms of life are developed from the lower forms, the lowest of which are not far removed from the physical elements with which the geologist and astronomer deal, has provided the biologist with a vista of time comparable to that of the more exact sciences. Thus he too can gaze into the past, though he does it through a microscope, and his discoveries are largely dependent on the degree of accuracy with which he reads the past development of the higher from the lower life-structures. It is on this hypothesis that he pursues his studies of all forms of life, confident that he is thereby making some contribution to the understanding of human life.

How much the biologist is concerned with the study of the

248

past is clearly revealed in the eagerness with which archaeologists, anthropologists, and paleontologists dog the footsteps of the geologist for occasional fragments of authentic past biology as this is revealed in skeletal, shell, bone, or fossil finds. So far the finds have confirmed the hypothesis of the biologists to such an extent that the geologist uses their dogma in reading his own past. And, with slight reservation, we can say of the biologist as we have of the geologist and the astronomer that the extent and value of his discoveries will depend in large measure upon the accuracy and fullness of his knowledge of the past. If science, then, upon which all technology depends, is so often seeking its discoveries in the study of the past, can the student of society disregard that past? To be sure, concerned as he is with the activities of man, he cannot summon a limitless past with the help of a microscope or a telescope, yet he possesses one advantage which the scientist lacks. The subjects of his concern have kept records which describe not only their acts but the feelings that prompted the acts, and also the hopes and fears, the wishes and dreams that man had, and has, for the future. But man was long in reaching the point at which he learned to keep these records. The period of recorded history is only a few thousand years, a pitifully brief time in the eyes of the biologist and scarcely visible against the span of astronomical time.

Some of us can still recall the mingled feelings with which we first read of Dr. Heinrich Schliemann's excavations at Troy, where he found the ruins of one city underlain with the ruins of still another, and further investigations have disclosed the ruins of some nine or ten cities on that same site. There was something staggering in the thought that a busy and flourishing society could so completely cease to exist, its cities falling in ruins, their buildings crumbling away, the whole so leveled to dust and overgrown with vegetation that a later society could build another city on the same site, perhaps entirely unaware that there had been a city there before.

If we could only console ourselves with the thought that this happened at Troy alone! But can we? Not so long ago travelers and archaeologists roaming through the thick tropical forests of Indochina came upon traces of architectural ruins. Clearing away something of the forest and excavating, they uncovered the magnificent temple of Angkor, mute evidence that in that region there had once flourished a civilization highly developed in art and technology. Archaeological investigation in central Asia has disclosed there also evidence of great cities which flourished centuries ago in the midst of well-developed civilizations equipped with both art and technology. And excavations in Central America, aided by the airplane observations of Colonel Charles A. Lindbergh, have revealed the existence of cities of the Mayan civilization on this continent.

Each of these discoveries has shown that a society had grown up, progressed far in a knowledge of art and technology, then ceased to develop, and finally declined until all its proud achievements were obliterated and the region in which they had flourished reverted to forest or desert and the society itself to a state of savagery or barbarism.

But all these illustrations come from prehistory; their story has been lost. Perhaps they represent merely accidental, sporadic developments. Could such things occur in a continuing society?

The oldest continuing societies of which we know are those of the Mediterranean world, Egypt and Greece and Rome. The pyramids and the great temple of Karnak are marvelous achievements both, whether viewed as technology or as art. Society has continued in those regions, but did it continue to develop that art and that technology? The best artists, writers, scientists, and philosophers of our own time still marvel at the excellence which the Greeks attained twenty-five hundred years and more ago. Did the Greeks maintain and continue that civilization? It is possible today to find shepherds herding their flocks in the midst of ruins of some of the finest buildings the world has ever seen.

And Rome? No society until our own day had advanced farther in technical lore than had the Rome of the Caesars and Augusti. Yet some centuries after Cicero, Caesar, and Virgil were gone the inhabitants of Rome were reduced to dragging marble columns and marble slabs from the old buildings to burn for the lime they might yield.

The story which the ruins of lost history mutely tell is fully confirmed by that of those civilizations whose history we know. Both continue to remind us that there seem to be limits to the progress which a society can make.

We who have seen the United States develop from the little settlements on the eastern seaboard to its present size, with a growth that varied from time to time but always moved forward, have great difficulty in accepting the notion of limits. We who in our own lives in the Middle West have seen the log cabin transformed into a skyscraper of concrete and steel, have seen the open fireplace yield to the automatic heating plant, have experienced the shift from candlelight to fluorescent and neon tubes, have seen new arrivals come by airplane where once they came by covered wagon or even pack train and canoe—we, I say, have difficulty in admitting that there can be limits to progress. And yet I think there are limits, and I venture, perhaps rashly, to define them.

The lower limit seems easy enough to fix. The difference between civilization and savagery is the learning of a single lifetime. I do not mean to imply that a savage society could by its own efforts achieve the height of civilization in a period of seventy years. But I do mean that an intelligent child of savage parents could be taught to be an efficient member of civilized society in less than a lifetime. I also mean that a child of even most intelligent parents, members of a highly developed society, could, if reared among savages, grow up a savage.

There is nothing speculative in these assertions. Such things have happened, though not frequently. The reason is simple enough. In the period of recorded history—the past few thousand years for which we have written records—man has changed little if at all. He has not changed outwardly, and it is not likely that he has changed any more inwardly. We are therefore safe in assuming that man was just as capable of learning at the beginning of recorded history as he is today, and conversely that he is just as capable of being a savage today as he was then.

The lower limit, therefore, may be described as a state of savagery, and it could be attained within a lifetime by even the most highly civilized society. That is the meaning of the successive cities on the sites of Troy, of Angkor, Karnak, and Chichén Itzá.

But is it possible to describe the upper limit to which society may progress? H. S. Jennings, a biologist at Johns Hopkins University, says, if I can paraphrase him correctly, that man today is such a mixture of strains that, even if the eugenists had their way and only the most superior individuals begot offspring, the proportion of superior people two or three thousand years hence would not be appreciably larger than it is today. For that reason I think we are safe in assuming that the people composing society over this period will be much the same as they are today, and as they have been through written history. This being so, the upper limit of the progress of society seems determined by the extent to which people—and nations—are willing to work together, each doing the particular service he is best equipped to do, each respecting the similar service of his neighbors, and all having regard to society in its widest sense.

This can be illustrated from the relatively simple and material field of industry. How long would it take a single individual, assuming that he knew how to do it, to manufacture a single automobile? Not merely assemble the parts, but actually make them out of the raw materials. Perhaps no single individual could do it. But if he could it would probably take him a lifetime. Yet consider what happened when Henry Ford organized his thousands of workers, each performing only a single operation. I do not have exact figures, but I am doubtless safe in saying that the output averaged a number of cars a year for every worker in the industry, possibly even as many as one car for every worker each working day. Whatever the exact figures may be, the illustration brings out certain principles: first, the slow progress made by *one* man attempting to do *all* parts of the work; and second, the phenomenally rapid progress made by a *thousand* men each doing *one* part of the common task.

# History in an Age of Technology

Admittedly the operation of society is much more comprehensive than making an automobile and the political, economic, and social systems essential to social progress are much less obvious and much more complex than a purely material creation such as an automobile. But the principles revealed in the case of the automobile would seem to apply in the societal sphere with even greater force. The upper limit of progress is determined, therefore, by the extent to which people and nations are willing to work together, each content to do a portion of the world's work adequately, and appreciating the importance of allowing others to do the same.

This is not only the upper limit of social progress; it is also the limit of technology itself. We sometimes forget that technology is the achievement of man, his creation, the tool with which he accomplishes some of the hopes and desires he has always felt. Without man's wish and willingness, there would be neither electric light nor radio nor telephone, neither airplane nor automobile nor railroad—in short, little to call our machine age.

I said, without man's wish and willingness. I omitted one, perhaps the most important, condition. People are not born willing and able to work together in this fashion. That is a cultivated virtue, the outcome of education. It is only through education, either formal or acquired by the process of living, that the individual learns to control his impulse to do as he pleases when he pleases. It is only through education that the individual learns that he can gain even greater comforts and pleasures by restraining his impulse than by yielding to it. It is only through education that he learns that by doing well only a few things and letting others do in similar fashion the few things which they do best, everyone can enjoy comforts, conveniences, pleasures, and joys such as the greatest monarchs of less favored societies could only envy. This education, then, is *an*, I might almost say *the*, essential condition for social progress.

And what is this education through which the individual acquires the willingness to check his impulses, to do well a few things, so that he may enjoy the greatest measure of comfort

# The Social Web

and pleasure? Not the least part of it, certainly, is a study of the social past with its panorama of societies which did have a large measure of such willingness and ability to work together and of societies which did not, of societies which attained a high degree of civilization and of societies which reverted to savagery. The more fully he learns to understand them, the reasons for their successes and failures, the more fully will he be willing to surrender his immediate and individual wishes in order to join in social progress, and the greater must be the technological development of his time. And the more widely this knowledge of history is disseminated, the more fully it is shared by the whole society, by everyone in it, the greater will be the opportunities for progress. A world society is possible only through continuous and universal education.

Thus we come in the field of the social sciences to the same conclusion that has been reached in the other sciences. Progress in social science is proportional to the fullness and accuracy of the knowledge of the past, and social progress is dependent upon the extent to which this knowledge of the past is shared by all the people. Therein lies the basis of the willingness of society to support such progress, upon which in turn not only technology but all the sciences depend. In this connection it is well to recall the remark of a recent writer that no branch of engineering is as hard as the engineering of human consent.

So we come to the paradoxical conclusion that what are generally regarded as the least scientific branches of learning are the most fundamental. This is one of the lessons which the forests over Chichén Itzá and Angkor, the sands over Troy and Palmyra, and the broken columns of the Parthenon and the Coliseum tell in such tragic fashion.

Does modern technology obviate the study of the past? I do not think so. Whether we view the question from the sentimental, the practical, or the scientific approach, technology demands an increased, rather than a lessened, study of the past. In fact, the greater the progress of technology, the more widespread must be the study of history and the other humanities to support it.

# History in an Age of Technology

It is precisely the enrichment of life and thought and purpose which a judicious reading of the past can supply that our stressful times demand. As we look at our troubled world, we are almost overcome by the urgency and the immediacy of its pressing problems. Perhaps the chief offering that history, the mother of all the humanities, can make to this generation lies in its capacity to enlarge the comprehension and sympathies of the human mind and spirit. The ripe and gracious quality of learning, the mature wisdom derived from an understanding of the implications of many diverse facts, must be more highly esteemed among us. A poised and disciplined judgment, centered not in the present moment alone, exigent though this be, is certainly one of the qualities our times demand. A broad diffusion of historical knowledge, producing a deep realization that other ages than our own have faced and made momentous decisions, whether for good or ill, must steady the thinking of us all.

If the historian cannot, like the physical scientist, attempt to measure "the true movement and the calculable order of the universe," he can, amid all the confusion, repeat as one of the sure lessons of history that answers to our strivings are not given but must spring from the imaginative daring of high intelligence. These answers must be created—and in our own day—from a fine fusion of the humanities with science and invention in a synthesis never before attempted. If we fail, our civilization, like others in the past, must perish before its own apathies and ignorances.

Nietzsche, in the best of all his essays, on the meaning and use of history, took a somewhat gloomy view when he concluded that only great minds could look at truth, as history reveals that truth, and yet retain hope and strength for pressing on. This thought was re-echoed with something of a smile by Santayana, poet as well as philosopher, when he reminded us "to see ourselves in the mirror of stars and infinity and laugh as we pass." This capacity is not the least of the results to be derived from long dwelling with the Muse of history. High courage of both kinds—of both Nietzsche and Santayana—our age demands, and history, wisely and widely read, can supply it to us all.

# INDEX

# Index

# History and the Social Web

260

clusions drawn, 133–34. *See also*
Renaissance
New York, 212
Niccoli, Niccolo, 107, 120, 124: interest in Humanism, 116–18
Nietzsche, Friedrich, view of history, 255
Norden, W., 59, 60
Normans, 61, 114: and medicine, 46
Notaries, Florentine, 140
Nurredin, sultan, 94

Odum, Howard Washington, 200
Odysseus, 118
*Or San Michele*, 155
*Orator*, 120
Orcagna, Andrea, 156, 158, 169
Ordinances of Justice, 149
Orleans, University of, 215
Orsini, Roman family, 113
Ostmark, 229
Otto of Freising, 79, 95, 109
Otto the Great, emperor, 111, 114, 210, 229
Ovid, 89, 179
Oxford University, 130, 178, 211

Padua, University of, 49, 51, 189: fame as medical school, 57; and Humanism, 126–27, 129; in Renaissance, 177–78
Pagolo, astrologer, 123, 126
Palazzo Vecchio, 184
Palmieri, Matteo, 121
Palmyra, 254
*Pandects of the Corpus Juris Civilis*, 125
Panofsky, Erwin, view of history, 178–79
Papacy: in thirteenth century, 37; warfare with Empire, 148; Babylonian captivity, 183, 184. *See also* Great Schism, Church
Papal states, 182
Paracelsus, Philippus Aureolus, 21, 58, 176, 216
Paré, Ambroise, 176
Paris, 81, 82, 130, 217: organization of university at, 49; Montagu College, 211
Paris, Matthew, 98, 99
Parthenon, 254

Paschal II, pope, 66, 71, 72
Pavia, (Italy), university of, 126, 128
Pazzi, Piero, and classical studies, 117–18
"Peace of God," 30, 32, 37: enforcement of, 33–34; success of, 35
Perseus, statue of, 127
Peter of Barcelona, archbishop of Tyre, 80–81, 82
Peter the Hermit, 92, 95
Petrarch, 108, 181, 182, 185, 215: hatred of doctors after plague, 52; and New Learning, 107, 110, 112–16, 119, 175; mentioned, 108, 124, 125, 189
Pharmacy, 176
Philip II, king of France, 114
Philip II, king of Spain, 210
Philip IV, duke of Burgundy, 211
Philip IV, king of France, 114
Philosophy, 176
Physiology, 176
Piacenza, Council of, 61, 72
Pico della Mirandola, 125, 179
Pierz, Franz, Benedictine father, 231
Pietro d'Abano, 51
Pisa, 61, 148, 149, 178: university at, 126, 127, 128; merchants of, 139; expansion of commercial empire, *1000–1300*, 140
Pisani, Andrea, 157
Pistoia, Italy, 124
Pitti, palace of the, 162
Plato, 121, 123, 175, 204
Platonic Academy of Florence, 176
Pliny, 38
Plutarch, 120, 121
Poggio Bracciolini, Gian Francesco, 107, 117, 185
Poitiers, battle of, 237
Politian (Angelo Poliziano), 125, 179, 180, 189
Politics, as subject of history, 244–45
Polo, Marco, 213
*Principe, il*, 121
Prior of the Holy Sepulchre, 87
Private warfare, ninth through eleventh centuries, 27–28
Prutz, Hans, 196
Psychology, contribution to history, 202, 205, 206
Ptolemy, the geographer, 38
Pulci, Luigi, 179, 180, 182

# History and the Social Web

## Index

William, duke of Aquitaine, 30
William of Montferrat, 87, 198, 199
William of Orange, 210
William of Tyre, 70, 109: on relative merits of Eastern and Latin medicine, 48–49; modern historians' judgment of, 79; origin and early education of, 80–82; becomes Amaury's chronicler, 82–84; undertakes tutoring of Baldwin, 83; duties and offices under Baldwin IV, 84–86; writing activity under Baldwin, 86–87; aspirations to patriarchate, 87–89; semi-retirement of, 89–90; conclusion of writings of, 90–91; death of, 91; guiding philosophy of, 92; arrangement of work of, 93; evaluated as historian, 93–96; value of work as source for crusading history, 96–97; effect on European historiography, 97–99; critical appraisal of work of, 195–99; quoted, 246

William the Conqueror, 210
Wilson, Woodrow, 210
Woolen industry, in Florence, 143–44
Worcester, earl of, 126
Wright, Louis B., 177
Wycliffe, John, 236

Ximenes, cardinal, 107, 130

York, England, library at, 108

Zoology, 176, 187